THE SIX WAYS OF KNOWING

By the Same Author

The Chief Currents of Contemporary Philosophy

An Introduction to Indian Philosophy
(Jointly with S.C. Chatterjee)

The Philosophy of Mahatma Gandhi

THE SIX WAYS OF KNOWING

A CRITICAL STUDY OF THE ADVAITA THEORY OF KNOWLEDGE

D.M. DATTA

MOTILAL BANARSIDASS
PUBLISHING HOUSE • DELHI
Email: mlbd@mlbd.in • Website: www.mlbd.in

2nd Reprint : Delhi, ***2021***
First MLBD Edition : Delhi, 2017
Second Revised Edition : 1960 (2014)
First Edition : Great Britain, 1932

ISBN: 978-93-91430-58-0 (Cloth)
ISBN: 978-93-91430-66-5 (Paper)

Printed & Published by
Rajendra P Jain *for*
Motilal Banarsidass Publishing House
A-44, Naraina Industrial Area, Phase I,
New Delhi–110 028 (INDIA)
Email: mlbd@mlbd.in
Website: www.mlbd.in

TO

MY TEACHERS OF PHILOSOPHY

AND

THE LATE RAJA SUBODHCHANDRA BASUMALLIK,
THE FOUNDER OF THE P. C. BASUMALLIK CHAIR

CONTENTS

PAGE

BOOK II

BOOK III

BOOK IV

PAGE

CHAPTER IV

CHAPTER V

CHAPTER VI

PREFACE TO THE FIRST EDITION

This is an age of international understanding. Races and nations which dwelt and flourished apart are now coming into intimate contact and gradually tending to evolve a world of common ideas and beliefs. In Science such a common world of thought has already been achieved. In Philosophy the ideal, though not realized, is fast dawning upon the minds of thinkers. For the fulfilment of this ideal—for the evolution of a world-philosophy—what is best in every system, Eastern or Western, modern or ancient, requires to be gathered and added to the common stock. Anyone who has a casual acquaintance with Indian Philosophy knows what valuable contributions it can make towards this common fund. Difficult as the task of interpretation is, some eminent scholars, both Indian and European, have already done valuable work in this direction. But much more yet remains to be done. This volume is an effort to that end. It tries to present, after critical analysis and evaluation, the contributions of *some* Indian thinkers in a special branch of Philosophy.

During the years 1925-28, the writer had the privilege of occupying the Praboth Chandra Basu Mallik Chair of Indian Philosophy at the Bengal National Council of Education. In Compliance with the wishes of the founder of this chair he was called upon to undertake some investigation in Indian Philosophy and publish the results of his labour. This volume represents his work in discharge of that duty.

He attempts to study critically some important epistemological theories of one of the chief schools of Indian Philosophy, namely, the monistic (Advaita) School of Vedānta. These theories mainly concern the question as to the nature and number of the ultimate sources of knowledge, and must be of great interest to students of modern European Philosophy, in which epistemology has come to occupy a central place. Western Philosophy has generally recognized two ultimate sources of knowledge, immediate knowledge or perception, and mediate knowledge or inference. But there has been a variety of opinions on this matter among the different schools of Indian Philosophy. Some hold that perception is the only ultimate source of knowledge. Some accept both perception and inference. Others add a third, testimony or authority, to these. Still others hold that comparison is an additional independent source of knowledge and should be combined with the above three. Others again contend that there is a fifth kind of knowledge, postulation, which is not reducible to any of the preceding. A few other thinkers hold that there is also a sixth type—non-perception—from which primary negative judgments are derived and which cannot possibly be reduced to any of the above. These views are not mere dogmatic assertions. Each school gives elaborate arguments for its own position. This book deals with the Vedānta standpoint, according to which there are six sources of knowledge. The conceptions of these different kinds of knowledge, with all the arguments given by the Vedāntins to prove their independence and ultimacy, are critically discussed here in the light of modern Western concepts, and the attempt has been made to present the conclusions to students of Western Philosophy in a clear and lucid form.

As the purpose of this work is to bring the problems, concepts and theories of the Vedāntins within the focus of modern Western thought, the method adopted is one of critical analysis, comparison and evaluation. Analysis has been necessary to isolate the epistemological issues from extraneous aspects with which they are often associated. It has been useful also in grasping accurately the significance of the Advaita view wherever ambiguity and vagueness seemed to be possible. It has been most necessary, however, in the study of the Śabda-pramāṇa (testimony). Comparison with Indian and Western theories has been necessary to understand the exact position of the Vedāntins with relation to that of other thinkers. Evaluation has been needed to ascertain the real merit of the Vedānta views on the grounds of reasoning. The adoption of this method has often necessitated the elimination of Sanskrit technical terms, the use of Western terms and concepts, the rearrangement of topics and the introduction of lengthy criticism—all of which have their justification only in the purpose of the work.

Throughout the book the writer has adopted the attitude of a student whose mind has been infected with doubts derived from the study of Western Philosophy, and who tries to understand, therefore, how far the Indian theories can satisfy his sceptical mind. For the audience, and every writer has some audience before his mind, he has imagined a tribunal of Western philosophers, mostly composed of anti-idealistic thinkers, with whom he tries to argue the case for Advaita-Vedānta as understood by him in order to carry conviction into their sceptical minds.

As to the value of such a study, it may be said that it tries to formulate in terms of Western Philosophy some important epistemological doctrines of Advaita-Vedānta, and to show by criticism that though they are generally neglected, they constitute when rightly understood valuable contributions to the Philosophy of the world. Its negative value consists in exposing the absurdity of certain commonly accepted theories of the East and the West, and in suggesting some problems that demand solution.

It may be necessary to note that words Vedānta and Vedāntin have been employed, in conformity with the common Sanskrit uses of the terms, to signify Advaita-Vedānta and Advaita-Vedāntin respectively for the sake of brevity, and they are to be taken in those senses except when any other meanings have been explicitly indicated.

It will be noted that the order in which the different pramāṇas (sources of knowledge) have been taken differs from the traditional order followed by the Advaita writers. Upamāṇa (comparison) and anupalabdhi (non-perception), which will appear to Western thinkers to be obvious cases of perception, have been considered after perception. Again, arthāpatti (postulation), which will appear to be nothing but inference, has been treated after inference. Śabda (testimony), therefore, has been placed last.

It may be necessary to mention here that the scope of the present work is limited to the consideration of the problems of *knowledge* (pramā) alone; consequently the problems of *error* (apramā) have not been included. This latter occupies a large field in Avdaita-Vedānta, and thorough justice to it can be done only in an independent treatise.

The writer would fail in his duty if he did not express his gratitude to all his teachers. He gratefully remembers first his early teachers, Professors Vanamali Chakravarty and Prabodh Chandra Sanyal, who first kindled in his mind the ambition to undertake a comparative study of Indian and Western Philosophy. He is indebted also to Dr. (now Sir) B. N. Seal, in whose versatile genius and incredible depth and width of scholarship his youthful ambition found a concrete embodiment and a source of lasting inspiration. He is grateful, further, for initiation into the original Sanskrit texts, to his teachers Mahamahopadhyaya Pandits Laksmana Sastri, Pramatha Nath Tarkabhushan, Ananta Krishna Sastri, and other learned Pandits.

He is specially indebted to the highly talented Pandit Jogendra nath Tarkatirtha, of the Sanskrit College, Calcutta, with whom he studied for about two years some of the more abstruse texts while writing this book.

For the critical method pursued in this work, he is indebted, more than to anybody else, to the silent, but profound thinker, Principal Krishna Chandra Bhattacharyya (now Professor, Calcutta University). For about three years he enjoyed the privilege of sitting at his feet discussing problems, removing doubts and reading texts. It is through the inspiring influence of this master mind that he picked up the rudiments of critical thinking, of which the present work is but an humble fruit.

Next to his teachers, the author is indebted most to the world-renowned thinker and writer Professor S. Radhakrishnan, of the University of Calcutta. From the very conception of the work till its completion Professor Radhakrishnan has most generously helped him by constant suggestion, guidance and encouragement. But for his kind encouragement and active sympathy the book would scarcely have been published in the present form. The writer has the greatest pleasure, therefore, in expressing his gratefulness to him. He would thank also the distinguished Sanskrit scholar Principal Gopinath Kaviraj, of the Government Sanskrit College, Benares, for kindly reading some portions of the book and encouraging him with his valuable opinion.

He must thank, further, though in an un-Indian manner his own brother and teacher Professor Suresh Chandra Datta (of the Government College, Gauhati), who has been through the manuscript, corrected many mistakes and made valuable suggestions which have enabled the writer to improve the book in many respects.

Finally he must express his deep sense of gratitude to the Bengal National Council of Education, under the auspices of which this work was done. He is specially thankful, however, to its learned Secretary, Mr. Hirendra Nath Datta, and its Superintendent Mr. Hem Chandra Das Gupta, for constant help and encouragement. But for the facilities offered by the Council, the author could scarcely have conducted the investigations embodied in this work.

PATNA COLLEGE, PATNA, INDIA, D. M. DATTA
June, 1930

PREFACE TO THE SECOND EDITION

It is a great regret that in spite of a persistent demand for the book in India and abroad, it had to remain out of print, since the destruction of stock by enemy action over London. Though, in view of the losses, the previous publishers, Messrs. George Allen and Unwin Ltd., were kind enough to write to me, as early as 24th June, 1946, relinquishing their rights to leave me "entirely free" to enable me "at once to approach another publisher", the difficulties created by the war also in India and my continuous pre-occupation with other works indefinitely delayed the necessary revision and re-edition.

Meanwhile requests for the book came from some Indian Universities which had recommended the book, and from foreign scholars, some of whom had to go to the British Museum Library and the Library of Congress to read it as 'a rare book, not lent out'. When the book was revised, Sir Jnan Chandra Ghosh, the former Vice-Chancellor of the University of Cacutta, was kind enough to go through some of the relevant correspondence, and the University undertook the publication of the revised edition in 1956. But owing to heavy pressure of work the University Press could print it out only this year.

In the work of revision I have tried to keep to the original plan and size of the book. I have been benefited very much by the extensive, scholarly criticisms and suggestions received from Professor Kalidas Bhattacharyya of Vishvabharati University. Professor Ganga Nath Bhattacharyya, an esteemed former colleague at Patna College, favoured me by going closely through the entire book, and suggesting many points for improvement. Professor Sudhindra Chandra Chakravarty of Vishvabharati and Atindra Mohan Gun of Calcutta Presidency College deserve my best thanks for reading some of the proofs. I must also thank Dr. Richard V. De Smet, S. J. (now a Professor at De Nobili College, Poona) who read the book at the British Museum, and used it for his Doctoral Dissertation for the Gregorian University, Rome, and reminded me repeatedly about the necessity of a second edition.

To my friend and former colleague at the University of Wisconsin, Professor William F. Goodwin, I am much obliged for lending me a copy of the first edition, bought by him second hand, but which had been previously owned and used by the late Professor George Santayana. Dreaming little that his copy will ever find its way back to the author in India, the great philospher made free and profuse comments on the margin, benefiting the author and also revealing himself as a keen, patient and critical student of Indian thought.

I am indebted to the staff of the Visvabharati Library for constant help.

I must thank finally the University of Calcutta, and the Superintendent and staff of the University Press for all assistance in bringing out this book, though late, yet in a suitable form.

SANTINIKETAN, WEST BENGAL, INDIA, D. M. DATTA
November, 1959

INTRODUCTION : PRAMĀ AND PRAMĀṆA

WESTERN Philosophy generally recognizes two sources of knowledge—Perception and Inference. But Indian Philosophy presents a variety of opinions on this matter. The Cārvākas admit only one source of valid knowledge—perception. The Bauddhas and some Vaiśeṣikas admit two sources—perception and inference. To these the Sāṅkhyas add a third—authority or testimony (Śabda). The Naiyāyikas admit a fourth way of knowing—comparison (Upamāna)—in addition to these three. The Prābhākaras again add to these four methods a fifth—postulation or assumption (arthāpatti). The Bhāṭṭas and the monistic Vedāntins recognise, however, six methods of knowledge, adding non-cognition (anupalabdhi) to the five already mentioned. We shall discuss here all the six methods of knowledge, as admitted by the Advaitins, one by one.

But before taking up the problems of our study proper, it is necesary to discuss in brief the Indian conceptions of knowledge (pramā) and the methods of knowing (pramāṇa), because they underlie all epistemological discussions.

The Sanskrit word jñāna stands for all kinds of cognition irrespective of the question of truth and falsehood. But the word pramā is used to designate only a true cognition (yathārthājñāna) as distinct from a false one (mithyā-jñāna). In English the word knowledge implies a cognition attended with belief. If, therefore, a cognition turns out to be false, belief in it is immediately withdrawn and as such it should cease to be called knowledge. Consequently knowledge, strictly speaking, should always stand only for a cognition that is true, uncontradicted or unfalsified. The ordinary division of knowledge into true knowledge and false knowledge should, therefore, be considered as an instance of loose thinking; the word true as applied to knowledge would then be a tautology, and the word false positively contradictory—false knowledge being only a name for falsified knowledge, which is another name for no knowledge.

If this logical meaning of the word knowledge be consistently and rigidly adhered to, knowledge will exactly correspond to the word pramā. Pramā is generally defined as a cognition having the twofold characteristics of truth and novelty (abādhitatva or yathārthatva and anadhigatatva).[1]

As regards the first characterstic, truth, all schools of the Indian philosophy are unanimous. Every philosopher holds that truth should be the differentia of knowledge or pramā. But views as regards the meaning of truth vary, and consequently the mark of a pramā is variously expressed. Broadly speaking there are at least four different views about truth.

According to one view the truth of knowledge consists in its practical value. A true congnition is, therefore, variously defined as that which reveals an object that serves some purpose (artha or prayojana) or leads to the achievement of some end,[2] or which favours a successful volition (saṃvādipravṛatya-nukūla). This view will at once be seen to resemble the modern pragmatic theory of the West. It is mostly held by the Buddhists, but other writers also occasionally support it.

Another view, that we find chiefly in the Nyāya works, regards truth as the faithfulness with which knowledge reveals its objects. True knowledge is, therefore, defined as that which informs us of the existence of something in a place where it really exists, or which predicates of something a character really possessed by it.[3] This view resembles the correspondence theory of Western realists.

A third view, which is incidentally referred to by many writers, regards truth as a harmony of experience (saṃvāda or saṃvāditva). A true knowledge according to this view, would be one which is in harmony with other experiences.[4] This view again resembles the Westerrn theory of coherence.

The Advaita school of Vedānta, however, favours a fourth view according to which the truth of knowledge consists in its non-

1 Vedānta-paribhāṣā, pp. 19 f. (Venkateṣvar Press, 1911).

2 Nyāya-vindu, chap. i.; "Tataḥ artha-kriyā-samartha-vastu-pradarsakam samyag-jñānam." and *Ibid.*: "Yataś ca arth-siddhis tat Samyag-jñānam." (Chowkhamba).

3 Tattva-cintāmani, Pratyakṣa (As. Soc. ed., p. 401): "Yatra yad asti tatra tasyānubhavaḥ pramā, tadvati tatprakārakā-nubhavo vā."and Tarka-saṃgraha and Dīpikā : "Tadvati tatprakārakaḥ anubhavo yathārthaḥ ." Gautama's avyabhicāri' is also similarly explained by Vātsyāyana (N. sūt. 1.1.4, Chowkhamba, 1925).

4 *Cf.* Tattvakaumudī (on Kār. 51) 'saṃvādyate'. Also *vide* Pramāna-vārttika-bhāṣya (Patna, 1953), pp. 3-4, "Pramāṇam avisaṃvādi-jñānam."

contradictedness (abādhitatva).[1] The correspondence view of truth cannot directly prove itself. The only way to prove correspondence is to fall back on the foreign method of consilience or coherence (saṃvāda)—that is to infer the existence of a real correspondence between knowledge and reality from the facts of the harmony of experience. But all that we can legitimately infer from the harmony of knowledge with the rest of our experience up to that time,is not that the knowledge is absolutely free from error, but that it is not yet contradicted. For we do not know that we shall not have in future any experience that can falsify our present knowledge. As regards the pragmatic test of causal efficiency (artha-kriyā-kāritva), the Advaitins argue that even a false cognition may, and sometimes does, lead to the fulfilment of a purpose. One of the examples[2] they cite to support their view is the case of a distant bright jewel which emits lustre. We mistake the lustre for the jewel and, desiring to get the mistaken object of our knowledge, approach it and actually get the jewel. In this case, therefore, the knowledge of lustre as the jewel—which is clearly a false cognition—leads to the attainment of the jewel and thereby satisfies our purpose, though eventually we come also to know that the initial cognition which caused our action was itself false. We can multiply instances of this kind. The hypothesis that the earth is stationary and the sun is moving has been working quite satisfactorily for ages; on the basis of this cognition many of our actions are performed and purposes attained. It is only its conflict with astronomical phenomena that enables us to detect its falsity.

It is found, therefore, that the pragmatic view of truth is not tenable. The correspondence view has ultimately to fall back on the consilience or coherence theory which, when subjected to strict scrutiny, has to yield the result that truth, as ascertained by it, consists only in its non-contradictedness.

According to the Advaitins, therefore, pramā or knowledge must have as one of its characteristics truth; and the truth of pramā consists in its content being uncontradicted (abādhitārtha-viṣayakatva).[3]

The second characteristic of pramā or knowledge is, as we have already

1 Vedānta-paribhāsā, pp. 19 f. and Advaitasiddhi (Nirnayasagara, 1917), p. 340 : " Bādhitaviṣayatvena hi bhramatvam, na tu vyadhikaraṇa-prakāra-tvena, tasyāpi viṣaya-bādhaprayojyatvāt,..."

2 Tattava-pradīpikā-Citsukhī, p. 218 (Nirnayasagar, 1915).

3 Vedānta-paribhāsā, pp. 19 f.

said, novelty. It is not sufficient that knowledge should be true, it is also necessary that the content of knowledge should be new or previously unacquired—anadhigata. On this point, however, not all authorities are unanimous; while some (e.g. Mīmāṃsakas)[1] consider it to be an essential part of the differentia of knowledge, others[2] think it unnecessary as unduly narrowing the scope of knowledge. The Vedāntists seem to be rather indifferent to this controversy and unwilling to take sides.[3] The material part of the controversy turns upon the question whether memory should be admitted to have the status of knowledge. If truth be the sole characteristic of knowledge, memory, in so far as it is uncontradicted or undoubted, has to be called knowledge. But there is a peculiarity about memory that deserves special consideration. The only claim of memory to belief lies in its explicit reference to a past experience which it professes to reproduce faithfully. A remembered fact is belived to be true just because it is regarded as identical with the content of a past experience which it claims to represent. This confessed and explicit falling back on the past experience means its self-abdication in favour of its archetype. Thus the question of treating memory as a distinct type of knowledge does not at all arise, being barred *ex hypothesi*. The only kind of knowledge is then the knowledge of the already unacquired. But though memory is not a distinct source of knowledge, it is still a distinct experience that has to be distinguished from knowledge and given a separte name. The experience which reveals the new (i.e. knowledge proper) is called anubhūti,[4] whereas reproduced knowledge is called smṛti.[5] Thus novelty comes to be considered an essential quality of knowledge.

If this be the conception of knowledge (pramā), the question then arises whether in the case of a persistent knowledge of the same object, our experience at every moment during that time can be regarded as knowledge. When I keep looking at a table for some moments continuously,

1 Prakaraṇapañcikā (6.3): "na pramāṇam smṛtiḥ."

2 Praśastapādabhāsyam : "vidyāpi caturvidhā, pratyaksa-laiṅgika-smṛtyārṣa-lakṣaṇā" (p. 94, Chowkhamba).

3 Vedānta-paribhāsā, pp. 19-20; (the author defines pramā in both ways so as to include or exclude memory).

4 Bhāṣā-pariccheda (Kārikāvalī with the com. Siddhāntamuktāvalī, Nirnayasagara, p. 232).

5 *Ibid.*

my experience of the first moment, as an acquisition of the "new", is of course to be called knowledge. But what about the experiences of the subsequent moments? Can they also be rightly called knowledge, seeing that they only reveal to me what has been already acquired at the first moment and lack there by the quality of novelty ?

This question is answered in the affirmative by all schools of thinkers. But different reasons are assigned in justification of this answer.

Some say[1] that in a persistent knowledge (dhārāvāhikajñāna), say of a table, the object is not the same at different moments, as it is ordinarily supposed to be. For even if we grant that the same table persists without any spatial change for a certain period, yet the inevitable temporal change has to be taken into consideration. In other words the table, the object of our knowledge, is determined both spatially and temporally to our consciousness. By perceiving its spatial properties we judge it to be big or small, high or low. Similarly by perceiving its temporal property we judge it to be "present". Without perceiving this timequality it would be difficult for us to distinguish present knowledge of a table, or its perception, from the past knowledge of a table or its memory. So the table as determined by the first moment of the persistent knowledge is not the same as that determined by the second moment. Every moment we have the knowledge of an object that is different from the object of the previous moment and is, therefore, as good as a new object. The definition of knowledge (pramā), therefore, applies to the case of a persistent cognition as well, the quality of novelty being present also in that case.[2]

This reply is regarded by others[3] as unsatisfactory. These thinkers, while admitting that the time-quality of a percept is also directly perceived, hold that in a persistent perception the different moments, which are infinitely small, are never perceived as such. What we perceive as "present" is not an atomic point of time but a finite span of time.[4] So it is difficult to say that in a persistent perception the time-quality of the object is perceived as new at every moment. The atomic moments (kṣaṇas) are obtained not perceptually, but logically, i.e. by a continuous conceptual

1 Vedānta-paribhāsā, Śikhāmaṇi and Maṇiprabhā on this topic.

2 Vedānta-paribhāsā. p. 20.

3 Kusumāñjali. "Kṣaṇopādhīnām anākalanāt," st. 4, p. 5 (As. Soc ed.).

4 Tattva-cintāmaṇi, Pratyakṣa, p. 380 : "kṣaṇānām atīndriyatvāt sthūlopādhimādāya vartamānatva-grahaṇāt."

analysis of the perceived span. Knowledge remains, therefore, the same during the moments composing this finite span of time, and consequently at each one of these moments, except the first, there is only a repetition of the old knowledge obtained at the first moment.

The disqualification that is pressed against memory is, therefore, equally present in the case of a persistent cognition, and the difficulty in including the latter in the definition of knowledge (pramā), while excluding the former, remains as great as before.

The solution of the difficulty, however, lies in understanding the exact sense of "novelty" (anadhigatatva) as present in the case of knowledge and absent in the case of memory. In memory novelty is said to be absent, in the sense that memory is wholly a reproduction of a past knowledge; it is solely caused by the impression of a past experience (saṃskāra-mātra-janya).[1] In a persistent knowledge the knowledge of the second moment is not a reproduction of the knowledge of the previous moment; it is caused not by the impression of the previous experience, but by the very objective conditions which cause the first knowledge. So while memory by its very nature falls back on a past experience, and entirely rests thereon for its validity, the knowledge at subsequent moments of a persistent cognition stands by its own right and makes a demand for its independent validity. It is in this important respect that memory has to be distinguished from a persistent cognition, and it is in virtue of this very important distinction that the one has to be excluded from the definition of knowledge and the other has to be included therein. This is the Nyāya solution of the problem.

The Advaitins however hold that in their theory of knowledge, such a problem or difficulty does not at all arise; no defence of explanation, therefore, is necessary, According to them, knowledge persists so long as fresh knowledge does not come to replace it.[2] Whether knowledge changes or remains the same can only be ascertained by determining whether the logical activity of the self, i.e. the judgment affirming the knowledge ("The pot is" or "The pot is perceived"), changes or remains the same.

This problem assumes that in persistent cognition there is separate knowledge at every moment (during the time of persistence), while the content or object of these distinct elements of knowledge is the same, and therefore, at every subsequent moment there is only a repetition or

1 Tarka-samgraha : "Saṃskāra-mātra-janyam jñānam smṛtih."

2 Vedānta-paribhāṣā, p. 26.

reproduction of the knowledge of the first moment. But this assumption is wrong. For if the object of the so-called different elements of knowledge be judged to be identical, they are themselves indistinguishable from each other, i.e. they are but one identical process of knowledge. Thus the question of repetition or reproduction does not arise at all.

This question and the Vedāntin's answer require the consideration of the fundamental problem how one perception is to be distinguished from another. One way of distinguishing one perception from another is, of course, the ascertaining of a distinction between their respective objects. This would mean that the characteristic that distinguishes one perception from another must remain in the object of that knowledge, i.e. the distinguishing characteristic must itself become the object of that very perception. But is this the sole way of distinguishing one perception from another ? The Vedāntins say "yes". But those who raise the original question seem to think that there may be some other way of making a distinction; as, for example, by the distinction of their times of happening. In such a case the time characteristic may not have been originally known as an element qualifying the object of the knowledge. At a subsequent time we may infer that as the knowledge persisted for a length of time which was composed of so many different moments, the knowledge of the first moment must differ from the knowledge of the second moment, since the two pieces of knowledge possess two distinct qualifications (viz. "of the first moment" and "of the second moment"). This would be distinguishing knowledge by an external adjective, while the former case consisted in distinguishing knowledge by an essential or internal quality. But it should be noted that a mere distinction based on an external mark does not argue separateness in existence. Edward VII as the King of England can be, for certain purposes, distinguished from Edward VII as the Emperor of India, or the father of George V; but this does not mean that the three as distinguishable must also be separate. Similarly the knowledge of the first moment, though in language or thought distinguishable from the knowledge of the second moment, is not necessarily separate from the second. In order that time-quality may serve as the basis of an inference as to the separateness of one knowledge from another, that quality must enter the knowledge itself as characterising its object. The perception of the table "now" is known to be different or separate from the perception of the table I had an hour ago, from the fact that the "presence" and "pastness" characterize respectively the object of the present perception and that of the past perception. In such a case the second perception contains a novelty (in virtue of its time-quality, viz. "presence") and is, therefore, a fullfledged knowledge.

To return to the original discussion, then, we find that even if "novelty" be regarded as an essential characteristic of knowledge, any real case of knowledge, such as persistent perception, or repeated perception, is not excluded from the definition of knowledge. A pramā or knowledge, therefore, can be accurately regarded as a cognition, the object of which is neither contradicted nor already known as an object (anadhigatā-bādhitā-rtha-viṣayam jñānam).[1]

The special source of a particular pramā or knowledge is called pramāṇa.[2] Pramāṇa is defined as the karaṇa of a pramā. A karaṇa is conceived as the *unique* or special cause through the *action* of which a particular effect is produced.[3] In the case of perceptual knowledge or pratyakṣa pramā, for example, a sense-organ (in the case of an external perception) or the mind (in the case of an internal perception) is said to be the karaṇa or instrumental cause. There are many causes, e.g. the mind, the sense-organ, etc., the existence of which is necessary for the production of perceptual knowledge of an external object. But of these, the mind is a cause the existence of which is common to all sorts of knowledge, perceptual and inferential; so it cannot be regarded as a special cause. The special cause here is the particular sense-organ involved in that perception, because it is not common to other kinds of knowledge; it is peculiar to external perception alone.

A cause,[4] to be called a karaṇa, must not be merely unique (asādhāraṇa) it must also possess some active function (vyāpāra). The contact of the sense-organ with its object is undeniably a cause (kāraṇa) of perception. It is also unique; the instrumentality of sense-contact is present in perception alone. But still it is not called the karaṇa of perception, because it is itself a function or action of the sense-organ and as such does not possess a further function (vyāpāra).

A pramāṇa is, then, such an active and unique cause (kāraṇa) of a pramā or knowledge.

1 Vedānta-paribhāṣā, p. 20.

2 *Ibid.*

3 "vyāpāravad asādhāraṇam kāraṇam karaṇam."

4 In the ordinary sense of a causal condition.

BOOK I

PERCEPTION (PRATYAKṢA)

CHAPTER I

PERCEPTION AND METAPHYSICS

Of all the methods of knowledge, perception is by far the most important, for the obvious reason that it is the most fundamental. It supplies the corner-stone of the philosophy of the world. In fact it is always found that a theory of the world either starts with a theory of perception or, if starting somewhere else, it has to offer a satisfactory account of perception that fits in with its assumptions. In India almost every school of philosophy has its assumptions. In India alsmost every school of philosophy has its own theory of perception, that either leads to or follows from its peculiar position in metaphysics. In the West, since the time that the critique of knowledge came to be regarded as the basis of the theory of reality, perception has received a peculiar homage, as being the source of the most undoubted part of human knowledge. It will be our task here to explain the Vedānta views on perception and critically judge their value in the light of parallel theories of other schools in India, as well as in the west.

It is extremely difficult to ascertain the exact relation between epistemology and metaphysics. Should epistemology be based on metaphysics or should metaphysics be based on epistemology ? Which of these two enquiries should precede the other ? Or is there no question of precedence at all, the two branches of knowledge being independent but supplementary to each other ?

In Western philosophy since the days of Kant, a decided right of precedence has been accorded to the problems and theories of knowledge, and metaphysics has come to be built on the results of epistemological analysis. This tendency still continues to dominate the philosophic speculations of the West, though in recent times protest against this method also has begun to be heard.[1] In Indian philosophy metaphysics has generally preceded epistemology. In most of the schools, the nature of reality and the possibility of knowledge have been ascertained on the grounds of the revealed texts, which have come to be regarded as the embodiment of spiritual experiences. Consequently epistemology has been confined to the investigation of the different sources of knowledge

1 D. C. Mackintosh : *The Problem of Knowledge*, p. 7. Also, W. T. Marvin in *The New Realism*, pp. 49 f.

(pramāṇas) and the problems of truth and error. The declared object of such epistemological investigation was the ascertaining of the true method of the knowledge of reality, which was almost always conceived to be the way to liberation. The Buddhistic thinkers, however, challenged this method. They owed no allegiance to the revealed texts and attempted a revision of metaphysics through the criticism of knowledge. Their enquiry, like that of Kant, ended mostly in agnosticism, in the conception of the impossibility and futility of metaphysics.

It is rash and precarious to pass a general judgment on the question of the relation of metaphysics to epistemology. In part, we think, metaphysics, as well as epistemology, can be and should be independent. In other respects, they are mutually interdependent. Epistemology, as dealing with the problems of mediate knowledge or logical reasoning, can be investigated independently of metaphysics to a great extent. Indeed, metaphysical thinking has to be carried on through reasoning, the validity of which can be known through epistemological criticism. But even there, the ultimate postulates of thought require to be justfied by a system of metaphysics which alone can compel its final acceptance. As regards the problems of immediate knowledge, also, we can proceed to a certain point independently of metaphysics. But when we come to the question of the possiblity of such knowledge or to the criticism of its value, no satisfactory conclusion can be drawn without metaphysical considerations.

Here we are concerned with the problems of immediate knowledge. The Vedāntins, as we shall presently find, freely draw upon their metaphysical theories in order to explain many of the problems of perception. To a modern student of philosophy this method would appear to be dogmatic. The theories of perceptual knowledge would be regarded as vitiated by gratuitous metaphysical assumptions, and consequently little or no value would be attached to the Vedāntic conclusions. But if we closely examine the modern epistemological theories of perception, it will not be difficult to find that in spite of their loud protests against metaphysics, epistemologists have tacitly assumed without criticism certain theories of reality, on the truth of which alone their epistemological conclusions can stand. If so, is it not far better to express the metaphysical grounds, and confess plainly and honestly that the final guarantee of these epistemological theories would come from the truth of the metaphysical assumptions ? In such cases metaphysics and epistemology have to be considered in relation to each other.

For Vadāntins, however, the inclusion of metaphysical considerations is doubly necessary. It is needed primarily as a necessary explanation that Vedāntic metaphysics owes to the problems of perception. Vedānta has to show that the problems of perception can be satisfactorily accounted for consistently with its metaphysics.

The second necessity of including metaphysics is to impart a thoroughness to the epistemological conclusion itself, which would otherwise remain vague, as depending on uncriticised and unacknowledged grounds.

In our present investigation we shall, while dealing with perception, freely refer to the metaphysical conceptions whenever they are found to underlie the epistemological conclusions. But we shall also try to estimate the value of the vedāntic conclusions by critically comparing them with those of other schools of philosophy of India, as well as of the West. This will help us also to understand the relative worth of the so-called dogmatic and critical methods of epistemology.

CHAPTER II

THE DEFINITION OF PERCEPTION (PRATYAKṢA)

The word Perception has come to be used for the Sanskrit word pratyakṣa. We have adhered to this general usage. It is highly difficult to translate a word of one language by a word of some other language, because in spite of the general conformity in meaning the two words have different associations which cannot be preserved in translation. In spite of this difficulty translation becomes inevitable, and for literary purposes it may not be of great harm. But in philosophy, where accuracy of expression is an esential need, the greatest care has to be taken in rendering one word by another. Confusion of association due to loose rendering often creates serious misconception, and invites unnecessary criticism which applies only to the translation and not to the original. In rendering Indian philosophy, which developed through a thousand years a peerless store of highly technical words with inextricable associations, it would have been best to retain the original terms, but for the fact that the crack-jaw Sanskrit words, if preserved, would add an outlandish look and an apparent stiffness to the matter and would prove an effective obstacle to the foreign readers already so few. In the present case, we shall follow a *via media*, using both English and Sanskrit words alternately, as far as possible. We use the word Perception for the Sanskrit word pratyakṣa[1] in this manner. How far the meanings of the two words coincide or differ will be evident from the discussion that follows.

1 The word pratyakṣa etymologically consists of the two elements prati (to, before, near) and akṣa (sense-organ), or prati and akṣi (eye). So in common parlance it has come to mean "present to or before the eyes or any other sense-organ," and hence "direct," "immediate," etc. It is contrasted with the word parokṣa, which means "away from the eye or any other sense," "mediate," "indirect," etc. It is primarily used as an adjective.

In philosophy it is used, broadly speaking, to indicate immediacy. It is used here both as a noun and also as an adjective. As a noun it stands for immediate knowledge. As an adjective it is applied to (1) knowledge (jñāna), (2) the object of knowledge (viṣaya), and also to (3) the way of knowing (pramāṇa). (Kṛṣṇanātha Nyāyapañcānana : Āśubodhinī, p. 27). In the first sense we have cases like pratyakṣam jñānam (immediate knowledge), or idam jñānam pratyakṣam (this knowledge is immediate or direct), In the second and third senses we have expressions like ayaṃ ghaṭah pratyakṣaḥ (this pot is immediately known), and idam pratyakṣam pramāṇam (this is a direct way of knowing, or this is direct evidence).

As regards the exact definition of pratyakṣa, however, there is a marked divergence of opinions among the different schools of philosophy. Leaving aside the various minute differences, we may broadly classify these different views into three types. We have first the Buddhistic view according to which percepton is an unerring knowledge of the unique particular.[1] We have, further, the large majority of views which consider perception as knowledge arising out of the contact of sense with an object.[2] Lastly there is the view of the Prābhākaras and the Vedāntins, and also a section of Naiyāyikas, who characterize perception as immediate knowledge.[3]

According to the Buddhistc view[4] the word pratyakṣa is to be confined to the knowledge of the unique (svalakṣaṇa),particular object that is given directly through the senses. The name, and the universal concept through which we generally interpret the particular, should not be included in perception, as they are supplied by out imagination (kalpanā).

This theory of perception is either a result of, or a step towards, the peculiar metaphysics of the Buddhists, who conceive reality as consisting of unique and momentary particulars. Other schools criticize this rather extraordinary view, and we shall have to consider it fully in someother connection. The main objection,[5] which may be mentioned here, is that the uninterpreted sensation of a pure particular is no knowledge at all and cannot, therefore, be regarded as pratyakṣa, which must at least be a kind of *knowledge*.

The more popular and general view is that pratyakṣa should be defined as knowledge derived from that contact of sense with an object—(indriyārtha-sannikarṣa-janyamjñānam). This view is subscribed to by Gautama[6] (the founder of the Nyāya schol), by Kaṇāda, the author of the Vaiśeṣikasūtras,[7] by Kumārila-bhaṭṭa,[8] and a great majority of other thinkers. All of them agree on this point, though they differ as to other

1 Nyāya-vindu. pp. 11-16, (Chowkhamba ed.).

2 Nyāya-sūtras, I. 1.4. Also Muktāvalī and Slokavārttika.

3 Prakaraṇa-pañcikā, Tattva-cintāmaṇi and Vedānta-paribhāsā.

4 Nyāya-vindu, *loc. cit.* and Pramāṇa-vārttika, pp. 245 f.

5 Prakaraṇa-pañcika (Chowkhamba), p. 49.

6 Nyāya-sūtras, I. 1. 4.

7 Vaiśeṣika-sūtras, and Praśastapāda-bhāṣya, on Pratyakṣanirūpaṇam.

8 Sloka-vārttika (Chowkhamba, Benares, 1898); "sat-samprayoge puruṣendriyāṇām...", Jaim. Sūt., I. 1. 4.

details, e.g. some think that the word pratyakṣa should be confined only to uncontradicted knowledge (avyabhicāri-jñānam),[1] while others think that this qualification is unnecessary and that pratyakṣa should be used as a generic name for perceptual knowledge as well as perceptual error.

This view is considered to be unsatisfactory by a third class of thinkers, of whom Gaṃgeśa, the famous Neo-naiyāyika, the Prabhākara school of Mīmāṃsakas, and the Advaitins are the most prominent. The objection raised by Gaṃgeśa and the solution offered may be summed up thus:–

The definition of pratyakṣa as knowledge obtained directly through the contact of a sense with an object is too wide, because this definition would apply even to the cases of inference and memory. For, in inference also we have the contact between the mind (which is the internal sense), and the subject of the inference (which here is the object). Similarly in memory also, there is a contact between the mind and the object remembered. If to obviate this difficulty we say that the mind is to be considered a sense only in the case of an internal perception, and not in the case of memory or inference, we shall be required to find the criterion of sense. What is sense ? If we say that sense is the cause of a perception, we shall fall into a vicious circle. Perception is to be determined by reference to sense, and sense again to be determined as the cause of perception. To avoid this circle, we have to define perception in some other way. Perception may be safely defined as immediate knowledge.[2] Or it may be defined negatively as knowledge that is not derived through the active agency of other knowledge.[3] Inference is not immediate knowledge, it is derived from previous knowledge; so also is memory. And when perception is thus determined, we may define sense in relation to perception.

The author of Nyāya-siddhānta-mañjarī also supports this view. According to the Prabhākara school also perception is immediate knowledge—Sākṣāt pratītiḥ pratyakṣam.[4]

The Advaitins, while agreeing that perception is immediate consciousness, differ from most other schools of thinkers on one essential

1 Nyāya-sūtras, I. I. 4.

2 Tattva-cintāmaṇi, Sannikarṣavāda-rahasyam : "pratyakṣasya sākṣātkāritvam lakṣaṇam."

3 *Ibid.*, "jñānākaraṇakam jñānam iti tu vayam."

4 Prakaraṇa-pañcikā, p. 51

point. According to the views set forth above, though perception cannot be defined in terms of sense-activity owing to the difficulty already mentioned, yet wherever there is perception, external or internal, the activity of some sense, external or internal, must be thought responsible for it. But the Advaitins think that this is not true. There is no necessary connection between perception and the activity of sense.[1] God has no senses, yet it is admitted by all who believe in the existence of God, that he has immediate knowledge of things. According to some Advaitins, who do not consider mind to be sense, we have in internal perception an instance of immediate knowledge independent of sense-activity.

In order to understand this view fully, it is necessary to consider the Vedāntic psychology of perception. But before we pass on to that topic, we may offer a few remarks as regards the definitions of perception stated above.

The Buddhistic view of perception differs from other views because of a fundamental difference as to which kind of knowledge is to be considered immediate. We shall discuss this matter fully later on. As regards the other two views, there is difference in formal definition, in spite of a general agreement as to which kind of knowledge is immediate. The second kind of definition, that attempts to differentiate perception on the grouds of its genesis, is, as Mill would say,[2] an accidental definition, or better, a mere "description". To say that perception is knowledge derived from the senses, is to leave its essence or connotation untouched. Considered thus, the third kind of definition, which calls attention to the essence of perception, namely its immediacy, is superior to the former kind and may be called an essential definition. "If we enquire," says Hobhouse, "into the common character uniting ideas of both kinds (i.e. simple ideas of sensation and reflection), we shall find it, not in their dependence on any sense-organ or on any special kind of physiological stimulus, but in their immediate presence to consciousness."[3]

1 Vedānta-paribhāṣā, p. 52.

2 *System of Logic*, vol. i, on Definition.

3 Hobhouse : *The Theory of Knowledge*, p. 15.

CHAPTER III

THE PSYCHOLOGY OF PERCEPTION

1. THE CONCEPTION OF SENSE (INDRIYA) AND ITS FUNCTION

The psychology of perception in Indian philosophy is peculiarly different from that in Western philosophy. It is chiefly due to the peculiar physical and physiological conceptions that were current at the time. But it is due also, to no small degree, to the way in which the psychological problem was approached.

In order to understand the psychological account of perception it is necessary and important to know what Indians meant by sense. It is difficult to get a clear account of the conceptions about sense, though they are always presupposed in many discussions. We have, however, a short but lucid account of these conceptions in Vivaraṇa-prameya-saṃgraha. We obtain there three different views of the senses (Indriyas).[1]

According to the Buddhistic thinkers,[2] indriyas or senses are the golakas or sense-orifices,—the eyes, the ears, the nose, etc., as visible to us. The Mīmāṃsakas,[3] however, do not accept this view. According to them, an indriya or sense is not the visible physiological organ, but is a peculiar capacity (śakti) of the organ. Most other philosophers, however, hold[4] that an indriya is neither the organ itself nor its capacity, but is altogether a different substance (dravya) having its locus in the visible sense-organ. If visible orifices or their capacities were indriyas, serpents that have no such physiological organs as ears could not hear. Besides, trees which have no marks of these sense-organs could not perceive. So an indriya is not to be identified either with a sense-organ or with the capacity of the sense-organ. It is a different material substance, though very subtle. It is composed of the same substance, the quality of which is sensed by it. For instance, the eye, which receives impression of rūpa or colour, which is a quality of light, is itself composed of the same substance as light. Similarly the nose which receives smell, which is a quality of

1 Vivaraṇa-prameya-saṃgraha, pp. 185-187 (Lazarus, Benares, 1893).

2 Ibid.

3 Ibid.

4 Ibid.

earth (Pṛthivī), is itself composed of earth; and similarly for the rest of the indriyas.[1]

The existence of an indriya is proved by inference. Every action presupposes some instrumental cause (karaṇa); therefore the act of perceiving also must have some karaṇa which is called an indriya.[2] The knowing self knows objects through the instrumentality of the indriyas. Why should we not conceive, then, that there is one indriya only ?[3] Because the nature of the object known requires that the sense through which it is known must somehow be attuned to it, or must be composed of the same fundamental substance that composes the object itself. And as the natures of objects, e.g. of sight, smell, taste, etc., are different, there must be as many different kinds of indriyas as well. The plurality of the indriyas can also be inferred from the different seats they have in the body and the different conditions under which they function.

As regards the mode of action of the indriyas, the Buddhists hold that senses need not come into contact with objects when they are perceived. In fact as sense, according to them, is only the physiological organ, it is absurd to think that the sense-organ, say the eye, should come into contact with the visible things which may be far away. So they describe the indriyas as aprāpya-kāri (or capable of working without reaching the object).[4]

Others think, however, that in receiving an impression an indriya or sense must come into actual contact with its object. From the Vedāntic standpoint Mādhavācārya establishes this view thus : If all the senses, including even those of touch and taste, could perceive objects without coming into actual contact with them, we would have been able to have the touch and taste of distant objects. But if it is held that not all, but only the visual and auditory senses, can receive impressions without actually reaching the object, then it has to be explained why we should not see a sight or hear a sound even after it has vanished. So it is reasonable to think that it is necessary for every one of the senses to reach the object and have contact with it, in order that the object can be perceived at all. This theory is stated by saying that every indriya is prāpyakāri (capable of working only on reaching the object).[5]

1 Cf. Empedocles' view 'like is known by like'.
2 Viv. pra. saṃ.
3 Ibid.
4 Ibid., p. 187.
5 Ibid., p. 188.

The question therefore naturally arises : If a sense must come into contact with its object, how can we explain the vision of a distant object, say a star, or the hearing of a distant sound ? Evidently, there is here no contact of the eyes or ears with their objects.

In reply to this question it is said that even in the case of sight and hearing contact between the sense and its object is possible, because the senses of sight and hearing are not the eyes and ears as we see them, in which case contact would have been impossible. The real senses are invisible subtle material substances that can expand and contract with great rapidity. When we see a distant star the visual sense, itself composed of light (tejas), shoots forward in long rays like the rays of the sun and reaches the object with lightning speed.[1] Owing to this high speed of the optical sense we seem to perceive simultaneously two objects, one of which is very distant and the other very near, although in fact there is difference between the times taken by the sense to reach the two objects.[2]

As regards the contact of the auditory sense with sound, there is a difference of opinion. The Naiyāyikas think that sound itself travels in waves[3] and thereby reaches the ears. But the Vedāntins hold that even in this case it is the sense that goes out to meet the sound-producing object. For they think that if sound itself came to meet the sense of hearing it would be impossible to distinguish the distance and direction of different sounds and locate their sources externally in space; of all sounds we would then say that they exist in our ears. What we feel, however, is that we hear the sound, say, of a distant drum—not the sound of our ears. It is reasonable, therefore, to think that the imperceptible sense of hearing goes out to reach the object, as in the case of sight.[4]

The account of the senses and their modes of action, given above, would appear very crude and dogmatic to the modern intellect. These theories were not arrived at *a priori*. They were based on experienced facts. But the facts which supply the basis of these theories also appear to us to be very crude. In the Nyāya-sūtras,[5] for example, we find that the peculiar light observed in the dark in the eyes of some nightroaming

1 Prakaraṇa-pañcikā, p. 44 (prak. 5).
2 Viv. Pra. saṃ., p. 187.
3 Kārikāvalī, p. 536.
4 Vedānta-paribhāṣā, p. 180.
5 Nyāya-sūt., 3, 1, 44 : "Naktañcara-nayana-raśmi-darśanācca."

animals (e.g. cats) is considered to strengthen the hypothesis that there is also such a light—some subtle substance in human eyes—which is the sense of sight. This imperceptible visual sense reaches its object through the help of external light (e.g. sunlight).[1]

In spite of their crudeness, these accounts possess a certain suggestive value. Coming into conflict with our accepted notions, they at least make us seek the grounds on which we stand with unsuspecting ease. In Western psychology we use the word "sense" without knowing exactly what we mean by that word. Is sense identical with an organ ? If so what is the meaning of the phrase "organ of sense," so often used in psychology ? Are the two words "organ" and "sense" only appositional here, as in phrases like "City *of* London" ? Is the same explanation applicable to the phrase "sense-organ" as well ? How are we also to understand the use of the word in connections such as "what was not in sense is not in intellect" ? It would appear from these various uses of the word that sense cannot be always identified with an organ. Its meaning would point to something other than an organ. But we miss in Western psychology an attempt to define the exact meaning—there is scarcely any discussion about it. The one outstanding feature that strikes even a cursory reader of Indian philosophy is the serious attempt to define the exact meanings of words and carefully use words only in the meanings so determined. In determining what exactly is meant by sense of indriya, the writers apply this uncommon zeal for accuracy. The question has been differently answered by different thinkers as we have already stated above. But in Western psychology we altogether miss the question and consequently also the answer. And though the answers given in Indian philosophy may have to be rejected in the light of the more developed theories of physics and physiology, the problem still remains, and demands an answer that will be more in consonance with modern scientific investigations.

As to the mode of action of the indriyas or senses, we find that the theories advanced require more than a mere passing notice. At first sight the view that senses go out to reach their objects would appear as absurd as the view that it is the sun that moves round the earth. But a little thought would show that the modern theory, that influences from objects reach our senses, is not so obvious or satisfactory as it seems, nor is the opposite

1 Ibid., 3, 1. 42.

Indian theory so absurd as it is thought to be. Difficulties are at least equally balanced on both sides. Let us see how.

It should be recognized at the outset that in determining the mode of action of the senses towards their objects, we move in a sphere where the positive sciences are of little help. The test of the adequacy of any theory advanced in this direction would mainly be the satisfactoriness with which it can explain the various aspects of the knowledge of objects. The relation between object and sense in the case of visual perception requires the most elaborate explanation, and in Western psychology it has been determined on the basis of the most up-to-date scientific researches. It would be best therefore to compare the Indian conception with Western one in this respect.

According to the Western theory, when an object is seen stimuli in the form of light-waves coming from the object affect the eyes, and in consequence of the action of the physiological apparatus in the eyes an image is formed on the retina; thereon some brain centres are stimulated and we have the vision of the object. The physical and physiological details involved here are perhaps beyond doubt. So far as it goes the account may be quite correct. But the question still remains whether it is a sufficient account of the origin of the knowledge of objects. For the present, we do not raise the question how physiological changes in braincentres give rise to knowledge. Our interest now is with the objective end of the process. The sense of vision here does not come into contact with the object, neither does the object come into contact with the sense. The object sends its influences, the sum-total of the action of which is represented in the formation of the retinal image. In the place of the object, therefore, we have its representative—the small inverted picture of the object, that is directly given to the organ of sight. But if this be the whole account, the mystery of how a small inverted image of the object on the retina makes us see the physical object, great or small, distant or near in the external world, is too great to be ignored by any enquiring unsophisticated mind. This difficulty has been realized by some idealistic thinkers of the West. But they have cut the Gordian knot by declaring, on the basis of such analysis, that what we directly see is not any physical object, but only a sensation. This has led them either to subjective idealism or to representationism. But we think that even subjectivism cannot escape this difficulty. Even subjectivists cannot deny the fact that what we see is not a small retinal picture inside our eyes, but something that is quite different from it in size and quality and at least appears to be there in space. And if what we actually see is to be declared a delusion, the process of delusion from the retinal picture to the seeing of the object has to be explained. Otherwise this physiological and physical account, as the basis of subjectivism, has to be abandoned. Thus we find that the problem cannot be evaded by any metaphysical or epistemological device. How to solve it then?

Though the solution of the problem cannot be so easily given, we can yet indicate the data which we have to utilize and also the direction in which the solution has to be sought for. From the side of knowledge, that we have the consciousness of an object outside us in space cannot be denied. From the side of the process the physical and physiological account, describing the formation of the retinal image, has to be accepted so long as the scientific basis of this account remains unchallenged. But as this mere image formed on the organ of vision, though correct, is yet inadequate to the vision of the object as we actually have it, we have to look for some other physiological process which would set up a more direct connection between our organism and the object. If so, it is improbable that the object can approach our organism. The probability lies then on the other side. An approach must be made from the side of our organism towards the object. Our sense must somehow approach the object itself. This direct approach will explain better the directness of perception, and it will simplify also the problem of external localization, to explain which the present psychological theories have to indulge in a series of happy guesses and conjectures. In this scheme the retinal picture also may have an useful place, as a guide through which we can find out its prototype outside us in space.

If we realize thus the inadequacy of the modern theory, and also the necessity of supplementing it further in the way proposed above, we shall be in a better position to understand the usefulness of the Indian theory, which not-withstanding its weak scientific basis may suggest to us a new direction of thinking from which a solution may ultimately come. The going-out of the subtle imperceptible senses may not then appear to be so absurd and misleading as it seems to be at first sight. The conception of an indriya or sense being composed of the same stuff as that the quality of which it can sense, would then point to the kinship of our physical organism to the external world, and the consequent fitness of it as a medium for receiving information of the external world. Light waves can affect our sense of sight, because this sense itself is composed of light. There is thus an unbroken continuum between our organism, the vehicle of our knowledge, and the external world, the object of our knowledge.

With these remarks, which are intended only to lessen the apparent absurdity of the theory of sense and its function, we may pass on to the consideration of the conceptions of mind and its place in perception, as found in Indian philosophy in general and Advaita philosophy in particular.

2. The Conception of Mind (Manas or Antaḥkaraṇa)

The Sanskrit word manas is translated by the English word Mind. Though the two words resemble each other in meaning to a great extent, yet there are important differences which should never be forgotten in translation. The word manas, like the English word Mind, is not used in the same sense by all schools of thinkers. The general and peculiar senses in which it has been used will become clear from the ensuing discussion.

In some respects, the conception of manas corresponds to the empirical view of mind in Western philosophy. It stands for mental states and function. Even when it is conceived as a positive substance, as by the Naiyāyikas, it is primarily conceived as an instrument—an internal sense through which we attend to inner and outer objects. The rational activities of the mind such as memory, comparison, etc., are ascribed to the self, ātman.[1] In most of the schools the phenomenon of recognition is used as a datum for inferring the existence of the rationl self—ātman.[2] Those who deny the existence of ātman, such as the Buddhists, do not ascribe the functions of reason to the manas; they deny altogether the existence of such a rational agent; for they think that all mental phenomena can be explained through association, and the hypothesis of an abiding self or reason is quite unnecessary. The Laukāyatikas are said[3] to consider manas as identical with ātman. But the ātman, for them, was nothing more than a by-product of matter.

Coming to the orthodox schools, we find that the Prābhākaras, the Bhāṭṭas, the Sāṃkhyas, the Naiyāyikas and the Vaiśeṣikas all agree in regarding manas as the internal organ of perception (antarīndriya) through

1 Nyāya-sūt, and Bhāṣya. 3, 1, 1, and 3, 1, 7.

2 Ibid.

3 Viv. pra. saṃ., 188

which we directly know, for instance, pleasure and pain and other mental states. As such they also agree in considering manas as unconscious. This view would serve as a striking contrast to the almost unanimous view of Western philosophy that consciousness is the specific characteristic of mind. The Indian thinkers regard consciousness as an attribute of, or as identical with, the ātman alone. Like the eyes, the ears and the nose, etc., manas also is an instrument, unconscious but very subtle; and through its instrumentality the ātman obtains the knowledge of objects. Though the activity of manas is chiefly felt in internal perception yet it is an indispensable factor in external perception as well. Kaṇāda, the author of the Vaiśeṣikas-sūtras, states that the proof of the existence of manas can be obtained from the fact that in cases of absent-mindedness we do not get knowledge, although an object, an external sense and the self are all present to co-operate with one another. This shows that the activity of some organ of attention is necessary for the production of knowledge. This inner organ is the manas.[1]

The non-spiritual character of manas or mind receives clear emphasis in the Sāṃkhya school, which considers it as an evolute of ahaṃkāra, which is ultimately derived from prakṛti, from which the entire physical world itself evolves. As such, manas belongs to the world of unconscious objects, and is sharply contrasted with ātman or puruṣa (i.e. self) whose essential attribute is consciousness.

The Vedānta view of mind is different from those of other schools in certain important respects.

First of all, manas, according to the Vedāntins, is not an independent reality. It is not regarded as a fundamental substance. It is only one of the many aspects or functions of antaḥkaraṇa (= inner organ) which is the generic term that would correspond to the word mind.

Secondly, according to most of the Vedāntins, manas is not an indriya or sense-organ.

Thirdly, it is not regarded as an invisible, infinitesimal substance (as in the Nyāya system), but is considered to be of medium dimension.

Each of these point requires special consideration. As regards the first, according to some Vedāntins, e.g. the authors of the Vivaraṇa, the Vedāntā-paribhāṣā, etc., antaḥkaraṇa has four different aspects or functions which are named : (1) manas; (2) buddhi; (3) ahaṃkāra; and (4) citta.

1 Saṃkara accepts this argument (vide his com. on Bṛhad. Upa., 1. 5. 3).

Manas represents the indecisive state of antaḥkaraṇa or mind as found, for instance, when we cannot ascertain whether an object in this or that. Buddhi stands for antaḥkaraṇa in its state of decision, as when we decisively know a thing as "this." Ahaṃkāra is the state of antaḥkaraṇa having some reference to the self, as in the judgment "I am happy." Citta is antaḥkaraṇa in its state of remembering, i.e. referring to a past event.[1]

The author of the Pañcadaśī,[2] however, distinguishes only two functions of antaḥkaraṇa, namely manas and buddhi (= vijñāna) and it is thought by subsequent writers that in his opinion citta is included in manas, and ahaṃkāra in buddhi. The author of the Vedānta-sāra also supports this twofold division, but according to him ahaṃkāra is subsumed under manas and citta under buddhi.

From a comparison on these different writers, it appears that all these Vedāntins are unanimous and positive as regards the meanings and functions of manas and buddhi. But opinions differ as to exact meanings of citta and ahaṃkāra and their relations to the other two functions. It should also be noted that in certain connections manas is also used in a wide sense as a synonym for antaḥkaraṇa, that is, in the sense in which it is used by writers of other schools.

But the most important thing to understand in this connection is the vedāntic idea of the nature of manas or antaḥkaraṇa. According to the Naiyāyikas, manas is a distinct dravya or substance, that is, as such, co-ordinate to other realities like the material elements, the self, etc. According to the sāṃkhyas also, as we have already mentioned, manas is a non-spiritual entity, that is co-ordinate to and independent of the self. According to the Advaitins, however, the self or ātman is the only independent reality; the material, the physical or the objective are but creations of ajñāna, i.e. ignorance or nescience. Antaḥkaraṇa is but a product of this primal, beginningless nescience, through a confused identification with which the self gets individuated. The self is caitanya (consciousness) itself, and consciousness is not a contigent product of any interaction between the subject and object—it shines in its own light; it is called svayamprabha or svayamprakāśa or self-shining.

In waking life, as well as in dreams, we do not find the ātman in its isolated state. The ātman appears to us as limited and circumscribed by

1 Vedānta-paribhāṣā and Āśubodhinī,chap. i.

2 6. 70 (Bangabasi edn., 1914), and Āśubodhinī, chap. i.

ajñāna, We often have a feeling of general ignorance, which is not like a feeling that arises out of the want of the knowledge of any particular thing; it is a more radical and positive feeling of the limitation of our knowing capacity. According to the Advaitins[1] this experience is a direct experience of our congenital ajñāna, which presents a resistance to the otherwise unthwarted freedom of the self-shining ātman. It is under the stress of this ajñāna that ātman assumes an objective attitude. Assumption of the objective attitude directly leads to its further self-limitation. It creates a breach in the one whole of caitanya, a dualism of the self and the not-self, the subject and the object, the "me"and the "not-me". This marks the consolidation of ajñāna into ahaṃkāra (egotism or self-consciousness), which, as we have already shown, is but a mode of antaḥkaraṇa. Henceforward the ātman behaves as the aham or the limited ego that has accepted the limitations of antaḥkaraṇa. Limitation necessarily creates the consciousness of an "other", a not-self that has to be known (or made the object of knowledge); it creates also a want which, for satisfaction, calls forth action. So it is said that avidyā or ignorance carries the seeds of vidyā (objective knowledge) and karma (action). Thus ajñāna as antaḥkaraṇa creates a finite centre of value and validity. As identified with it the ātman has to know everything through it; and knowing through it, it has to know objectively.

The history of every Jīva[2] of finite centre is kept distinct from that of every other such centre by his ajñāna, which records the impressions of all past experiences. It is by appropriating this particular ajñāna that one Jīva realizes its distinctness from another Jīva and forgets its unity with the pure consciousness that underlies all. This act of the appropriation of ajñāna on the part of the ātman, or rather this confused mutual identification that takes place between the ātman and the ajñāna, is called adhyāsa. This confusion reigns supreme in all our waking hours and even in dreams, where the play of ahaṃkāra or egotism (or behaviour as the limited self) dominates all our knowledge, feelings and actions. This is evident from the use of the first person singular "I" (aham) that we make in all these stages. We say, "I desire," "I know," "I feel happy," and the like.

1 Citsukhi, chap. i.; Advaita-siddhi, pp. 548 f.; also Viv. pra. saṃ. "Pratyakṣam tāvat aham ajñaḥ," p. 12.

2 Jīva = individual self

If these exhausted the whole of our experiences we should scarcely know the self as anything other than the limited "I," that functions either as the subject (as pitted against an object) in knowledge, or as the agent, or the cause of some volition, or as the enjoyer of some feeling. Fortunately, however, we have in our dreamless sleep a novel experience that challenges any hasty generalization that our ordinary experiences tempt us to make. In such deep sleep we do not experience the obsession of our habitual egotism or ahaṃkāra. We do not distinguish ourselves from any not-self. The dualism of the "I" and the "not-I" (aham and idam) vanishes altogether. But it is a mistake to consider that in such a state consciousness also ceases to be. The memory we have after such a sleep generally reports that we slept comfortably and did not know anything then. The Advaitins say that this memory points back to the actual existence of some pleasant experience—a blissful consciousness which shows the intrinsic nature of the ātman in its isolation from objects. This objectless blissful consciousness is the ātman's own light. The absence of egoism (ahaṃkā ra) and dualistic objective knowledge which mark the activity of antaḥkaraṇa show clearly that in suṣupti (i.e. dreamless sleep) there is a lapse of antaḥkaraṇa itself. Not that ajñāna (i.e. ignorance) is altogether absent in this state. If ajñāna perished altogether we should have a memory of omniscience, but on the contrary we remember that we did not know anything then. The memory of this ignorance, therefore, points to the existence of ajñāna in suṣupti as well. But the peculiarity of this state lies in the fact that in spite of the existence of ajñāna, there is a temporary lapse of adhyāsa, or the mutal identification that ordinarily takes place between the ātman and the ajñāna. The ātman does not appropriate the ajñāna, but simply lights it up just as a lamp in a solitary desert shines through the encircling mass of gloom. In want of this adhyāsa the ajñāna does not crystallize into antaḥkaraṇa, so that there is neither any differentiation, nor any determinate knowledge. As we return from dreamless sleep to dreams or to the waking stage, confusion comes back and with it antaḥkaraṇa reappears. Thus in interpreting even this undifferentiated consciousness (nirvikalpaka-jñāna) of a deep sleep, we divide it into terms of our differentiating consciousness (savikalpaka-jñāna), and say "*I* had a pleasant sleep, *I* did not know anything then"—expressions that are couched in the ordinary dualistic subject-predicate form which characterizes the sphere of determinate knowledge.[1]

1 Viv. pra. saṃ.. I. I; p. 61.

From this rather lengthy discussion, then, we can easily gather the vedāntic conception of antaḥkaraṇa, its origin, its lapse and the nature and range of its activities. From the metaphysical standpoint there is, as we have just tried to show, a vast difference between the vedāntic view and those of other schools. Whereas others hold the antaḥkaraṇa or mind to be independent of, and also as real as, the ātman or the self, the Advaitins think it is derived from the primal illusion or ajñāna from which the self suffers. Antaḥkaraṇa has no existence independently of the self, and even as dependent on the self it exists only so long as the self is not cured of this dogging distemper through an intuition of its real nature. But even metaphysically there is this agreement between the Vedāntins and other orthodox thinkers, that according to all of them mind is not self, it is unconscious.

From the practical point of view, the vedāntic antaḥkaraṇa (or manas, as it is also sometimes used for antaḥkaraṇa) discharges almost all the functions that are ascribed to manas by other schools. But whereas others consider determinate knowledge, desire, volition and memory to be attributes or functions of ātman, the Vedāntins think they are the functions neither of the ātman itself, which is pure indeterminate consciousness, nor only of antaḥkaraṇa which is a mode of ajñāna; they are regarded as products of the mutual association (adhyāsa) between ātman and antaḥkaraṇa, which is responsible for all deteminate activities. So these activities disappear when there is temporary dissociation between ātman and ajñāna in deep sleep, or there is complete destruction of ajñāna in the state of realization.

There is a little difference of opinion as to the proof of the existence of mind. The non-advaitins in general prove its existence by inference, as we have shown in a previous connection. But according to the Advaitins, mind is directly perceived. In their view antaḥkaraṇa is but a mode of ajñāna, and ajñāna, we have already seen, is directly revealed to the self in dreamless sleep and even in waking life in our experiences of general ignorance. Besides, pleasures, pains and other modes of the antaḥkaraṇa are directly known by the self.

In the Brahma-sūtras,[1] however, we come across an attempt at proving the existence of antaḥkaraṇa. The argument advanced is substantially the same as that of Kaṇāda already referred to. It is said that if the self, the

1 Brahma-sūtras, 2, 3, 32.

senses, and the object were the only three factors in knowledge, knowledge would be present always or never, so long as all these three are constantly present to co-operate together. As this is not the case—as knowledge sometimes takes place and sometimes does not, in spite of the presence of these factors—we are forced to admit the existence of a fourth variable factor, which is mind. Govindānanda, the author of the Ratnaprabhā, a gloss on the commentary of Śaṃkara on the Brahma-sūtras, says in this connection, that though antaḥkaraṇa is a direct object to the self (Sākṣin) and though its existence is proved on the testimony of the Upaniṣads, still such an inference is necessary only to convince those who neither admit the perceivability of antaḥkaraṇa nor accept the authority of the Śrutis.[1]

The second point of divergence between the Advaitins and the non-advaitic thinkers relates to the question whether mind is an indriya or not. We have seen that according to almost all non-advaitic thinkers, with the exception of some Buddhists, mind is an internal sense-organ—an indriya. An indriya, as we have already explained in another connection, is conceived as the karaṇa or the instrumental cause of perception. The Naiyāyikas and some others, who admit the existence of an abiding self as the knower of all knowledge, consider mind to be the instrument which is employed by the self, the agent, in internal perception. The reason why some Buddhists reject this theory perhaps lies in the fact that they do not admit the existence of an abiding subject; the empirical mind conceived as the stream of consciousness (vijñāna-santāna) is in their view the highest reality of consciousness. And in the absence of the agent (the ātman) the necessity of an instrument also vanishes; consequently mind is not conceived as an indriya or an instrument of knowledge.

Though the Vedāntins admit the existence of a permanent self, which in self-consciousness behaves as the knower or the subject, yet even among them there are some who do not regard manas or antaḥkaraṇa as an indriya or an instrument of this subject. In the Upaniṣads, the manas is mentioned in many places as distinct from the indriyas. In the kaṭha Upaniṣad, for instance, it is said : "Higher than the indriyas are the subtle elements (out of which the indriyas are made) and higher than these is the mind."[2] Again in another place,[3] the self is compared to a charioteer, the body to a chariot,

1 Ratnaprabha on Brahma-sūtras, 2. 3. 32.

2 Kaṭha, 3, 10.

3 Kaṭha, 3, 4.

the intellect (buddhi) to the driver, the manas to the reins and the indriyas to the horses. In the Muṇḍaka Upaniṣad[1] also it is said : "From this are derived the vital air (Prāṇa), the mind and all the indriyas." But in the Smṛtis (e.g. in Manu-saṃhitā), the mind is generally described as one of the eleven indriyas (the five sense-organs, the five motor-organs and the mind). The Vedāntins, as is well known, primarily count upon the testimony of the Śrutis—the Upaniṣads in special. They sometimes call in the evidence of the Smṛtis, but only because they think that they faithfully represent the views of the revealed texts. Where any conflict arises between a revealed text and a Smṛti, the attmept is first made to explain it away, and failing that the authority of the revealed text is upheld as against that of the Smṛti. The anomaly noticed above calls for such an explanation. Śaṃkara, while commenting on the Brahma-sūtras (2.4.17), incidentally states that though according to the Śrutis mind is not an indriya, according to some Smṛtis, however, it is an indriya. He thus simply notices the difference of opinion, without trying either to reconcile the two opinions or reject one in favour of the other. In that particular context any further discussion, however, would have been out of place. But if his silence was due to the obviousness of the conclusion that can naturally be expected on such a conflict, his opinion,.of course, should be understood to be the same as that of Śrutis.

Among the later writers, however, Vācaspati Miśra, the author of the Bhāmatī and Govindānanda, the author of the Ratnaprabhā, both tend to interpret the vague statement of Śaṃkara to be in favour of the view of the Smṛtis that manas is an indriya. In doing so, they necessarily so interpret the Śrutis as to remove the conflict. They think that in the Śrutis the mention of manas separately from the indriyas does not mean that manas is not an indriya. It is only a peculiar manner of speaking, as is found in some other phrases like "the cattle and the bullocks" or the "Brāhmaṇas and the Parivrā jakas," where the latter, though included in the former, are separately mentioned only for the sake of special emphasis. The author of the Pañcadaśī[2] also mentions manas as an internal sense-organ (antarindriya).

1 Muṇḍaka, 2, 1, 3.

2 Pañcadśī, 12-18.

The author of the Vedānta-paribhāṣā,[1] however, rejects this view. He places the testimony of the Śrutis in the fore-front, and interprets also certain statements of the Bhagavadgītā and other Smṛtis in accordance with the Śrutis and emphatically asserts that manas or antaḥkaraṇa cannot be regarded as an indriya. The author of the Vivaraṇa also holds this view.

It would appear that these discussions turn more on ascertaining opinions than on the consideration of epistemological issues. It is the latter that interest us most in the present connection. From the epistemological point of view two important questions have to be answered. The first question is : "Understanding an indriya in the sense ascertained above, is there any difficulty in regarding manas or antaḥkaraṇa as an indriya ?" The second question is : "Has the answer to the first question any special relation to the vedāntic position in general ?"

As to the first question, it should be noted that the meaning of "indriya," as used in the phrase "the eleven indriyas," is not the same as that referred to above. In this phrase, indriya is used in the wide sense of a karaṇa—an instrument of knowledge or conation in general. In this general and vague sense there may not be much objection to calling mind an indriya. But as we have already seen, the word as used in epistemological discussions has a narrower meaning. It is used in the sense of an instrumental cause or perceptual knowledge only. The Naiyāyikas and many others think that pleasures, pains, etc., are perceived by the self through the instrumentality of the mind, and consequently mind is an indriya. Even if we assume the premises as well as the conclusion of this argument we have to face some difficulties. The function of mind is not exhausted in internal perception alone. Its activities are present in external perception, as well as in inference, imagination, memory, etc. So the mind, as a whole, cannot be regarded as an indriya; in part it is an indriya and in part it is not. This difficulty is realized by the Naiyāyikas[2] themselves, and in works like Tattva-cintāmaṇi and Siddhānta-muktāvalī, we find that attempts are made to remove the doubt as to when the mind is to be regarded as an indriya and when it is not to be so regarded. That mind is not to be considered an indriya in the case of external perception, can be understood from the definition of the indriya discussed already. Indriya must be a karaṇa—an

1 Vedānta-paribhāṣā, pp. 49f.

2 Tattvacintaāmani : "smṛtya-numityā-dan ca manaso na indriyatvena hetuivam . . .". P. 550.

instrumental and special active cause. In an external perception the external sense involved is the special cause, whereas mind is a cause common to this and other modes of knowledge. So mind cannot be an indriya here, *ex hypothesi*. The difficulty, however, arises in cases of inference, memory, imagination, etc., where mind can be regarded as a karaṇa, or special instrumental cause, and, therefore, an indriya. The Naiyāyikas, however, say that in these cases, though mind is a karaṇa, it is not yet an indriya. Though this assertion may be aribitrary, the motive is obvious; if mind be regarded as an indriya, these modes of knowledge also have to be called perceptual, as being derived through the instrumentality of a sense; and a *reductio ad absurdum* would follow.

It would appear, then, that these arguments move in a circle. An indriya is defined as the source of immediate knowledge, and immediate knowledge as that derived through an indriya. As the two conceptions are made mutually interdependent it is difficult to understand exactly their specific characters. This difficulty is realized by Gaṃgeśa,[1] who revises the old definition of perception in terms of indriya and offers an independent one, namely, "Perception is knowledge that is not derived through the instrumentality of other knowledge"—jñānākaraṇakam jñānam.[2] Again, he defines indriya in a roundabout way so as to make it independent of perception. An indriya is said as to be "the locus (or medium) of contact (or relation, conjunction) between the mind and an object when that contact is the cause of knowledge other than memory."[3] But even in the light of this new definition, the conception of mind as an indriya is not altogether free from difficulty. In the case of external perception, the contact of the mind with an external object is established, it is true, through sense as the medium. But in the case of internal perception also we are to suppose (according to the definition) that the contact of the mind with an object, say a pleasure, is established again through the medium of the mind. Thus even in internal perception we are required to distinguish between mind as a term of the relation and mind as the medium of relation, which latter alone would be called the indriya. But is there any ground for believing that even in internal perception the mind requires a medium for reaching the object ? Even if we assume that there are two

1 Tattvacintāmaṇi, p. 552

2 Ibid.

3 Tattvacintāmaṇi : "Indriyatvam ca smṛtyajanaka-jñāna-hetu-manas-saṃyogāśrayatvam," p. 550.

distinct modes, corresponding to these two distinct aspects of the mind, the difficulty still remains. For if the first mode cannot reach the object independently, how can the second one, which is equally mental, reach it ? Why should not the second also requre a third and that a fourth, an so on *ad infinitum* ? So it would appear that this distinction is absolutely artificial. It is based on the unwarranted supposition that an internal perception should correspond to an external perception in every respect, factor for factor, and consequently that even here also there must be some indriya to serve as the medium, even though the necessity of a medium is not evident here as in the case of external perception. Thus we find that there are not sufficient grounds on which mind can be regarded as an indriya even in the sense in which Gaṃgeśa defines it. As soon as we realize the special character of internal perception, and admit that here the mind can independently reach its object, as the Naiyāyikas also must ultimately admit, the necessity of calling mind an indriya disappears.

We can now answer the second question, namely : Has the answer to the first question any special relation to the vedāntic position in general ? By summing up all that has been already said, we find that there are two reasons which make it necessary to regard mind as an indriya. The first reason is that if mind be not an indriya we cannot regard internal perception as perception; perception in this theory being derivable only through sense. The second reason is that if mind be not an indriya, there is nothing that can serve as the medium of the contact of mind with its object in internal perception. According to the Vedāntins perception, as we have already mentioned, is to be defined not as knowledge derived through sense, but as immediate knowledge; according to this view immediacy, and not sense-origin, is the intrinsic characteristic of perceptual knowledge. Thus the first reason carries no weight with a Vedāntin. The second reason also does not appeal to him, because in his opinion the object of an internal perception such as pleasure is a mode of antaḥkaraṇa or mind itself, and as such it is directly revealed to the self without the help of any further medium; it is, therefore, said to be kevala-sākṣibhāsya (an object to the unaided self). We find then that arguments that might compel others to consider mind to be a sense, have no force for the Vedāntins. There is also another important point to consider. In the vedāntic theory knowledge or consciousness, as we have said, it not a product. The antaḥkaraṇa can thus be regarded only as a factor in the modification of the already existing consciousness, and not as an instrument in the generation of knowledge as the Naiyāyikas and others suppose it to be. It appears to us, therefore, that though some Vedāntins hold with the majority of the thinkers of other schools that manas or antaḥkaraṇa is an indriya, the opposite theory as advocated by the authors of the Vivaraṇa[1] and the Vedānta-paribhāṣā is more in consonance with the general outlook of the vedāntic school.

As to the third point of divergence, whereas the Naiyāyikas consider mind to be of the infinitesimal order of dimension (aṇu-parimāṇa), the Vedāntins consider it to be of medium dimension (madhyama-parimāṇa). It is customary in Indian philosophy to discuss the dimension (parimāṇa) of every substance. Three orders of dimension are distinguished, namely the infinitesimal (aṇu), the medium (madhyama) and the infinite (parama-mahat). The infinitesimal are the partless, indivisible substances, e.g. the atoms. The medium are conceived as having parts. The reason why the Naiyāyikas think that mind is an infinitesimal substance is that mind can take note of only one object at a time; had it been not partless and atomic, we could know through the different parts of the mind different things at a time. The Vedāntins, however, hold that mind is a finite substance which has parts, because it is a created substance, and every created substance must necessarily be composed of parts. This proof they think, is too conclusive to allow any surmise to the contrary.

We thus arrive at the conception of mind as obtained in Indian philosophy in general, and in the vedāṇtic philosophy in particular. We shall now try briefly to understand these conception in the light of parallel theories of Western philosophy.

In Western psychology mind is conceived both as a subject and an object. In self-consciousness the mind is said to become its own object. In Vedānta philosophy, as is evident from the foregoing discussion, the difference between mind as the subject and mind as the object is conceived to be a fundamental difference in quality, and to be too great to justify the use of a common appelation for both. Consequently the two are regarded as two distinct entities and not two aspects or functions of the one entity, mind. Mind as subject is the self—the ātman—and the mind as object is the manas or antaḥkaraṇa.[2]

The principle of this distinction, however, has come to be recognized in contemporary Western philosophy by some idealists as well as by some

1 i.e., Pañcapādikā-vivaraṇa by Prakāśātman.

2 It is to be remembered, however, that manas is a product of nescience, and, therefore, only an *apparent* substance, that is illusory *sub specis aeternitatis*

realists. The Italian idealist, Gentile,[1] has laid the greatest emphasis on the "subject" that is never the "object," the subject that is known not as an object, but through the enjoyment of "a certain feeling of life." This pure subject would then correspond to the ātman of Indian philosophy in this respect. But it should be noted that the subject is called mind—not self. Some realistic thinkers also, though from an opposite motive, distinguish the two aspects of an experience, the act and the object. Lloyd Morgan calls the former "ing" and the latter "ed." Alexander[2] also follows the distinction. According to him, also, the former (e.g. perceiving, imagining, thinking, etc.) are mental, mind or consciousness being known only through self-enjoyment. The latter class or the "ed" includes percept, image, thought, which are called objects; they are known through contemplation. In this theory, then, mind as enjoyed would resemble the Indian ātman, whereas mind as the object of contemplation (which is declared to be non-mental) would resemble manas or antaḥkaraṇa of Indian Philosophy.

3. The Function of Mind (Antaḥkaraṇa) in Perception

In the the foregoing pages we have developed the vedāntic conceptions of mind (manas). We are now in a position to ascertain its function in perception.

According to the Vedāntins, in the perception of an external object the mind (manas or antaḥkaraṇa) goes out to the object through the indriyas, the senses. The senses, as we have already seen, are not conceived as passively receiving the stimuli that happen to come from the object, but are thought of as themselves going out to reach the object. The blind senses move, however, under the impulse and guidance of antaḥkaraṇa—rather the ātman as identified with antaḥkaraṇa. The senses, therefore, act as the vehicle of the movement of antaḥkaraṇa towards the object. On reaching the object the antaḥkaraṇa is identified with it, just as the water, going out of a tank through a drain to a tub, assumes the form of the tub on reaching it. But the mere fact of antaḥkaraṇa assuming the form of the object does not explain the knowledge of the object. Antaḥkaraṇa, as we have seen, is on a par with the material, the unconscious. So the

1 In *Mind asPure Act.*

2 *Space, Time and Deity*, vol. i. pp. 11-12.

modification of an antaḥkaraṇa, by itself, cannot amount to knowledge. The vṛtti or the mode of antaḥkaraṇa is illuminated by the ātman, the cit, which is there as the observer (Sākṣin) of all changes. In all empirical experiences the antaḥkaraṇa and the ātman remain identified or fused together, just as in a red-hot iron ball, fire and iron remain indistinguishably blended together. Hence a change of antaḥkaraṇa can enjoy the light of the self that is indistinguishably identified with it, and thus knowledge becomes possible.

In this explantion of the process of perception there are three points that require critical consideration. They are (1) the going out of the antaḥkaraṇa to the object; (2) antaḥkaraṇa's assuming the form of the object; (3) the relation of the vṛtti and its object with the self (ātman). We shall deal with them in this order.

As to the first point, we note that the mind is said to go out like a material object. We have already found that mind, as antaḥkaraṇa or manas, is regarded by almost all Indian thinkers as a natural object, only of a subtler type; and that the Vedāntins consider it to be also finite in dimension; the movement of the mind is thus not to be regarded as metaphorical, but actual. In Western philosophy the mental was formerly regarded as opposed to the spatial, and movement of the mind in space was regarded as a direct contradiction. In the theories of some modern realistic thinkers, however, the opposition between the mental and the material or spatial has been considerably minimised. Some thinkers (like Russell)[1] consider matter and mind as but different arrangements of the same neutral particulars. Some others (like Titchener)[2] hold the theory of psycho-physical parallelism according to which also mind and matter—the psychological and the physical—are not two different types of existents, but two parallel aspects of the same experience. Some others again (like Alexander)[3] consider both matter and mind as the evolutes of one primary stuff, viz. space-time. In the light of these new theories, then, neither the commonsense view of mind as found in its location and the description of its swift motion, etc., nor the vedāntic theory of its going out, would appear so absurd as it would seem to be in the light of the old Cartesian notions.

1 *Analysis of Mind.*

2 In *Text Book of Psychology.*

3 *Space, Time and Deity.*

But even while admitting in the light of the foregoing notions that the movement of the mind in space is not absurd or impossible, one may yet doubt whether in the case of perception the mind need necessarily be thought of as going out to the object. In Western philosophy, even those who do not hold (with Locke) that the mind is a *tabula rasa* on which external influences write their impressions, or with Russell[1] that in perception the standpoint of the observer is the "passive point," whereas that of the object is the "active point," but hold with the idealists that in perception the subject also is active as much as the object, do not admit the necessity of the mind's going to the object. In their view the activity of the mind does not consist in collecting impressions from outside but in receiving them when they happen to come, converting them into knowledge or experience and adjusting them to the environment. So the vedāntic theory will scarcely be accepted by any section of Western thinkers. Those who take the mental and the physical to be closely allied in character, either consider mind to be non-substantial and consequently incapable of motion, or consider it to be passive in the case of perception. Again, those who consider mind to be active in perception either consider mind to be absolutely non-spatial, and consequently its movement in space positively contradictory, or take the activity of mind to consist only in working up the raw material of impressions supplied by the senses. The Indian view, specially advocated by the Advaitins, that even in the collection of raw materials mind co-operates with sense, requires special explanation. A complete removal of all doubts about the vedāntic view would lead us beyond the limited scope of this enquiry. We shall present only a few considerations which will indicate broadly the necessity and plausibility of the vedāntic hypothesis. To the ultra-empiricists, who have a few descendants still surviving, we try to carry no conviction, since their theories have been sufficiently exposed and refuted by a long line of philosophers. Our remarks will be addressed only to those who admit that mind is capable of spontaneous activity of some kind. Now these thinkers generally hold that in perception the mind shows no activity prior to the activity of the senses, except perhaps in the few cases where perception is preceded by a positive will to perceive. What we should like to point out, however, is that even in such contrary cases as the sudden prick of a needle or the unexpected sound of thunder, the mind takes the lead.

1 *Analysis of Mind*, p. 130.

Not that in such cases there is any definite volition of the ordinary kind, preceding sense-impression. What we mean is that even in such cases attention, though chiefly engaged in someother direction, is in part, however small, left available for use even in this so-called unexpected direction. Otherwise sense itself would be incapable of receiving the touch or the sound, as often happens in deep sleep or rare cases of the total absorption of attention or total absent-mindedness. The ordinary view that the senses act first and then the mind, rests on the gross notion that the physiological organs are the senses and that affection of these organs means impression on the senses. But this notion cannot be ultimately upheld. Changes in the physiological organs due to external stimuli may be possible even in dead organisms, which however have no resultant knowledge. *Senses are senses in so far as they are the channels through which the mind seeks or tends to know the extrnal world.* The vibration of nerve-ends, the transmission of nerve-energy or the creation of chemical changes are all significant in so far as they represent the activities of the mind in its attempts to approach the external world. In Western psychology those who consider knowledge to be the product of physiological changes raise the puzzle how the physical can end in the mental. In fact however, in the process of perception, the mental is not the terminus of a preceding physical process. The activity of the mind is present from the very initial stages, though it may not always be conscious of its activity. At the terminating point of knowledge the activity of the mind only attains consummation and fruition of a long unconscious process. At every moment of our normal waking life, the mind flows out through the various channels of the senses. When I am reading a book, my mind may be chiefly engaged in the apprehension of its contents, it may be chiefly operating through the eyes and the particular region of the brain necessary for this work, but it does not even then totally forsake the other channels, through which, perchance, the sound of thunder or the prick of a pin, not previously anticipated consciously, may be received. So even in these rare cases of unexpected knowledge, there is a previous adjustment—however vague and general—on the part of the mind to receive an impression; the process of knowledge, therefore, is initiated by the mind though not with a conscious will.

But even if it be admitted, on the strength of the grounds stated above, that in perception mind acts prior to sense by pre-adjusting attention to the object, it may yet be asked whether it is not sufficient for the mind to attend to its object from within the organism without going out to the object. In reply, it may be said that when we perceive an external object our attention is directed not to the physiological changes caused by the object within the organism but to the object itself, outside in space. And in fixing attention on an object mind comes into direct contact with it. In this respect popular conceptions are in the right. Unsophisticated people always think and speak of mind as wandering from object to object moving with the speed of lightning, being present somewhere and absent from somewhere else. These descriptions agree with our direct experience and can also stand the test of philosophical criticism. The general Western view is that in perception, mind does not go out to the object, but only receives the stimuli coming from the object. It seems strange that even throughgoing realists do not challenge this customary analysis, in consistency with which our knowledge of the external world can at best be an inference; representationism being the only logical conclusion of such a theory of perception. But without direct contact with the external world we could hardly have even an inference about it from its supposed physiological effects. To take the case of visual perception, it is extremely doubtful whether from the retinal pictures of external objects we could construct the external world of three dimensions as we have it now. Some Western psychologists make elaborate efforts to explain how from the distribution of light and shade in the retinal pictures we obtain, through inference, the world of three dimensions. What we should like to emphasize, as regards such an account, is that without previous knowledge of the external, the mere distribution of light and shade or other local signs would remain mere qualities of pictures painted on a level screen. No Herculean effort of inference could make us project our internal percepts into external space and see them in their real order, magnitude and dimensions. The vedāntic view that mind goes out to meet its object in perception is, therefore, not at all unreasonable, supported as it is by common sense as well as philosophical speculation. The knowledge of the external world is explained by this theory far more simply and easily than by any alternative theory mentioned above. This will be more evident when we consider the second point of our discussion, to which we pass next.

The second point to be noted is the vedāntic statement that the mind takes the form of the object on meeting it. To Western thinkers this part of the theory would appear most difficult, if not positively grotesque. But on closer consideration it will be found that this theory also does not altogether lack the support of good reasons. To those who are acquainted with the history of modern Western psychology, the problem of the acquisition of the form of percept must be well known. According to the commonly accepted Western theory, when an object, say a tree, is perceived, different parts of the tree send their respective stimuli, and thus different sensations are obtained. The difficulty therefore arises as to how, from these different unitary sensations, we acquire the knowledge of the object as a whole in all its form and dimensions. The structural school has sought to meet this difficulty by supposing that the individual sensation atoms, with their respective intensities, local characters and other peculiar properties, arrange themselves into a compound that thereby produces in the mind, also, the form of the original external object. They have further attempted to formulate laws of association, fusion, colligation, etc., according to which the atomic sensations combine to form the mental compounds. But this theory rests on a belief in some mysterious coincidence and ignores, as James pointed out, the differences and uniqueness of the various grades of mental phenomena. It has, therefore, naturally met with opposition from different quarters. Various attempts have been made to avoid the difficulty of the automatic combination of blind sensations. The functional school, headed by Stout and others, has admitted the existence of a purposive mind with the power to adjust itself to different situations. The "Act psychologists" led by Brentano, again, have distinguished the act from the contact of a mental phenomenon, and have taken the act to be the unifying and combining principle. Some again, like Ward, have thought it necessary to admit the existence of a self. But though these theories have in different ways partially solved the difficulty of the blind and chance combination of sensations, by positing an intelligent and purposive or unifying principle, the fundamental difficulty of the atomistic or structural view has been left untouched. For starting, as they all do, from the individual piecemeal sensations arising out of the impressions created by the stimuli sent by external objects, they can scarcely arrive at the object as it is actually perceived, even with the help of such an internal principle. Two more important attempts to escape these difficulties have been made. The behaviourist school has cut the Gordian knot by altogether throwing overboard the introspective method which has been considered the source of all these puzzling questions; they have destroyed the fears of subjective spectres by withdrawing attention from the direction in which they are to be met. But a more reasonable approach has been made by the group of German thinkers associated with Werthimer, Koffka and Köhler, who comprise the famous *Gestalt* school of modern psychology. These thinkers have substituted the synthetic attitude in the place of the analytic, which has been regarded as the parent of all the confusion and difficulties besetting the atomistic theories. In their view the form of the object as we perceive it is not a subsequent construction out of primary piece-meal atomic sensations; the form is given in experience as a whole structure—a *Gestalt ab initio*—and it is only by subsequent conceptual analysis that we arrive at the elements. In the place of the "smiple stimulus of psycho-physics" they speak of a "stimulus situation" or a "stimulus whole" or a "physical *Gestalt*." "In regard to the physiological conditions, the *Gestalt* school maintains that local processes in the sense-organs or in the cortical centres cannot explain psychic wholes. For instance the perception of movement cannot be explained in terms of after sensations. The local and the brain processes must be structural wholes real in character. No part of the excitation reaches consciousness before the whole does."[2] There arises thus the "conception not only of a psychic *Gestalt*, but also of a physical *Gestalt* and a physiological *Gestalt*." Proceeding a step farther, we can even "speak of one *Gestalt*, the total situation, including the physical, the physiological and the psychical,"[3] the three *Gestalten* being but three phases of one and the same situation.

Though the vedāntic view may appear crude in the light of the ruling ideas of Western psychology, it may yet receive some support from the criticism and theories of the *Gestalt* school, the purport of whose views on the knowledge of forms is given above. It will be noted that unlike other psychologists, the *Gestalt* school speaks of the physiological Gestalt which consists of the whole form of the object, a whole that is not a compound constructed out of many simply separate stimuli, but obtained as a whole from the very beginning.[4] And according to the Vedāntins also

1 For information about this School I am indebted to : (1) An Article "On Gestalt Theory" by Sengupta in *Indian Journal of Psychology*, vol. ii, No. 2. (2) Two articles on "Psychology of Gestalt" by Harry Helsone, *American Journal of Psychology*. (3) Articles by Koffka and Köhler, in *Psychologies of 1925* (The school is widely known now—2nd ed.).

2 "On Gestalt Theory," (Sengupta), *Indian Journal of Psychology*. Vol. ii, No. 2. p. 64.

3 Ibid.

4 Cf. "A percept is not a sum of independent elements, nor a mental combination of such, but primarily a unitary structure." Koffka, "Psychical and Physical Structures," *Psyche*, July, 1924, p. 81; quoted in *Indian Journal of Psychology*. vol. ii. No. 2, p. 63.

the antaḥkaraṇa, which may be regarded as an instrumental and intermediate principle standing midway between the object and the self,[1] receives the perceived object as a whole by assuming its form. The mode of the antaḥkaraṇa (antaḥkaraṇa-vṛtti) having the form of the object can be to a certain extent compared, then, to the physiological *Gestalt*, with this difference, that whereas the vedāntic vṛtti is regarded as the result of the interaction between the mind and its object, the physiological *Gestalt* (or the psychical) is not considered to be the result of such interaction. The physical, the physiological and psychical being but three phases differentiated out of a single fact, interaction is altogether meaningless according to the *Gestalt* theory. The point on which we cite the evidence of this new theory is, however, the existence or formation of a physiological and a psychical *Gestalt* or *form*, corresponding to the form of the object (the physical *Gestalt*) in the case of perception.

But this point can also be demonstrated in an independent way, through a study of the character of images. Images are commonly regarded as purely mental. But their objective character and especially the physical characteristics of extendedness, etc., which some images possess, make it difficult to call them mental in the sense in which thinking, feeling, willing or even perceiving can be called mental. In consideration of this fact, some philosophers (Russell, Alexander) have tried to class images with the physical. Alexander thinks that the memory image of a table is the physical table itself seen through the distance of space and time.[2] This view is as untenable as the opposite views. If images cannot be classed with the purely mental, because they are known as objects through contemplation, whereas the latter are known in enjoyment and never as objects, neither can they be classed with common physical objects. For though images are found to possess the spatial properties of extension, objectivity, etc., as ordinary physical objects do, there are yet important differences which cannot be overlooked. Space as sensed and space as imaged are by no means one and the same, as Alexander seems to think; the former is public and is forced on the mind, whereas the latter is uniquely private and bears the sense of being created. Whereas the mind feels fettered in sensing an object, it feels a greater freedom in imaging an object—in willing it into and out of existence or even in changing its

1 Vide Pañcapādika-vivaraṇa (Lazarus, Benares, 1892), p. 70

2 Alexander, *Space, Time and Deity*, vol. i, pp. 24-25.

form and position at pleasure. These considerations alone should stand in the way of identifying images with physical objects. But there are many other difficulties. Even speaking of a memory image alone, we may have the image of an object that exists no more (as the image of a dead person), or we may have the image of an object presented in a previous perceptual illusion. In these cases it will be extremely difficult, if not impossible, to place the images outside the sphere of private experience and identify them with a physical object. But when we come to constructive imagination our difficulties in identifying them with physical objects increase still further.

We are thus forced to conclude that images can be classed neither with the purely psychical—the self, or the mental act, or the "ing,"as it may variously be called—nor with the purely physical such as tables and trees. We must place them midway between the two. In other words, we are to recognize that between the purely psychical and the purely objective there is a region that partakes partially of the nature of both, though it can be wholly identified with neither. This intermediate region extends, as it were, across the gulf that otherwise seems to separate the mental from the physical—the self from the not-self—and renders the whole of existence from the psychical to the physical continuous. The antaḥkaraṇa with all its modifications might be considered as belonging to this region. From the standpoint of Vedāntic metaphysics, the antaḥkaraṇa is but the subject in its objective attitude—the lapse of the ātman from pure, undifferentiated experience into the sinful duality of seeking an "other." It marks, therefore, the transition of consciousness from pure subjectivity towards objectivity. It serves as a mediating principle through which the subject knows its object.

If we understand antaḥkaraṇa to be made of the same stuff as that of images, there will be little difficulty in understanding the view that the antaḥkaraṇa can assume the forms of objects. For images of tables, chairs and trees, etc., are always found to possess the forms of these objects. At the time of perception, however, the object and the mode of antaḥkaraṇa that receives its form (i.e., the image of the object in the antaḥkaraṇa) remain identified, and then we know only the object and not its image. But when the object, is somehow removed from sense, we are left with the image alone in memory. It is thus that we have the experience of an image distinct from the object — though even then the image, as the copy, may not cease referring to the object, the original. This image or the antaḥkaraṇa-vṛtti is found to possess the form of the object perceived in the past, and it is through this mode (vṛtti) that we remember the object. But how can I have now in my mind the image of the past object which is no more presented to my sense ? The only reasonable answer to the question is that there is a certain principle that somehow records the form of the object when presented to sense, and it is through a reproduction of this record that I can call back to mind the form of the object at a subsequent moment. Antaḥkaraṇa would then be identical with this inner principle. From all this it will appear that the vedāntic theory, that in the perception of an object the antaḥkaraṇa takes the form of the object, is not at all unreasonable; there are, on the contrary, some very good reasons that place it on a fairly strong basis.

In the preceding pages we have inquired if the two points in the vedāntic psychology of perception, namely, the going out of the antaḥkaraṇa to the object and its assuming the form of the object, can be supported by any arguments based on the concepts of Western philosophy. We have found that the vedāntic ideas on this matter cannot be so easily brushed aside as crude or gross, as on first sight they may lead us to think; there are on the contrary some important considerations which confirm them. This concludes the psychological consideration of the vedāntic views of perception. The third point we promised to consider, viz., the place and function of the self in perception, will be dealt with in the next chapter, as this enquiry will lead us beyond the range of psychology proper into the domain of metaphysics and epistemology.

We should only add that the antaḥkaraṇa functions not only in perception and memory, but also in all other forms of mental dealing with objects, such as judging, inferring, imagining, forming ideas on the basis of words heard, and so on. In every one of these cases, there is an objective mode of the mind (antaḥkaraṇa-vṛtti). The only thing which is self-manifest, and does not need a mental mode, but on the contrary, illumines even the mode, is consciousness (cit) itself. But even the identity judgment of the Upaniṣad, namely 'I am Brahman,' which helps the self to realise its identity with the pure, self-manifest consciousness (=Brahman), has to be understood first with the help of a mental mode, a vṛtti of the antaḥkaraṇa, in the form of a judgment, though ultimately it ends in a non-relational subjective realization of selfmanifest consciousness that no longer needs the mode.

CHAPTER IV

THE PLACE AND FUNCTION OF THE SELF IN PERCEPTION

Perception involves a relation between the knowing self and its object. The conception of this relation is determined by the conceptions of the self and of the object. In vedāntic metaphysics the self, as well as the world of objects, has been variously conceived by different thinkers. Consequently the combination of each conception of the self with each of the conceptions of the objective world gives rise, theoretically, to one type of relation between the self and the object; and there would arise as many new contingencies as the number of such possible combinations. Some eminent writers (Madhusūdana Sarasvatī,[1] Brahmānanda Sarasvatī[2] Appayadīkṣita[3]) have reduced these contingent relations to three general types. We shall follow this general plan instead of going into the complicated and somewhat uninteresting details of the different conceptions of the individual self and the world and the possible combinations arising therefrom.

The three types of relations result from the three different ways in which an individual, and consequently the world, are conceived to be constituted. One class of thinkers holds that the knower, the individual self, is finite and limited; it is, therefore, neither all-pervasive (sarvagata) nor the ground or material cause (upādāna) of the phenomenal world. A second class of thinkers regards the individual self as allpervasive and unlimited, but not as the material cause of the world. A third class of thinkers again maintains that the individual self is both all-pervasive and the ground of this universe. Let us consider these views one by one, with the nature of the relation between the self and the object in perception resulting from each.

To understand these theories we must clearly understand the meanings of infinitude and all-pervasiveness, and finitude or limitedness, in regard to the self. We should bear in mind that pervasion and limitation cannot be applied in ordinary senses to the self, which is always conceived to be non-spatial. To the self limitation comes by way of objectivity; a self is

1 Advaita-siddhi, pp. 478 f.

2 Gauḍa-brahmānandī on the above.

3 Siddhāntaleśa-saṃgraha, chap. I.

limited in so far as it has an "other" —a not-self—to oppose it. From the epistemological standpoint the existence of an "other" means also a possible source of ignorance about that other. Thus limitation virtually means ignorance on the part of the self. In terms of will, again, limitation comes to mean external determination. Now the Advaitins, as is well known, unanimously hold that the ātman, the self, is in truth the same as the Brahman—the Absolute. But the absoluteness of the ātman is a dream that is not realized in our ordinary experience. The self as the "Ego," the "I", has somehow come to appear as an individual—a jīva—and seems to have lost its absoluteness. The question, however, arises as to what degree or extent the jīva appears to have lost its absolute character. In other words, what are the nature and degree of this apparent bondage or limitation? To answer this question, one has to analyse the concept of the "Ego" or the "I" (aham), the ātman in its apparent bondage.

The first and the most obvious result of this analysis will be the conception of the Ego as a limited determined individual, which is but only out of many individuals. In support of such a conclusion it may be pointed out that the word "I," which connotes the individual self, is used to distinguish the self from all not-selves. So the very meaning of the word implies the existence of other realities and thereby proves the finiteness of the Ego. Again, the Ego is the object in self-consciousness, and as such it may also be said to be a determinate object. Lastly, the existence of many such selves can be easily inferred from the fact that the word "I" is used by different persons. The uses of such personal pronouns as "you," "he," "she," also point to this conclusion. The use of the first person plural—"we—" puts the conclusion beyond all doubt. The individual self is, therefore, found to be limited and finite.

Obvious and inevitable as this common-sense view may seem to be, it is not altogether unassailable. While admitting that the use of the word "I" implies the existence of an object from which it is distinguished, it may yet be maintained that the self is never known to exist side by side with the object in any such spatio-temporal relation as that in which two objects, like a chair and a table, can be said to exist. The distinguishing of the self from the object does not necessarily imply that the self and the object are both made the objects of the differentiating act. In distinguishing a chair from a table both become determinate objects of our consciousness, as the judgment "*This* chair is not *this* table," clearly shows. But in the case where the self is distinguished from an object, say the body, only the latter becomes the object of our knowledge and can be determined in space and time and specified as "this." The self is, however, known, in such a context, negatively; and the judgment expressing this negation would be "*This* (object) is not the self," and not "This object is not *this* self." Thus though found to be confronted with an objective world that is distinct from it and outside it, the Ego is never found as an object existing *pari passu* with other objects. The existence of objects therefore does not necessarily limit the self as two objects, like a chair and a table, limit each other. On the contrary, the ego being distinguished from all objects is found to be distinct from the finite—the determinate. It should be described therefore as infinite and unlimited. The plurality of individuals or egos, also, is not so easily established as commonsense thinks it to be. Number can be used only of determinate objects and not of the self, which defies all objectivity. That different persons use the word "I" only means that by these subjectivity is shared alike; that is to say, that ultimately the same self is identified with and functions through different organisms. As identified with or appearing through these different centres, it also appears as different. Consequently there arise the appearances of the many selves, even as the sun reflected in different mirrors appears to be many. Of the personal pronouns again, "you" and "he" or "she" are not on a per with "I". The former are used of persons known objectively, and consequently their subjectivity or selfhood cannot be known as such. The existence of other minds can be imagined only through a projection of our own minds into other centres. It is an act of sympathetic imagination which scarcely amounts to objective knowledge. Nor does the first person plural necessarily imply the plurality of selves. On the contrary the fact that "I," "you" and "he" can together function as "we," shows that the range of subjectivity or selfhood can be widened beyond the usual "I," to include other centres which generally lie outside the pale of subjectivity. In the concept of the "we," then, we have an instance of the possibility of the same selfhood combining or running through the many centres which appear to be different. It is because I realize the existence of another mind only through a projection of myself that it is possible to absorb it again into subjectivity in the consciousness of the "we." The most convincing evidence of the same individual functioning or appearing as different egos can be found, however, in our daily experiences in which we split ourselves up into an "I" and a "thou" and sit in judgment upon ourselves. In a moment of self-condemnation we often say : "*I* am ashamed of what *thou* hast done." Thus the common-sense view of the multiplicity of finite and individual subjects comes to be replaced by the view of one universal subject, appearing through many centres which are mistaken to be independent subjects. The world of objects is *given* to this subject and is independent of it. The individual self is thus found to be all-pervasive or infinite, but not the creator or cause of the objective world.

The process leading from the first or common-sense view of the ego to the second, just stated, may now be carried a step farther. It may be said that the ego or the knowing self is not merely universal, but is also the ground of the objective world; that though the self is independent of its object, the entirely depends on the self for its existence; that if the self is really infinite there cannot be an objective world independent and outside of the self.[1]

These three views, which we have tried to deduce independently from an analysis of the concept of the ego, would represent the three different conceptions of the self and the object, held by different schools of vedāntic thinkers, as previously outlined. It is now necessary to pursue the relation of each of these conceptions of the self with the object and with the process of sense-perception.

According to the first view (i.e., that the individual self is finite and limited), the objective world comes to acquire an existence outside and independent of the individual self. Thus the perception of an object on this view means that a connection, previously non-existent, is set up between the knowing self and its object. This connection is established through the mediating principle, the antaḥkaraṇa. Now it should be remembered that according to the vedāntins all determinate existences, the individual self as well as the world of objects, are but the illusory determinations of the same consciousness—the self-shining Brahman. On the view under discussion the object, being independent of the individual self, shines not through the light of the self, but through that of Brahman itself that underlies the object.[2] In other words, that the object appears or reveals itself means that the absolute consciousness reveals itself as the object. The question therefore arises why the same consciousness should

1 *vide* Ānandabodha-bhaṭṭārakācārya's Nyāya-makaranda, Kṣetrajña-bheda-nirāsa, and jñeya-bheda-nirāsa.

2 Cf. Advaita-siddhi, p. 479.

reveal itself now as a table and again as a tree, or why when the distant tree or the table presents its visible qualities, we do not also feel its tangible qualities or have its smell. In order to explain this *casual and selective nature of perception,*[1] the advocates of this view must affirm that consciousness, as object, appears only in the form in which it affects the antaḥkaraṇa. Though the consciousness underlying the self and the objects is the same, the two appear to be different owing to two different modes that determine the same consciousness differently in the two cases. The determining factor in the case of the knowing self is the antaḥkaraṇa, and in the case of the object the particular group of properties which qualify it into that peculiar object; both these sets of determinants are again ultimately constituted by ajñāna. In the case of perception, then, the antaḥkaraṇa by going out and assuming the character of the object removes to *that extent* the distinction between the two sets of differentiating factors, peculiar to subject and object respectively, and thereby establishes and identity between consciousness as subject and consciousness as object. The advocates of this theory maintain, therefore, that the necessity for the going out of antaḥkaraṇa to the object lies in the *revelation of an identity* existing between the self and the object (abhedābhivyakti).[2]

The author of the Vedānta-paribhāṣā subscribes to this view. He discusses at some length the causes that constitute immediacy (pratyakṣatva). Since we shall have occasion to consider this view later on, we may pass on to the second view referred to above.

According to the second view the individual self is not finite; it is universal. But its universality does not mean that all objects, at all times, are present to it as such. Just as a logical concept (like "Cowness")[3] in spite of its universality applies only to the individuals subsumed under it and not to other individuals, so the individual self in spite of its universality lights up only those objects which appear to it through the medium of the antaḥkaraṇa. But there is a sense in which the self can be said to be universal in a more unrestricted sense. The self is aware of all objects at all times; some being known positively and other negatively. That the self knows objects directly presented to it is of course obvious. But even in the cases of objects which are not positively so presented, the self can be said to

1 Technically called Pratikarmavyavasthā.

2 Advaita-siddhi, *loc. cit.*, and also Siddhāntaleśa-saṃgraha, chap. I.

3 Advaita-siddhi, p. 479.

know them, though not as present but as unknown. On being aware of an object for the first time the self remembers that it was not aware of it before. This memory clearly implies that even before the presentation of the object there was a consciousness of its non-presentation to consciousness. Thus the self may be said to be always aware of all objects, both presented and not presented to consciousness. Hence the vedāntic dictum—"Everything is lighted up by the witnessing consciousness, either as known or as unknown."[1]

The recognition of the truth of this does not, however, amount to the annulment of the vast difference that exists between the awareness of an object as known and the awareness of an object as unknown. We can for ourselves distinguish three stages or grades of the awareness of an object. They are illustrated in the three distinct experiences which we have for instance (1) in trying to imagine a face without success, (2) in successfully imagining it and (3) in perceiving it. At the first stage of awareness, the face is only a possible object, objectivity of the face a mere promise. The face is, therefore, an object that is yet unknown. At the second stage, the possibility is clearly demonstrated, the foretaste of the object being given in the image in *mere* thought. At the third and the last stage, the promise of objectivity is actually realized, in perception.

Now in the second stage there is accommodation on the part of the subject to receive the object, but still the object does not reveal itself. This only shows that a mere will to know, on the part of the self, does not amount to knowledge; other conditions for the revelation of the object must also be fulfilled. These conditions are the going out of the senses, and through them of the antaḥkaraṇa, to the object and so forth. As the antaḥkaraṇa assumes the form of the object, the self identified with the antaḥkaraṇa comes to have a direct tinge of the object. This objective tinge of the subject is called ciduparāga (the tinging of the pure consciousness), and it is held that the neccessity of the going out of the antaḥkaraṇa lies in effecting this tinge (ciduparāga). This, then, is the significance of the perceptive process in the second view. The author of the Vivaraṇa and some others advocate this position.

According to the third class of thinkers, the self is infinite and is also the ground of this world. It is easy to see, then that on this view the individual self becomes identical with God as immanent in the world.

1 "Sarvam vastu jñātatayā vā ajñātatayā vā sākṣi-caitanyasya viṣaya eva." —Vivaraṇa, p. 13.

Everything, therefore, is not only a possible object to the self, but has its being in the self. The question why in that case all objects should not be always perceived, does not present any real difficulty. Our ideas are admitted by all to be nowhere else than in our mind, yet we find that an idea may be present to consciousness at one time, absent at some other time (when it is forgotten) and again come back to consciousness (When it is remembered once more). Though all ideas are equally present in the self, they must struggle with one another to come to the focus or float up to the surface of consciousness. So even within our self there exist forces that can prevent an idea from attaining consciousness. These forces constitute the veil of ignorance. From what we can learn about such ideas, it becomes easy to see that even the so-called external objects may be within the self and yet may not be always perceived. It is only when the antagonistic forces are removed and the veil of ignorance is lifted that a particular object floats up to the surface of consciousness. It is held, therefore, that the activity of the antaḥkaraṇa in the case of perception consists in rending the veil of ignorance (āvaraṇā-bhibhava).[1] This, then, is the interpretation of the perception of the perceptual process according to the third view.

We have considered, one by one, three types of vedāntic theories about the self and the world, and also the explanations they offer as to the relation of the self to the object in perception. To judge the relative merits of these three different types of theory we should discuss in detail the metaphysical theories of the self and the world, which would lead to an unnecessary digression. We may leave this matter with the remark that the Ego, the "I," as it is used in different contexts, yields when analysed such a wide latitude of meanings, from the mere physiological organism to the pure subject that transcends all objectivity, that in forming a philosophical conception of the self, any one of the different aspects may be considered as fundamental and the rest may be explained as secondary, derivative and illusory. Thus from an empirical point of view, each one of the resulting theories may be regarded as a possible hypothesis. So far as the vedantic theories presented here are concerned, it is necessary to point out that in spite of their differences there are some points of unity as well.

Whatever be his theory of the Jīva or the individual self, every Vedāntin holds that in all knowledge there is present the self-shining

1 " Jīvasya jagadupādānatve āvaraṇābhibhavārthā " —Siddhāntavindu quoted in Advaita-siddhi, p. 479.

transcendent light of consciouness which imparts to the object its character of immediacy. Consciousness in this aspect its character of immediacy. Consciousness in this aspect or context is called the Sākṣin or the witness. It is so called because it is conceived as the impartial spectator which takes no part in the ever-changing process of knowledge, but only lights it up or passively witnesses it. However individualized, finite, and determinate the self or consciousness may appear to be, it retains yet this aspect of transcendence. In consequence of this unanimous assertion of the existence of the witnessing light of consciousness, we also discover a common point of agreement among the different views as to the function of the antaḥkaraṇa in perception. For the three different views referred to above, namely the theories of abhedābhivyakti, ciduparāga and āvaraṇābhibhava, are found when analysed to contain the common element that perception takes place only when the object is brought into connection with the self or the witnessing consciousness, either by the revelation of an identify between the two through a removal of the differentiating factors, or by the tinging of the self with the form of the object, or by the removal of the veil of ignorance that hangs between the self and the object. The nature of the relation that is established between the witnessing consciousness or the self, as the passive observer (Sākṣin), and the object perceived, is admitted by all to be one of adhyāsa, i.e. erroneous identification of the one with the other. We shall critically consider these points on which there is general agreement among all vedāntic thinkers.

The understanding of these views in the light of Western philosophy is beset with many difficulties. There are first of all many theories of consciousness, from an identification of it with mere physiological processes to the flat denial of its existence. Secondly, there are the many conflicting theories about the relation of the mind to the object of perception advanced by those who admit the existence of consciousness. To make the vedāntic theories appear at all plausible we have, therefore, to consider these antagonistic views. In the present connection we can do this only partially and summarily.

The predominant theories minimizing the facts of consciousness are almost all inspired by theories of biology and evolution. If evolution is to be true there must be an unbroken continuity from protozoa to man; if the animal is to be regarded as the true ancestor of man, the human mind no less than the human body has to be explained as a mere development out of, or a more complex organization of, what existed in the forerunner.

Thus the human mind has come to be considered as a mere refinement of instincts and reflexes. Introspection, which has been regarded as the method that reveals the existence of forms of consciousness higher than those found in lower animals, has necessarily to be rejected as spurious and misleading. Russell has called in the eyidence of psycho-analysis to show that others can know more accurately about our hidden desires through the study of our behaviour than we ourselves can through introspection. It has been generally assumed, therefore, that the human mind cannot be studied through introspection. But must be studied exactly in the same way as the animal mind, that is through the behaviour of man towards his environment.

Against this standpoint we may say that even if the theories of evolution be true, and there be really an unbroken continuity running through all the stages of evolution of the living world, it does not necessarily follow that the earliest stage should exhaustively explain all that apears at any later stage. From the unbroken continuity that can be found in the colours on the spectrum, one cannot argue that green is nothing but red or yellow. In fact, in spite of continuity there may be and really is the emergence of the new and the unique which cannot be explained away. Man has much in common with lower animals and that may serve as the link of continuity. But at the same time nothing but prejudice can prevent us from recognizing the existence of a whole range of high and complex thought, emotion and volition which are uniquely distinct from the mere instincts and reflexes of the lower stages. As regards the ban on introspections, we may say that it is not based on sound reasons. There are, it may be true, the few cases of repressed or unconscious desires which cannot be known through introspection; but from this it is extremely rash to generalize that we cannot know any of our mental states at any time in any other more direct way than by the study of external expressions or behaviour. On the contrary we directly experience, every moment of life, fine shades of emotion, volition and intellection which have little or no external expressions, and the existence of which would remain altogether unknown had there been no direct awareness of them. The study of behaviour is of great value for the knowledge of the mind of animals and also of human beings, but it is folly to exaggerate it and make it the only method of psychology. In fact, however, behaviourism itself implies the existence of a more direct way of knowing mentals facts. For behaviour is important not merely as a compound of some physical movements, but as expressing some meaning which it is supposed to possess. But this very search for a meaning in behaviour implies that the behaviour as the sumtotal of physical movements cannot be regarded as ultimate, that there is something behind them; and it is *that* something, non-physical, which is really the object of enquiry. If so, the question at once arises as to how that "something meant" comes to be sought for in the merely physical movements. This question can be answered only by confessing that we have in our own case for the first time experienced simultaneously external behaviour, and also a corresponding conscious state as something existing over and above the former. It is because we have a direct experience of this connection between the physical and the mental that, in other cases, where the one is given we seek its counterpart. So it would appear that behaviourism, if pressed to express its grounds, has to admit both the existence of something other than the merely physical, and also the existence of a method, other than behaviourism, of being aware of that something. In other words, both consciousness and a direct experience of it have to be conceded their rightful places.[1]

To come to a second class of thinkers, who while not denying consciousness altogether, deny that it is an entity, James may be considered as the sponsor of this line of thinking. "Undeniably," he says, "thoughts do exist. I mean only to deny that the word stands for an entity, but to insist most emphatically that it does stand for a function. There is, I mean, no aboriginal stuff or quality of being constrated with that of which material objects are made, out of which our thoughts of them are made, but there is a function in experience which thoughts perform and for the performance of which this quality of being is invoked. That function is knowing."[2] According to James both thoughts and "material objects" are derived from a third and primal stuff which he calls "pure experience." This experience itself sometimes functions as the subject and sometimes as the object. More recently the American realists and Bertrand Russell[3] also, to some extent, have advocated this theory of neutral stuff (or particulars or entities) being, by different arrangements, responsible for the appearances of the mental as well as the physical. A more or less similar view has recently been held by Morton Prince,[4] who has shown that if we realized the up-to-date scientific theory of the ultimate nature of matter as energy, there would be no difficulty in conceiving the

1 *Cf.* the modern emphasis on 'insight' by the Gestalt school.
2 *Essays in Radical Empiricism*, pp. 3-4.
3 In *Analysis* of Mind.
4 "Why the Body has a Mind" *Mind*, January 1928.

possibility of matter and mind being only different organizations of the same ultimate stuff. He calls his view scientific monism.

It is necessary to consider how far Vedāntins can accept or reject these views. As rigorous monists Vedāntins hold that thoughts as well as material objects are derived from a common stuff, called caitanya (i.e., consciousness). Just as James holds that the same stuff functions in certain contexts as the subject and in other contexts as the object, Vedāntins also hold that the subject (pramātā), the object (viṣaya), and knowledge (jñāna) are all only differentiations of the same caitanya. This caitanya may also be called "neutral" in so far as it partakes of the nature of neither thoughts nor objects. Besides, like the realists, the Vedāntins also credit neither objects nor our thoughts of them with the reality of self-subsisting entities. While James calls them "functions," and some of his followers call them "convenient fictions," they in a sense come very near the Vedāntins who regard them as facts possessing only practical value (vyāvahārikasattā). But a closer enquiry would reveal a great difference existing between "neutral stuff" and caitanya. The realists neither clearly define the nature of the neutral stuff, nor indicate how the determinate orders of existences come to function either as thought or as matter. James conceived the primal stuff to be "pure experience." But his successors realized that he had thereby come dangerously near the idealists; so they recoiled to indecision by withdrawing the definite word "pure experience" and keeping it mystically vague under the uncertain name of a "neutral" stuff.[1] But we feel that if the realistic position be pushed to its logical conclusion, the vedāntic theory may not appear to be very far from it.

It may be asked, for instance, how from the same neutral particular we have, as Russell says, by different groupings mnemic (or mental) phenomena and non-mnemic (or Physical) phenomena. Russell has introduced the imagery of a sensitive photographic plate to explain the work of the human brain in the presence of which mnemic phenomena arise. But this imagery carries no conviction whatever. For though both the brain and the plate may resemble one another as recording impressions, still there is all the difference of the mnemic and the non-mnemic between the two cases which itself requires explanation, and therefore remains unexplained by the imagery. Thus either the conception of neutral stuff must be abandoned or, accepting this conception as necessary for the explanation of perceived phenomena, the evolution of these phenomena

1 Russell : *Analysis of Mind, passim.*

from the primal stuff must be confessed to be inexplicable. The second alternative, which alone can help the realists to retain their theory, would then be on a par with the vedāntic conclusion that the evolution of the phenomena of thoughts and objects from the same caitanya is inexplicable (anirvacanīya). But another question, more pertinent to our present topic, can be addressed to the advocates of this theory of neutral particulars. How are the neutral particulars known to exist? This question does not seem to be considered seriously; yet it is of the supreme importance. For unless we have knowledge about these neutral entities, that is more definite and more certain than the knowledge of ordinary objects, we can in no way persuade ourselves to reject our deep-rooted common belief in the existence of the physical and mental entities, in favour of a belief in the existence of this new-fangled stuff. The ordinary physical and mental phenomena are the only things that we know of either through perception or through inference. We cannot even conceive of anything which is neither physical, nor psychical, nor partially both. The neutral stuff in its isolation would therefore appear to be not only indeterminate but also inconceivable. How is it possible then to speak about the inconceivable? Realists dare not cross this yawning chasm lest they go beyond their depths, leaving behind them the *terra firma* of objective certainty. Kant had to face the same difficulty in speaking of the reality lying behind phenomena—*das Ding an sich*. But he frankly confessed its unknowability.

The Vedāntin however does not experience this difficulty. To him the neutral reality, which appears now as the object and now as thought, is caitanya—the *self-shining truth*. Thus though it can never be known (that is, as an object) and can therefore be called "unknowable" (after Kant), yet it is possible to refer to it. The admission of the immediacy or self-manifesting character of the fundamental reality enables the Vedāntins to declare that thoughts and objects—the two most obvious popular categories of existence—are not ultimately real, and possess only a practical value. What is most interesting to note is that though the realists fail to justify the existence of the ultimate reality (i.e., the neutral stuff), being unable to show how it is known or spoken about, yet they are very emphatic in declaring the falsity of the popular entities in favour of this half-conceived hypothetical stuff. But the Vedāntins, though declaring firmly that the ultimate reality is immediately present to consciousness (sākṣāt aparokṣāt brahma), calmly assert that the falsity of the entities of popular belief is only an anticipation or promise which can be realized after a sustained effort (sādhanā) of recovering from the hypnotic spell under the influence of which the world has come to appear as such. So long as this effort is not crowned with success, the value of the popular empirical categories of subject and object, self and not-self, mental and physical, remains practically unaffected.

The only object of introducing the foregoing discussions, however, is to bring out the immediacy or self-manifesting nature of the ultimate reality, caitanya. Caitanya has been previously translated as "self-shining consciousness" for want of a better expression. But this rendering may create a certain misconception against which we should guard. Consciousness is identified with the mental and contrasted with the physical. But caitanya, as we have seen, is the reality, which, in its isolation, may be truly described as neutral both to mind and matter; it is the *fundamentum*, through the illusory differentiation of which we have the dualistic world of objects and their knowledge. From this it would follow also that while consciousness, as identical with knowledge, is always conceived to be "about" some object, "caitanya," as the undifferentiated reality, does not necessarily imply the existence of some object. In its isolated character it may be described only as self-shining. This characteristic of caitanya, in its pure aspect, is not altogether absent in the stage of differentiation. It is in virtue of this fundamental quality that an object appears and the subject knows. Appearance and knowledge are but the two differentiated sides of the same neutral fact of immediacy. In other words, the appearance of caitanya as object to caitanya as subject, or the knowledge on the part of caitanya as subject of caitanya as object, has to be credited to the fundamental self-manifesting characteristic of caitanya.

When these ideas are applied to the concrete case of the perception of an object we must say, then, that the fact of the self knowing the object means that the object is somehow brought into connection with the witnessing or self-shining caitanya, which is really the nature of the self. To put the same fact in another way, we may say that though the individual self functions for all practical purposes as a limited ignorant entity, its real or transcendent nature of being a self-shining principle is demonstrated in every act of knowledge which is characterized by immediacy. This, therefore, is the meaning of the assertion—to explain which all these discussions have been necessary—that, according to Vedāntins in general, there must be in every perception some connection shown between the object and witnessing self or sākṣin.

The question however arises why, if the self as well as the object is in reality the self-manifesting caitanya, the self sometimes perceives the object and sometimes does not do so. To answer this question Vedāntins ask us to remember that for the sake of logical demonstration, we start with the empirical facts of the casual appearance or non-appearance of objects and the casual knowledge or ignorance of the subject, and we obtain the conception of caitanya (as underlying both the subject and object) as an explanation of these facts of experience. Thus, to ascertain the causes of the casuality of knowledge and appearance, we have simply to study the empirical conditions under which we have, or have not, perception. What these conditions are, according to the Vedāntins, we have already discussed in detail while considering the functions of the indrioyas and the antaḥkaraṇa. The meaning of these empirical conditions has only to be interpreted in a way that fits in with the conception of the self-shining caitanya, which we have seen has to be accepted on philosophical grounds. The author of the Vedānta-paribhāṣā tries to give a complete interpretation of the facts of immediacy (pratyakṣatva) from his own standpoint.

The word pratyakṣa (immediate), as we have noticed already, can be predicated both of an object (viṣaya), e.g., the table is pratyakṣa (or immediately perceived), and of the knowledge (jñāna) of an object, e.g., the knowledge of the table is pratyakṣa (immediate). The conditions which lead to the perception of an *object* (viṣayagata pratyakṣa) are that the antaḥkaraṇa must go to the object through the indriyas and assume the form of the object, so that either the differentiating factors which create and division between the subject and the object may be removed, or the veil of ignorance hiding the object from the subject may be removed, or the subject may be tinged with the form of the object—whichever of these three views, explained already, may be thought satisfactory. It should be made clear that an *object* is immediately known only in that form of it which antaḥkaraṇa assumes, and not in any other form. To illustrate, when we *see* a table it is immediately known only as a coloured object, not as an object having a touch, smell or weight; these latter forms the antaḥkaraṇa does not assume in this particular case, in which it approaches the object through the sense of vision which cannot reveal these other forms. When an object is known through inference it is not known immediately, because the antaḥkaraṇa in this case does not go out, through a sense, to the object to assume its form.

As to the immediacy of an element of *knowledge* (jñānagata-pratyakṣa), we must remember that according to the Vedāntins, as to many other thinkers, knowledge, as knowledge or as a mental act, is always immediate. Even an inference or a mere idea must be regarded as immediate (pratyakṣa) or self-evident *as an act* or mental process. The ordinary distinction between mediate and immediate knowledge altogether vanishes when knowledge is looked upon from this point of view. The distinction, however, is highly useful and is based on the conception of knowledge as a concrete unity of both act and object, and not as a mere abstract act divorced from the object. Looking at knowledge from this point of view the Vedāntin upholds, then, the useful distinction between mediate and immediate knowledge. Knowledge, thus considered, would be immediate when its *object* is immediately known. So we find that the conditions for the immediacy of the *knowledge* of a pot also would be the going out of the antaḥkaraṇa to the pot through the senses, and its taking the form of the object, etc., so as to result ultimately in establishing an identity between the subject and the object, or in removing the veil hanging between the subject and the object, or in imparting to the subject the tinge of the object—whichever of these three alternatives be thought satisfactory.

The Vedāntaparibhāṣā chooses the first alternative. According to it consciousness, the Reality underlying everything, is empirically delimited, in three ways, as knower (pramātā), knowing process (pramāṇa) and the object known (viṣaya). The *object* is immediately known when the inner organ (antaḥkaraṇa) flowing through a sense out to the object assumes its form, and removes thereby the separation between the knower and the known (i.e., between the consciousness delimited by the antaḥkaraṇa and the consciousness delimited by the object). As the same process leads also to the unification of the knowing process (i.e., consciousness delimited by the antaḥkaraṇa's modification or vṛtti) and the object, this *knowledge* also becomes immediate.

We have tried to indicate in this chapter the general and special conceptions of the self and its function in the perception of an object. All our discussions in this connecion have turned upon the explanation of one main point, namely that the self in its transcendent aspect of self-shining caitanya is responsible for the immediacy that we experience in perception; that it is the light of the self-luminous self which imparts immediacy to the object and the knowledge of the object.

CHAPTER V

OBJECTS OF PERCEPTION

We have discussed so far the vedānitic views regarding the process of the acquisition of perceptual knowledge and the parts played therein by the indriyas, the manas and the ātman. In the present chapter we shall consider what objects of knowledge are regarded by the Vedāntins as immediately known. It will be evident that a general reply to this question can at once be given from the results of the preceding chapters. We can say that only that object is perceived or immediately known which the antaḥkaraṇa can reach, so as to establish a direct relation between the knower and the object. But though this answer may possess a theoretical value, it is of little practical help in determining whether a particular object is immediately known. For the going out of the sense or antaḥkaraṇa is not itself a perceived fact; it is a hypothesis designed to explain the fact of immediacy; and as such it already implies the knowledge of the immeidacy of the object. So the general reply, though possessing some theoretical value, is of little practical help in determining whether a particular object is known perceptually or not; it also involves a *petitio principii*. We have to return, then, to the other alternative, namely that the immediacy of the knowledge of an object must itself be immediately known. In other words the quality of immediacy must be intrinsically patent in the knowledge of the object itself. But even this principle, however flawless in theory, is not always so easy of application. This will be evident from the many instances to be discussed in this chapter. Here we shall consider the knowledge of some particular objects, such as time, universals, relations, etc., and try to ascertain whether such objects are directly or immediately perceived. In Indian philosophy two kinds or stages of perception have generally been distinguished; one has been called nirvikalpaka and the other savikalpaka. We shall presently see what these two concepts mean for different schools of thought, and what the objects of these two kinds of perception are; after considering these and the objects revealed through them, we shall have a complete idea as to the objects known in perception.

I. Indeterminate (Nirvikalpaka) Perception

We take nirvikalpaka pratyakṣa first. It is best to begin with the views of the Nyāya school, as stated by its great exponent Gaṃgeśa in his classical work, Tattva-cintāmaṇi,[1] or by Viśvanātha in his Siddhānta-muktāvalī.[2] It is held by these thinkers that when perception takes place at the very first moment, we do not have the knowledge of an object *characterized* by any predicate or character (such as, 'This is a pot,' or 'This is blue'), but apprehend some unrelated elements (e.g., pot, potness, blue, etc.). So in this primary stage pratyakṣa is to be regarded as nirvikalpaka or indeterminate. When the non-relationally apprehended elements are differentiated and related in the form of a judgment (e.g., 'This is a pot'), we have a pratyakṣa (perception) that may be called savikalpaka—relational or determinate. The existence of the primary stage (i.e., nirvikalpaka pratyakṣa) is not, however, directly experienced;[3] but it can be logically proved to exist as a necessary presupposition of our determinate knowledge of the object. The determinate perceptual knowledge, in which something is perceived as a pot, implies that we ascribe to the presented thing the attribute of potness. But this substance-attribute relation cannot take place before the elements related are perceived. We may therefore reasonably assume that prior to the determinate perception of the pot as a pot we must have a nirvikalpaka or non-relational knowledge of pot and potness.[4]

Some thinkers, [5] however, especially the grammarian philosophers, contend that since language enters into the very texture of all kinds of knowledge without exception, knowledge that is worth the name must be always determinate. The possibility of the existence of an indeterminate stage of knowledge, such as nirvikalpaka pratyakṣa, is therefore, necessarily ruled out.

The Mīmaṃsakas, on the other hand, refute this view and assert the existence of nirvikalpaka pratyakṣa. Kumārila, the founder of the Bhāṭṭa

1 Pratyakṣa-cintāmaṇi, Nirvikalpaka-vādaḥ.
2 Siddhānta-muktāvalī (Nirnayasagar) on Kār, 58.
3 "Jñānam yan nirvikalpākhyam tad atīndriyam iṣyate," loc. cit.
4 Siddhānta-muktāvalī, loc. cit. and Jagadīśa's Tarkāmṛta.
5 Cf. Bhartṛhari's dictum "Na so asti pratyayo loke yaḥ śabdānugamādṛte. Anuviddam iva Jñānaṃ sarvaṃ śabdena bhāsate," Vākyapadīya, 1-124, (Benares Sana. Series).

School, says in the Ślokavārtika : "There exists some primary indeterminate knowledge of the pure object, a knowledge that is like that of children or the dumb; neither any particularity nor any generality is then perceived; the individual which is the substratum of them is then known alone."[1] And Pārthasārathi-Miśra, the author of Śāstradīpikā, holds that in the nirvikalpaka stage the object is indefinite (mugdha) and multiform (anekākāra), whereas in the latter stage it becomes definite and presents only one form.[2]

The Buddhists not only admit the existence of nirvikalpaka pratyakṣa, but also assert that it is the only kind of pratyakṣa or immediate knowledge that we really possess.[3] According to them the object, as we immediately perceive it, is something unique (svalakṣaṇa). In the succeding stage of savikalpaka jñāna or determinate knowledge, we supply from our mind names, universals, etc., which are therefore not to be mistaken either as existing in the object or as being immediately known.[4]

To this the Mīmaṃsakas[5] reply that, in the primitive indeterminate stage, the object cannot be known as something unique. For if it is so known it will be known *as* a particular that can, by no means, be said to be indeterminate. Thus, immediate knowledge of this kind should really be considered to be determinate (savikalpaka) and not indeterminate (nirvikalpaka), which would give us the knowledge of neither generality nor particularity.

Before dealing with the Vedānta views, it is necessary to understand more critically the suggestions already considered. Their general meaning seems to be sufficiently clear. But when we try to ascertain what precisely is the nature of the object in the nirvikalpaka stage, this apparent clearness is lost in the uncertainty of possible alternative interpretations. The difficulty arises because we can conceive that, prior to the fully developed perceptual judgment about an object, there may be not one but many stages in the awareness of the object. We may first have a mere unmeaning sensation in which the object is presented as an uninterpreted, unanalysed fact. We may then have a bare apprehension of what Hobhouse calls

1 Śloka-vārtika, Pratyakṣa-sūtra. Kār. 112.

2 Śāstradīpikā, p. 41. (Tarkapāda, Nirnayasagara, 1915).

3 Nyāyavindu, pp. 11-13.

4 Ibid., pp. 13-16.

5 Prakaraṇa-pañcikā, pp. 54-55.

"the present" which, having a slight tinge of meaning, is something more than a blind sensation, but is not yet a developed perception. Lastly the perception may develop, and we may have the judgment itself. But the judgment also may have two stages : first, it may be unattended by any verbal image or expression, and afterwards attended by these symbols so as to gain the form of a proposition. Further, the development of knowledge through all these stages may be either conceived realistically, as an unfolding or definite discovery of what was given at the very first stage, or idealistically, as the increasing contribution to the object, on the part of the mind, of characteristics not primarily present in the object. If we try to understand the nature of the object in nirvikalpaka pratyakṣa in the light of such searching analysis, we find that the conceptions of the different schools, or of the same school in different places, do not absolutely coincide. The Buddhistic view, as discussed above, is at once easily differentiatied, by its idealistic bias, from the realistic views of the Naiyā yikas and the Mīmāṃsakas. According to the Buddhists it is only the unique particular that is *given* in the nirvikalpaka stage which, for them, is co-extensive with perception. The universal, relations, etc., are considered by them as *a priori* contributions subsequently made by the mind. The Naiyāyikas, on the contrary, think that attributes, universals, relations, etc., are all given to the mind even in the nirvikalpaka stage, and no new element previously absent is contributed by the mind in the savikalpaka stage. The real difference between the two stages, according to them, is that in the latter the mind interrelates the elements given in the former as unrelated (viśakalita).

The views of the Mīmāṃsakas seem in many respects to be identical with those of the Naiyāyikas. But there seems to be a marked difference also between them. At least two facts enable us to draw such a conclusion. First, we find that the Mīmāṃsakas compare nirvikalpaka pratyakṣa with the perceptual knowledge possessed by children or dumb persons. Now, though we may believe that the knowledge possessed by a newborn baby may be more or less confused, unanalysed and indeterminate, we have no reason to think that a dumb adult also has a similar knowledge of objects. On the contrary, it is reasonable to think that a dumb person possesses not merely determinate perception of objects, but also judgments of perception; only such judgments may not be expressed by word-symbols. It is reasonable to conclude from this that, according to the Mīmāṃsakas, any perception short of a perceptual judgment *attended with linguistic symbols* may be called nirvikalpaka pratyakṣa. This interpretation appears all the more likely when we remember that the Mīmāṃsakas try to establish the existence of nirvikalpaka pratyakṣa by refuting the views held by the grammarians.[1] As we have already pointed out, the grammarians hold that as knowledge without language is impossible, and since language has always definite determinate meanings, there can be no nirvikalpaka-jñāna. The Mīmāṃsakas answer this objection by pointing to the existence of knowledge without language in the cases of dumb persons and try to argue that as in these cases there is no use of language, knowledge can be indeterminate.[2] There is additional evidence to show that the nirvikalpaka pratyakṣa, as viewed by the Mīmāṃsakas, was of a more developed character than that of at least the later Naiyāyikas. While the great Naiyāyika Gaṃgeśa says that knowledge of the nirvikalpaka type can neither be true nor false, since it does not possess any practical use,[3] the Mīmāṃsakas, on the contrary, hold that practical efficiency is not absent even in such knowledge; for, they say, animals as well as children have nothing but nirvikalpaka pratyakṣa, and yet they act on the knowledge they have.[4] From all this it would appear that the concept of nirvikalpaka-pratyakṣa, as held by the Naiyāyikas, partly resemble that of the "sensation" of Western philosophy. At this stage there is neither any meaning nor any judgment, but a blind fact that is not, however, considered to be indefinite. It is clearly a pre-judgment stage. But according to the Mīmāṃsakas the object in nirvikalpaka-pratyakṣa cannot be said to be altogether meaningless, since it possesses at least as much meaning as can evoke some behaviour towards it. Judgment also need not be altogether absent in this stage, if it be possible to have judgment without language. According to this view, the only feature that differentiates a nirvikalpaka jñāna from a savikalpaka perception is the indeterminate, indefinite, indecisive character of the former as contrasted with the determinate definite and decisive character of the latter. So the difference here is reduced to that between obscurity and clearness, which is ultimately a

1 Siddhāntacandrikā on Śastradīpikā, p. 40.

2 Loc. cit.

3 Tattva-cintāmāṇi, Pratyakṣa-khanḍa, p. 402: "Nirvikalpakañca pramāpramā-bahirbhūtameva vyavahārānangatvāt."

4 Siddhānta-candrikā on Sāstra-dipīkā, P. 40: "Tiraścām bālānāñ ca nirvikal-pakenaiva sarvo vyavahāraḥ."

difference of degree rather than one of kind. According to the Naiyāyikas, however, there is a real qualitative difference between the two. Though the substance, attributes, universals, etc., are all present in the nirvikalpaka stage, as much as in the savikalpaka one, they appear discrete and isolated in the former, whereas they are strung together in the substantive-adjective way in the latter.

We are now in position to consider the vedāntic views on the matter.

According to the Vedāntins, knowledge is savikalpaka if it consists of the predication of one content to another in a substantive-adjective way. But knowledge in which such a relation is absent is nirvikalpaka. So far as the theoretical definition or explanation of the term nirvikalpaka is concerned, the Vedāntins are not very far from the other schools which maintain that the substantive-adjective relation is absent in the content of nirvikalpaka perception. But in the application of this definition to concrete instances the Vedāntins part company with their comrades. For they hold that a nirvikalpaka perception should not necessarily be confined to the pre-judgment stage, because they think that among judgments themselves there are some which exhibit all the marks of a nirvikalpaka-jñāna,[1] and that these nirvikalpaka judgments can even be expressed in language. Illustrations of such perceptual judgements are to be found in cases of the recognition of an identity arising from the perception of an object for a second time. When on perceiving a man for the second time we say, "This is that Devadatta," we have a perceptual knowledge or judgment that is nirvikalpaka, since the predicate does not here bear an adjectival relation to the subject. Though we primarily start here with two different contents, we finally arrive at an identity through the negation of the difference between the two. In other words the purpose of the judgment here is not to assert any adjectival relation, but to assert an identity. Hence it can rightly be called nirvikalpaka or non-relational. In Book VI we will discuss fully the nature of identity-judgments, and it is premature to consider at this stage objections that can be raised as to the possibility of such judgments.[2] Here it is necessary to notice only one possible objection. While granting in anticipation that such a judgment does not express any adjectival relation but an identity, and also that the knowledge expressed

1 Vedānta-paribhāṣā, p. 89 : "Tatra savikalpakam vaisiṣṭ yāvagāhi jñānam yathā 'Ghaṭam aham jānāmi.' " . . . Nirvikalpakantu saṃsargānavagāhi jñānam yathā 'So yam Devadattaḥ.' "

2 Cf. also author's article on "The Import of a Proposition in Vedānta Philosophy," *Philosophical Quarterly*, January 1929.

in it is nirvikalpaka, one may yet ask, "Why is such knowledge called perceptual? Is it not rather a case of recognition or memory?" To this the Vedantins reply that as the judgement is based here on the perception of the object, there is no reason why we should not call it perceptual. In other words the identity, as asserted in this case, is neither remembered nor inferred but directly perceived, just as the man is perceived. It may be observed that the Vedāntins' contention in this respect is quite sound. The form of a judgment expressing a remembered identity would resemble "The man whom I saw yesterday is the same as the man whom I saw the day before."

It may be objected that even the judgment "This is Devadatta," though based on the perception of Devadatta, is partially based on memory. The judgment would not be possible if we did not remember that particular man with some particular attributes and that he was called Devadatta. We may answer this objection by saying that the dependence on memory, found in this particular case, can be shown to exist in most perceptions; it is therefore no peculiar feature, that may be regarded as vitiating this particular kind of perception and not affecting other kinds.

We find, therefore, that giving nirvikalpaka its proper meaning, we have no difficulty in thinking of a recognition judgment like "This is that Devadatta," as expressing a nirvikalpaka perception.

While all vedāntic writers are at pains to demonstrate the non-relational (nirvikalpaka) character of these judgments, none of them seems to be interested in what other schools call nirvikalpaka-pratyakṣa. We do not find any definite statement whether or not the Vedāntins believe in the existence of the nirvikalpaka stage as conceived by the naiyāyikas or the Mīmāṃsakas. The Vedāntins are found neither to refute nor to support the contentions of other schools as to the existence of a primary awareness of an indeterminate or unmeaning object prior to the developed perception of it. Writers of other schools such as Rāmānuja[1] (the author of Sribhāṣya) and Pārthasārathi-Miśra[2] (the author of Śāstra dīpikā), however, state, by way of refutation, a view, which they ascribe to the Advaitins. According to this view, there is in nirvikalpaka-pratyakṣa the awareness of existence (sattā) alone. This existence becomes afterwards differentiated, in savikalpaka-pratyakṣa, through the activities of the mind.

1 Srībhāṣya, Mahāpūrva-pakṣa, "... nirviśeṣa-sanmātra-brahma-grāhitvāt pratyakṣasya." (p. 21, R. V. & Co. ed., 1909).

2 Śāstra-dīpikā, p. 40, and Nyāyaratnākara on Śloka-vārtika, Pratyakṣa-sūtra, Kār. 114, et seq.

This view seems to be taken from a theory which a certain section of Advaitins hold in another context. When asked as to how the Advaitins can maintain the position that reality is one and the phenomenal world is false, in defiance of perception which bears testimony to the plurality and reality of the world, a particular group of Advaitins, like the author of Tattvaśuddhi,[1] reply that perception really gives us the knowledge of pure existence (sanmātram) and not of particulars which are but subsequent creations of our imagination (kalpanā). This extreme view, which almost borders on that of buddhistic idealists, is countenanced neither by Śaṃkara nor by any of his great followers. The difficulty sought to be evaded in this manner is removed by them in some other ways, the discussion of which is unnecessary in this connection. In epistemology Śaṃkara and many of his followers advocate a theory of direct realism, which chiefly distinguishes the Advaitins from their opponents, the idealist Buddhists. In fact Śaṃkara firmly asserts in one connection "In every act of perception we are aware of external objects like the pillar, the pot, the cloth and the floor."[2]

This positive evidence, coupled with the negative—namely that Advaitins illustrate nirvikalpaka-pratyakṣa usually by examples of recognition-judgments and not by those ascribed to them by the Mīmaṃsakas and Rāmānuja—enables us to conclude that at least the greatest thinkers of the Advaita school did not actually hold the view which, in the version of opponents, appears to be their common contention. In the absence of any positive statement from the Advaitins themselves, it is best to refrain from any criticism of this view in the present connection, in which we are solely concerned with the conception of nirvikalpaka-pratyakṣa. We shall conclude by noting simply that in the Advaita writings we miss a clear account of the nature of the object in the stages prior to the developed perception of it. Like other thinkers, the Advaitins also distinguish between nirvikalpaka-pratyakṣa and savikalpaka-pratyakṣa. But while for others the distinction means one between undeveloped or indefinite perception and developed or definite perception, for Advaitins it means a distinction between perception of the identical (or the non-related) and perception of the related.

1 Siddhāntaleśa-saṃgraha, p. 357 (Jīvānanda's edn.). *Vide* also Maṇḍana's Brahmasiddhi, pp. 58 and 70 (Madras edn.); and Advaitabrahmasiddhi, p. 22 (Cal. Univ. edn.).

2 Brahma-sūtra bhāṣya, 2, 2, 28.

2. Determinate (Savikalpaka) Perception

We may now consider the objects of savikalpaka perception. From what we have shown in the preceding section, it appears that according to the Vedāntins all perceptions except those that constitute identity judgments come under the savikalpaka class. According to the Naiyāyikas and also the Mīmāṃsakas, this form of perception is a development out of the rudimentary nirvikalpaka stage. But this is not necessarily the case with the Vedāntins, as we have just shown. For the identity judgment "This is Devadatta," which Vedāntins consider to be an example of the nirvikalpaka type, really follows the determinate (savikalpaka) perception of the man, Devadatta. Thus we have here the case of a savikalpaka perception preceding and not succeeding a nirvikalpaka one. To enquire about the objects of savikalpaka perception from the vedāntic point of view, then, we have to enquire about the objects of all perceptions except those of identity. We shall undertake this enquiry in the present section.

If we have understood the vedāntic account of the psychophysical process leading to perception, we can roughly judge what should be considered an object of perception by the Vedāntins. The form of an object and also its colour, touch, smell, taste and sound, can be immediately perceived. The antaḥkaraṇa can approach these objects through the five senses, and consequently there is no difficulty in perceiving them. As regards the knowledge of the weight (gurutva) of an object also, there is a general agreement between the Vedāntins and most other schools, though this opinion would appear somewhat curious to Western thinkers. The weight of an object is held to be always inferred (nityānumeya) and never perceived. The reason for such a view is to be found in the fact that Indian thinkers recognize only five senses (indriyas) of external perception, and the muscular sense of modern psychology is not considered to be a sense at all. The weight of an object comes, therefore, to be inferred from the fact of its falling down when left unsupported. So far there is more or less general agreement among Indian philosophers. But beyond these matters there is little unanimity of opinion. When we come to time, universals, relations, etc., we find that while some writers think that they are immediately known others believe that they cannot be so known. It is necessary to consider these cases one by one. Let us first consider the knowledge of time.

3. Perception of Time

The Vaiśeṣikas and the Naiyāyikas maintain that time cannot be an object of perception. For according to them a substance (dravya) to be perceptible must possess a non-infinitesimal dimension (mahattva) and a manifest form (udbhūtarūpatva). Atoms cannot be perceived, because they are of the infinitesimal order of dimension. Again ether (ākāśa), time (kāla), etc., cannot be perceived because they lack visible form.

The Mīmāṃsakas[1] and the Vedāntins, however, hold that the formless character of time is no hindrance to its being perceived. According to them the conditions of perception, as laid down by the Naiyāyikas and the Vaiśeṣikas, need prove no stumbling-block. Laws should subserve facts; facts must not be sacrificed nor even distorted for the preservation of any preconceived law. If the conditions formulated by the Naiyāyikas and others do not accord with any particular case of perception, we must conclude that these conditions are the results of hasty generalization, and therefore need revision. That time is immediately perceived is an undoubted fact. On seeing a pot, we say, "we see the pot *now*." We cannot explain the quality of the presentness (vartamānatva) of the object, pot, in any way other than by holding that time-quality is as directly revealed through the sense of perception as the pot itself. This direct experience, otherwise inexplicable, enables us to conclude that time is an object of perception, and that its perception can take place through the senses.[2] If time were not perceived along with the perception of the object, we should always doubt whether our knowledge, were about a present, past, or future object.[3] "In every act of knowledge, there must be a consciousness of time."[4] This is a common dictum of the Mīmāṃsakas, and Vedāntins also subscribe to it.

It is necessary, however, to understand the exact sense in which time is said to be perceived. Time (kāla) as perceived is not thought of either as an empty form from which all events have been abstracted, nor as the series of events present, past and future stretching from infinity to infinity. It is absurd to think that time conceived in any one of these ways should be dirrectly perceived through the senses. The time that is said to be perceived is the present time which subsists in the object as an element

1 Śāstra-dīpikā, p. 45, and Siddhānta-candrikā thereon.
2 Vedānta-paribhāṣā, p. 20.
3 Sikhāmaṇi on the above.
4 The dictum is : "Na so asti pratyayo loke yatra kālo na bhāsate."

qualifying it. It is not unreasonable, therefore, to think that time as a quality of the perceived object is revealed to us through all the senses which are thought responsible for the perception of the object itself. The naiyāyikas, however, conceive time as an eternal substance that is a sort of holdall for all the phenomena of the universe (jagatām āśrayaḥ). It is natural, therefore, that they should consider time to be imperceptible (atīndriya). It is true that the Naiyāyikas speak of two kinds of time: the infinite, eternal time (mahākāla), which is an undivided whole, as well as finite time (khaṇḍa-kāla), measured by the duration of an object or an action. But the latter is conceived more or less as a convenient fiction having only a practical value. A finite time is nothing more than the one undivided time appearing finite, because known or measured through the finite duration of an object or an action.[1] Hence we find that finite times are often spoken of as ghata-kṣaṇa (pot-time), paṭa-kṣaṇa (cloth-time). The standard for the measurement of finite time is, according to the Naiyāyikas, the apparent daily motion of the sun (sūrya-parispanda)[2] round the earth. The unit of time is called a kṣaṇa and is equivalent to $\frac{2}{45}$ of a second.[3] According to the Naiyāyiaks, then, the perceptual judgment "The pot is present" (Idā nīm ghaṭaḥ) implies that a connection has been set up in knowledge between the pot and the contemporaneous motion of the sun or the kṣaṇa. But the question arises how the pot and the motion of the sun could possibly be brought together. This puzzle, the Naiyāyikas[4] affirm, can be removed only by supposing that there is one time which holds together the finite duration of the pot and the solar motion and is able, therefore, to bring about a relation between the two. Thus, by inference we arrive at the conception of the one undivided time, as the locus (ādhāra or āśraya) of all generated events.

We do not find any attempt, on the part of the vedāntins, to meet the contentions of the Naiyāyikas. We may however offer a few remarks of our own on this matter. In his conception of time as an eternal substance and as the locus of all phenomena, and especially as a generator of all the generated (janyānām janakaḥ), the Naiyāyika resembles to an interesting degree one of the modern realistic thinkers, Alexander, who also conceives

1 Kārikāvalī. kār. 45, and Muktāvalī thereon.

2 Ibid.

3 Seal's *Positive Sciences of the Ancient Hindus*, p. 148: "In the Nyāya-Vaiśeṣika school the day of twenty-four hours (solar) is stated to contain 30×30×30×18×2×2 units of time (kṣaṇas). The Nyāya unit of time therefore measures $\frac{2}{45}$ of a second."

4 Siddhānta-muktāvalī on Kār. 45.

time (combined with space) as an ultimate stuff out of which everything else has evolved. Alexander also thinks that time is not "apprehended" by the senses, though "our experience of space and time is provoked through the senses." It should be noted, however, that Alexander admits the existence of an intuition of space and time prior to sensations; and it is through intuition that they are "immediately apprehended."[1] The Naiyā yikas, as we have found, would grant neither the sensation of time nor any intuition of it. The knowledge of time is wholly a matter of inference, though based on the experience of the near and the distant in time, the "now" and the "then," or the "before" and the "after."[2] This peculiar position of the Naiyāyikas does not seem to be ultimately tenable. If we had no immediate knowledge of even finite times or durations (as "now," "then," "present" etc.), we should altogether lack the experience of the near and the distant (in time), and consequently inference would be altogether impossible. It is possible to construct inferentially one universal time only when we already have the experience of finite times, and not otherwise. The Mīmāṃsakas and the Vedāntins are, therefore, right in holding that time, as present, is immediately apprehended. And when an object is apprehended through any sense its time-character also may be similarly apprehended. Sadānanda, an Advaitin, says in his Advaitabrahmasiddhi that time is perceived through all sense.[3]

It is interesting to enquire, however, whether time or the present is conceived by Indian thinkers to be an atomic point or an extended span. This question, to which in Western philosophy James has drawn much attention, is not explicitly and systematically discussed in any detail. But still we often come across incidental references, from which it is possible to infer definitely the views of Indian thinkers on this question. In the Tattvacintāmaṇi of Gaṃgeśa we come across an incidental remark which runs as follows : "Since points of time (Kṣaṇāh) are imperceptible, the present (vartamāna) is known through a finite or measureable (sthūla) determinant (upādhi)."[4] Again in Nyāyavārtikā-tātparyya-tīkā we have

1 *Space, Time and Deity*, vol. ii, pp. 144-8.

2 Siddhānta-muktāvalī (on Kār. 45.). which observes that the necessity of admitting the existence of time is to explain our experience of temporal distance and nearness (partvāparatva).

3 p. 22 (Calcutta University ed.).

4 Pratyakṣa-cintāmaṇi, p. 380: ". . . kṣaṇānām atīndriyatvāt, sthūlopādhim ādāya vartamānatva-grahāt. . . ."

the incidental remark : "because the atomic points of time are never perceived by us who have these eyes of flesh."[1] Substantially the same remark occurs in Kusumāñjali as well : "because the kṣaṇas as time-determinants are not perceived."[2] All these remarks show clearly that Indian thinkers were aware of the difficulty that arises if atomic instants of time are thought to be the objects of perception. The "present" as known is sthūla (finite), not sūkṣma (infinitesimal). As to the length of the duration of this "present" time, the Vedāntins appeal again wholly to experience. It endures so long as the experience of the "now" is not succeeded by an experience of the "then"—so long, in other words, as the self judges it to endure.[3]

4. Perception of Universals, Relations, etc.

We come now to the consideration of the knowledge of universals, relations, etc. The Naiyāyikas have discussed these matters fully and accurately, The Vedāntins accept, on many points, the views of the Naiyā yikas tacitly without any further discussion, so that we have their views explicitly stated only on the points on which they happen to differ from the Naiyāyikas. It is best, therefore, to start with the views of the Naiyāyikas and point out where the Vedāntins deviate from these.

According to the Naiyāyikas, there are two kinds of perceptions—ordinary (laukika) and extraordinary (alaukika). An ordinary perception is that in which there is an ordinary relation between object and sense. An extraordinary perception is one in which no ordinary relation between the object and any sense can be traced. We take ordinary perceptions first.

The Naiyāyikas differentiate six kinds of ordinary relation (sannikarṣa) between object and sense as being responsible for the perception of six kinds of objects. A substance like a "pot" is perceived through the contact of the particular sense with the substance. This relation is direct and is called saṃyoga (conjunction). In the perception of a quality, say a blue colour, inhering in the pot, there is no direct conjunction between the sense and the percept. The relation here is indirect; there is first the relation of conjunction (saṃyoga) between sense and the substance, pot and then the relation of inherence existing between the blue colour and the pot. This relation is, therefore, called "inherence in the conjoined"

1 Nyāya-vārtika-tātparya-ṭīkā, p. 21 (Chawkhamba, 1925).

2 Kusumāñjali, st. 4, p. 5: "Kṣaṇopādhīnām anākalanāt" (As. Soc. ed.)

3 Vedāntaparibhāṣā, pp. 20-8

(saṃyukta-samavāya). Again the blueness inhering in the blue colour is also perceived. Here the relation is still more indirect–the links being sense-substance-inhering quality-universal inhering in the quality. This relation is called "inherence in the one inhering in the conjoined" (saṃyukta-samaveta-samavāya). In the perception of sound, however, the relation between the sense and the object is said to be one of simple inherence (samavāya). Sound is a quality inhering in the ākāśa and an ear itself is conceived as ākāśa in a limited form. So that the relation between sound and the ear is the same as that between sound and ākāśa, which is a relation of inherence. The universal, soundness (śabdatva), inhering in sound is perceived through an indirect relation between the sense and the object, and this relation may be called "inherence in the one inhering" (samaveta-samavāya). Lastly non-existence of a particular object in a particular locus is perceived through the relation of the sense with what is adjectival to the locus, with which the senses have direct conjunction. Non-existence is then known as adjectival to the locus. This relation is called "adjectivality to the conjoined" (saṃyukta-viśeṣaṇatā).[1] Samavāya also is perceived in the same way, as an adjective to its locus.[2]

Let us consider now what the Vedāntins think of this account of the Naiyāyikas. Almost all the objects that are held to be perceivable in the above account would be held by most of Vedāntins also to be perceivable. That a substance like a pot, and the qualities, say colour, etc., belonging to it are held to be directly perceived we have already pointed out. The universal, potness, in the substance, pot, as also the universal, blueness, in the quality, blue, are also perceived. Sound is perceived, of course; so also the universal, soundness, inhering in it. Vedāntins object, however, to the perception of non-existence, and assert that the knowledge of non-existence (even in a perceived locus) is a quite unique kind of knowledge that has to be classed apart. As to samavāya the Vedāntins do not admit its existence at all.

We have to note, however, that even in the preceding instances, where the Vedāntins agree with the Naiyāyikas with regard to the perceivability of the objects, they do not admit the Nyāya account of the nature of the relations obtaining between the particular senses and the objects. This difference is ultimately due to the difference that exists between the metaphysical conceptions of Nyāya and Vedānta as to the status of

1 Siddhānta-muktāvalī on Kārs. 59-61.

2 The Vaiśeṣikas do not accept however the perceivability of samavāya; vide Praśastapāda's Padārtha-dharma-samgraha

substance, quality, relations, universals, etc. To understand this point it is necessary to consider, in passing, the views of these two schools about these entities.

According to the Naiyāyikas the categories of realities are seven—substance (dravya), attribute (guṇa), action (karma), universal (sāmānya), particularly (viśeṣā), the relation of inherence (sāmāvāya), and non-existence (abhāva). All these are considered to be distinct realities. Attributes and actions have their locus in the substance with which they have a relation of inherence (samavāya). Universals have their locus in particulars to which they bear the same relation of inherence. There are two principle relations according to the Naiyāyikas : saṃyoga and samavāya. Saṃyoga is the relation of the collocation or conjunction of two terms that were previously unrelated or unconnected, *e.g.*, the relation between the table and the floor. Samavāya is the constitutive or inherent relation that exists, for example, between the whole and its parts, between attributes or actions and their substance, and between a universal and its particulars. Of these two relations, Saṃyoga is considered by the Naiyāyikas to be an attribute (guṇa) of the terms related, but samavāya is not taken as an attribute, but as an independent category by itself.[1]

It will be seen that the views of the Naiyāyikas have a striking resemblance to those of the contemporary Western realists like Russell. Just as the neo-realists hesitate to call entities like relations, universals, etc., existents, and invent for them the new world of subsistents, the Naiyāyikas also hold that a universal (sāmānya), the relation of samavāya, and particularity (viśeṣa) as well do not possess common existence (sattā), though each has a unique nature and being.[2] Things like tables and chairs are, according to the Naiyāyikas just as to the mordern realists, a mosaic of the many entities— substances, attributes (colour, size, etc.), action (movement), universals (tableness, blueness, etc.), etc.— held together with the relation of inherence which is also a discrete entity. In perceiving a thing, say a chair, an unprejudiced mind should perceive a particular, its attributes, its contact with the floor, etc., the universal, chairness, etc., and also the relation (of samavāya) riveting together all these discrete entities.

1 Vide Kārikāvalī. While Samavāya is counted as one of the seven "padārthas," Saṃyoga is counted among the "guṇas."

2 Ibid., Kār. 14. It is observed that only the first three "padārthas" (namely dravya, guṇa and Karma) possess the universal existence. (sattā). The other three entities have each a unique being of its own (svātma-sattva), acc. to Praśastapāda.

Naturally enough Vedāntins do not accept this Nyāya view of entities. Śaṃkara criticizes this theory in details in his commentary on the Brahma-sūtras.[1] and establishes the view that an attribute, an action, a universal, particularity, etc., exist in the substance not as discrete entities, but as elements or aspects which are not distinct from the substance. In oder to prove this contention, he criticizes the Nyāya-Vaiśeṣika view of relations. The Naiyāyikas and the Vaiśeṣikas think that attributes and substance, actions and substance, universals and particulars, are held together through another entity, namely, the relation of inherence or samavāya. Śaṃkara says that it is difficult to defend the conception of this new relation. The necessity of admitting this new relation evidently lies in the fact that the relation between a whole and its parts, or attributes and their substance, or a universal and its particulars, is far too intimate to be classed with the ordinary relation of saṃyoga. If this intimacy is rightly understood, the conception of samavāya is found to be necessary. We can never experience or even think of an attribute apart from a substance, a universal apart from a particular, and so forth. As a matter of fact an attribute is always experienced as inseparable from a substance; so also a universal from a particular. It is true that they are distinguished, admits Śaṃkara, in words. But that shows a difference only in meaning and not in existence.[2] The same objects, says Śaṃkara, may be called by different names, according to its many internal and external aspects. The identical individual, Devadatta, may be differently called a man, a Brāhmaṇa, a youth, etc. If the attributes and substance, universals and particulars, are found to be inseparable in existence, there is no necessity whatever for the conception of the foreign entity of a samavāya relation for holding them together. On the contrary it is reasonable to think that attributes, universals, etc., are identical with the substance in which they are experienced to reside. The conception of a relation like samavāya existing independently of the terms presents other difficulties also. If a relation is as independent an entity as the terms related, there arises the necessity of a second relation to connect the first relation with each of the terms, and the second relation may

1 Brahma-sūtras, 2, 2, 17.
2 Brahma-sūtra-bhāṣya, 2, 2, 17.

similarly be shown to require a third, and that a fourth and so on *ad infinitum*.[1] Thus, the logical analysis of the conception of a relation, as a co-ordinate entity, leads us to an infinite regress (anavasthā). In more recent times Bradley also criticizes 'relation' on similar grounds.[2]

When the conception of the relation of samavāya is abandoned, the entire superstructure of Nyāya metaphysics collapses. A thing can no longer be viewed as a mosaic of independent entities. It is one whole which presents the different aspects of attributes, universals, actions, etc., under different organizations (saṃsthāna).

This is how Śaṃkara refutes the Nyāya theory of entities and propounds his own view from the vedāntic standpoint. In the course of the foregoing discussion we have trodden a ground on which some of the most decisive battles have been recently fought in the West between idealists and realists. And we are aware that the arguments advanced by Śaṃkara to refute the realistic theories of things and relations, as held by the Naiyāyikas, will be far from being convincing to the students of contemporary Western philosophy. It is not pertinent to our present topic to discuss the many objections that might be raised. We can offer in this connection only a few critical remarks.

To bring this discussion within the focus of modern Western philosphy we must examine what the Vedānta and Nyāya views amount to in terms of the current conceptions of internal and external relations. It is generally known that while idealists stand for the internality of all relations, realists object to this position and favour the externality of relations. But when we come to examine the particular sense in which the words "internality" and "externality" are used, and the extent to which the views are advocated, we miss precise statements. Most realists, like Moore,[3] consider their task to be finished with the mere refutation of the general proposition of the idealists, viz., "All relations are internal." As their main interest is to save realism from the danger of idealism which, they think, automatically follows from the internality of the cognitive relation, which again becomes inevitable if the general proposition of the internality of all relations is granted, they are content to show that there are at least some relations

1 Ibid., 2, 2, 13.
2 *Appearance and Reality*, pp. 17f.
3 *Philosophical Studies*, pp. 276 f.

which are not internal, and consequently that the case for idealism remains unproved. Some realistic thinkers like Perry,[1] however, have gone beyond this negative view and have positively held that while some relations are external, all relations are not external, since there are cases of internal relations as well, such as logical implication, organic unity, etc. Realists like Russell, holding the extreme independence of relations, may, however, be inclined to hold that all relations are external. But these different views cannot be understood fully and critically unless we ascertain the exact sense of the word "external" or "internal."

The proposition, "A relation is external," may mean that a relation exists independently of the terms related. Its existence is on a par with the terms related. It may mean secondly that a relation certainly has existence, but while it does not exist as a mere quality of the terms, neither does it exist altogether independently of the terms, just because all things in this world are mutually interdependent. Again thirdly it may mean that a relation is certainly different from the terms but does not, like the terms, exist; it only subsists. Fourthly it may mean that a relation is different from the terms, but this difference concerns significance, and not necessarily existence. A negation of each one of these four senses of external relation may yield a corresponding sense of the term internal relation.

We do not know if any Western realist will be prepared to go to the extent of holding the externality of relations in the first sense. The second sense is accepted by Alexander.[2] The third sense will be accepted by those realists who advocate the theory of "subsistence." As to the fourth sense, though we do not find any realist who accepts it in so many words, yet implications of such a sense can be traced in the views of some.

But coming to Indian thinkers, we find that the Naiyāyikas hold a position that cannot be wholly identified with any of the four views distinguished above. As regards saṃyoga, the Naiyāyikas accept the first part of the second view, in so far as according to them this relation (being a guṇa) has *existence* (*sattā*), but they reject the second half, as they conceive saṃyoga as a guṇa or quality. As to the relation of samavāya again, the Naiyāyikas reject the first part of the second view, as samavāya lacks *existence*, but accept the second part, since samavāya is not a quality

1 *Present Philosophical Tendencies*, p. 244.
2 *Space, Time and Deity*, vol. i, pp. 249-250.

(which directly belongs to a substance only), it relates even a quality to its substance, and even a universal to a quality. Naiyāyikas might, therefore, accept the third view in so far as samavāya, in lacking *existence* but still possessing a distinct and positive reality, might be said to subsist. But they cannot subscribe to this view wholly because saṃyoga, being an attribute, has existence (sattā).

It is clear, therefore, that we cannot class the views of the Naiyāyikas off-hand with any of the stereotyped Western views of the internality or externality of relations.

To return to the view of Saṃkara, to understand whom we have introduced these discussions, we can say that he accepts the view of externality in the fourth sense, namely that a relation is external *in so far as it has a significance or meaning* (though not existence) different from that of the terms. But this view is so tame and moderate that very few realists would like to call it an external view. They would rather stigmatize such a view as internal.

But our chief interest here is not so much to find out whether Śaṃkara's view would be called by the one name or the other, as to judge its intrinsic value. For this purpose we must decide whether the externality of a relation in any of the first three senses is tenable. The first sense, that a relation has an existence which is independent of the related and is on a par with the being of the related, represents the extreme view which brings the theory of externality almost to a *reductio ad absurdum*. There are few realists who will seriously advocate such a view. The other two views, namely, those of the dependent existence of a relation and the subsistence of a relation, are the only ones that are at all plausible. Let us consider these two views one by one.

As to the first, it may be said that the conception of the dependent existence of a relation is not at all intelligible. We can understand the meaning of dependent existence when it is said, for instance, that the leaves of a tree exist, but their existence is dependent on the existence of the trunk. In such a case we can directly know the existence of the leaves as distinct from that of the trunk. The distinction is given in experience and we start with the two existents, finding out subsequently on further thought that the existence of the one is dependent on that of the other. But in the case under discussion, we never perceive or know the existence of a relation (as distinct from the related) in any such way as we know the existence of the terms. When, for instance, we perceive the existence of a book *on* a table, we do not know the existence of a book, a table, and the relation "on" connecting the two. We perceive only the two terms, the book and the table. Similarly in case of a whole and its parts. And if the existence of the relation as a distinct entity is not perceived, the question of its being dependent or independent does not at all arise. But it may be said, "Even if a relation may not be perceived as an entity just as the terms are, may it not be reasonable to admit its existence on other grounds?" To this we may reply that if there are sufficient grounds to necessitate the acceptance of the separate existence of a relation, we must believe in its existence. But we do not see any grounds that can stand much scrutiny. The first and most obvious ground might be thought to be the fact that a relation has a name that distinguishes it from the terms. Now distinction by name may be thought to imply distinction in existence, only if we grant that corresponding to every meaningful word there must be an existing object, or that meanings are also existents. We are aware that there are some modern realists who are prepared to accept such a view. But if consistently held this view would ultimately lead us to a very absurd position. If every meaningful word denotes an existent we are to believe, as Śaṃkara points out, that the same man, as father, as brother, as servant or as master, etc., is really not one existing thing, but a multiplicity of different existing things. And once the sameness or unity of the man is dissolved into a multiplicity, we are faced with the puzzle as to how to combine the many existents into the one practical unity of the object, or how the many come to be associated together. Besides, if meaning always involves existence we have also to believe in the existence of a golden mountain, a unicorn and all sorts of things having names. We are aware that some realists, like Alexander, will readily accept the challenge and go further to admit the existence of even illusory objects. But we think that one can hold such an extreme view only if he is ready to ignore the difference between "the real" and "the imaginary," "the true" and "the false," and thereby undermine the possibility of philosophy itself, or if he has recourse to the theory of the different grades of existence, in which case the distinction between the real and the imaginary, the true and the false, is preserved as such in substance, though not so much in name, and consequently the distinction between the merely meant and the meant existent is virtually preserved. A relation, therefore, is not on a par with the terms in point of existence.

A second ground might be urged for the acceptance of the existence of a relation as distinct from that of the terms. It may be said that if a relation had no existence, we should fail to recognize any distinction between such facts as "a horse before a cart" and "a cart before a horse," where the terms are the same in both cases and it is only the difference in relation that makes the distinction in sense. Is it not necessary, therefore, to admit the existence of a third entity, a relation over and above that of the two terms?

To this we may say that the existence of a third entity, a relation, in no way makes such facts more intelligible, and consequently it is not absolutely necessary to admit its exsitence. Let us see why. Even if we admit that in addition to the two entities, the horse and the cart, there exists a third entity, the relation of "beforeness," we do not explain the difference a whit. For the relation "beforeness" is present in both cases. In order to explain the difference we must also take notice of another element, namely, the *direction* of the relation. And if consistency is to be preserved, the arguments advanced for maintaining the existence of a relation as external to or additional to that of the terms should force us to maintain the existance of this direction as something additional to that of the relation. We shall thus have a fourth entity in the direction. To explain a simple relation we shall, by this faulty method of analysis, be landed in the insoluble difficulty of conceiving four entities and the different relations to relate them, and finally to an infinite regress. If the direction of the relation be conceived as included in the relation itself, then in the same way we may also be allowed to include relation in the being of the terms. If, again, to avoid the infinite regress, it be urged that a relation though an existent entity does not require another relation to relate it to each of the terms, and that it is the very nature of such an entity to relate, by itself, two or more terms together, we may pertinently ask, what prevents us from thinking that the terms also can come into relation by themselves without the help of a third entity? In fact, the simplest explanation of the matter seems to be such a hypothesis. But before we can accept it, we must see whether we can explain the facts we noticed before, namely the distinction between the two statements, "a horse before the cart" and "a cart before the horse," without admitting the existence of the third entity, the relation.

The necessity for the interposition or addition of a third entity or relation arises from the narrow, exclusive conception we entertain about the terms. To illustrate, we first conceive of the horse or the cart as an entity having some intrinsic, non-relative properties alone; and when such an entity, is brought into relation with another similar entity, we find that something, over and above the essential properties of the two terms, remains to be explained; then to that something we give the name of relation. But if we widen our outlook and think of the entity as possessing, in addition to its essential, non-relative, intrinsic characteristics, other extrinsic, relative characteristics which it may have in the infinite situations in which it may be placed, then we can easily dispense with the existence of the third entity, a relaion. In other words, if we think that a "horse" is an entity in which there are not only the essential properties of "horseness," but also infinite other characteristics which it is found to possess in the infinite relations that it may enter into with other objects, we shall not require any entity like a relation to explain the horse in any one of the different situations in which it may stand. A thing thus comes to be conceived as an identity of some intrinsic and extrinsic forms or aspects. Different words are then found to denote differently the same thing in different aspects.

From what has been shown above it is found that the externality of a relation, in the sense of its dependent existence cannot be justified. As to the other possible view, namely the subsistence of a relation, we may say that in so far as this view recognizes that a relation does not possess the same sort of being as the related terms it is sound, while in so far as it advocates the conception of a relation as something independent of or additional to the terms, it exposes itself to all criticisms that the former view has to face.

A relation, then cannot be thought either to have any recognizable existence dependent or independent in addition to that of the terms, or to subsist outside the terms. A relation has no existence apart from the terms, and the only independence that it may possess is to have a separate name. We find then that Śaṃkara's view of relations is sufficiently reasonable. Consequently his view of a thing, as the unity of the various intrinsic (svarūpa) and extrinsic or relative (bāhyarūpa or sambandhirūpa) aspects, is more reasonable than the Nyāya conception of a thing as the mosaic of discrete entities externally related.

To return to the question of the perception of universals, attributes, relations, etc., from which we diverted our attention to the foregoing discussions, the Vedāntins, while agreeing with the Naiyāyikas on the perceivability of these objects, differ from them on the point of the relationship of these objects with sense. The view of the six kinds of contact (sannikarṣa) which, we found, the Naiyāyikas hold in order to explain the perception of different kinds of object, substance, quality, universals, etc., appear to be quite unnecessary as soon as the Nyāya view of things is abandoned. According to their own conception, the Vedāntins find that one kind of contact which takes place between a substance and its particular sense is sufficient to explain the perception of universals, qualities, relations, etc., which are indistinguishably identical with the substance.

There is one obvious objection that can be raised against this theory. It may be said that if universals, qualities, relations, etc., are identical, in existence, with the substance, and if the same kind of contact be thought responsible for the pereption of all these aspects of the substance, why should we not perceive all the aspects of the thing every time that we perceive it?

The Vedāntin easily meets this objection by saying that according to him the cause of the perception of a thing is not merely the contact of the sense with thing. There is also the factor of the anthḥakaraṇa assuming its form. Thus in spite of sense-contact, a thing may not be perceived if anthḥakaraṇa does not assume its form. That is to say, if a thing has *n* number of aspects and if sense comes into contact with the thing, all the *n* aspects do not necessarily become objects of perception; only those aspects will be perceived to which attention may be directed at that particular time. So the objection does not tell at all against the vedāntic view, though it may present a serious difficulty to the Naiyāyikas, for whom sense-contact is the dominant factor in perception.

The perception of a universal requires special notice. The Vedāntins, though holding with the Naiyāyikas that in the perception of a particular (say a table) the universal (e.g. tableness) is also perceived, differ very widely from the Naiyāyikas as to the conception of the universal, tableness, perceived. According to the Naiyāyikas the universal has an eternal, timeless reality. It bears to the many particulars a relation of inherence—samavāya. The Vendāntins do not believe either in the eternity of a universal or in its inhering as a discrete entity, in the particulars. According to them a universal, tableness, is nothing but the common attributes (anugata-dharma) of the many particular tables. So the relation between the universal and the particular is nothing but identity. The perception of the universal, tableness, is then nothing but the perception of those attributes of the table which are common to all other tables of experience. It is a perception that is only a part of the perception of the table itself, and does not imply any additional mysterious relation (between itself and the sense) like saṃyukta-samavāya (inherence in the conjoined) as the Naiyāyikas think.

As to the perception of attributes and actions, the Naiyāyikas give a detailed list of those that are taken to be objects of perception. Of attributes, separateness (pṛthaktva), number (saṃkhyā), division (vibhāga), conjunction (saṃyoga), proximity and distance—temporal as well as spatial—(paratva and aparatva), viscidity (sneha), fluidity (dravatva) and quantity (parimāṇa) are held to be perceptible. Of actions those are said to be perceived which have their locus in perceptible substances.[1] We do not find the views of the Vedāntins positively stated on these points. But judging from their general position we may say that Vedāntins (except of course of the type of Śrīharṣa and Citsukhācārya) would not object to the perceivability of most of these attributes and actions. As to the perception of the attribute difference, however, Vedāntins would not agree with the Naiyāyikas, since they think that non-existence as well as difference is known through a distinct method of knowledge called anupalabdhi. We shall have occasion to discuss this method separately in Book III.

Another point that calls for attention is the knowledge of similarity. The Vedāntins hold that similarity also can be perceived under cartain conditions. Knowledge of similarity is perceptual only when the subject judged to be similar is itself an object of perception. To illustrate, if on perceiving a cow A we know that this cow is similar to another cow B we perceived in the past, then our knowledge that A is similar to B is perceptual. But the knowledge that B is also similar to A is not held to be a case of perception, as B is not itself perceived. This latter knowledge is classed apart as a distinct kind of knowledge called upamāna, of which also we shall have to speak in some detail later.

1 Bhāṣā-pariccheda, kārs. 53-56.

To sum up the results of this section, we may roughly say that according to the Vedāntins a substance is perceived, and along with it and as inseparably identified with it are perceived universals (i.e. common attributes), relations (of the saṃyoga type), similarity (as possessed by the perceived object), and many other attributes of the substance which are ordinarily thought to be perceptible by other philosophers. But the above statement needs a little qualification, which we should mention here. This view is one which can be gathered from the writings of Śaṃkara and the majority of his followers. But there are a few Vedāntins like the author of the Tattvaśuddhi who would apply a destructive dialectic to show that even in perception we have nothing more than a knowledge of pure being (san-mātram).

5 The Nyāya Theory of Extraordinary (Alaukika) Perception

We have discussed the objects that are regarded by the Advaitins as immediately known through perception, determinate and indeterminate. This really completes the Advaita account of perceptible things. Still, further discussion under this topic is necessary to consider the cases of objects which some later Naiyāyikas regard as immediately perceived, though the Advaitins do not accept their view. These cases are described by these Naiyāyikas as alaukika-pratyakṣa or extraordinary perception.

We said in a previous context that the Naiyāyikas divide perception into two classes : ordinary (laukika) and extraordinary (alaukika). The cases of perception we have considered so far are ordinary (or laukika); in each of these there is, according to the Naiyāyikas, a relation (sannikarṣa) between the object and some particular sense. But in addition to these there are, the Naiyāyikas think, instances of perception where we cannot trace any such ordinary relation between the object and any sense. These cases are therefore called alaukika or extraordinary. There are, it is held, three kinds of extraordinary perceptions—namely sāmānyalakṣaṇa, jñāna-lakṣaṇa and yogaja. We shall state the Nyāya view on each of these and along with it discuss the grounds on which Advaitins differ with Naiyāyikas.

We take up sāmānya-lakṣaṇa first. Some Naiyāyikas (such as the authors of Tattvacintāmaṇi, Bhāṣāpariccheda, etc.) hold that we perceive not only a vyakti or individual, but also a class of individuals.[1] In perceiving a pot we perceive, as already shown, the universal potness (the generic property of pots) as characterizing the particular pot. This perception of the universal, potness, amounts, according to these thinkers, to the perception of all pots as possessing this universal. We find, therefore, that in perceiving a particular we virtually perceive also all particulars of that class. The difference between the perception of the particular directly presented to sense, and that of the remaining particulars of the class not so presented, lies in the fact that while what is directly presented is perceived as possessing the class characteristic plus its peculiar individual characteristics, the particulars not so presented are perceived as possessing the class characteristic alone. Such perceptions of a class can take place, as would appear from the above, only when the universal (potness) is itself directly presented to sense through the presentation of at least one particular of the class—one pot—and never when the universal is known mediately, through memory or inference. In such a case, then, the perceptual knowledge of the universal (sāmānya-jñāna) does the duty of sense-contact (pratyāsatti) in causing the immediate knowledge of the class. Hence this kind of perception is named sāmānya-lakṣaṇā-pratyā satti, which literally means contact through the knowledge of the universal.

The most important ground for accepting this view is that in such an inference as "Wherever there is smoke there is fire; there is smoke in that mountain; therefore there is fire on that mountain;" we have a general proposition ("Wherever there is smoke there is fire") expressing a universal relation between the middle term, smoke, and the major term, fire. The question arises as to how such a general connection between all smokes and fires comes to be ascertained. In our experience we can ascertain only that a certain case of smoke, say that in the hearth, is a case if fire. But how can we go beyond that particular experience case so as to be able to arrive at the general proposition "All cases of smoke are cases of fire"? If our perception is confined to particular facts alone, all that we can legitimately assert is that "This case of smoke is this case of fire"; and even by repeating this perception in different cases we get only a series of particular propositions of the same kind and never the desired general proposition. Nay we can go a step farther to say that if

1 Tattva-cintāmaṇi, Anumāna-khaṇḍa, pp. 283-293, and Bhāṣā-pariccheda, Kār. 64.

our perception were confined to the particular presented smoke alone, we would not even have the problem, "Is all smoke attended with fire?"[1] And without such a problem we would have no motive for repeating our observation or experiment in order to find out whether the connection between smoke and fire was invariable or only casual. Thus the chances of our obtaining a general proposition would be all the more remote. The best way out of this difficulty is to admit that while perceiving the smoke in the hearth, we perceive the class characteristic (sāmānya), i.e. the universal "smokeness," and through that perceive also all smokes as possessing this "smokeness".

The second ground in support of this view concerns the knowledge of the absence of a class of things. We pass such judgments as "There is absence of cowness in this horse." This judgment means the same as the simple judgment, "This horse is not a cow." Nobody would question the validity of such a judgment. But how is it possible? If our perception were only of the presented particulars we could legitimately say only "This horse is not any of the cows hitherto perceived." The assertion of the absence of cowness amounts to the denial of the existence of cows in general, and as such it presupposes the knowledge of all cows. To account for the validity of such judgments, we must admit that we have knowledge of a class of objects as well as of the particular members of that class. But how can we get such knowledge? Not through ordinary sense-presentation, for all the members of a class are scarcely ever presented to the sense of any one observer; nor through inference, for inference already presupposes the knowledge of a class. It is convenient, therefore, to hold that when any one member of a class is presented to sense, we have, through the universal inhering in it, a perceptual knowledge of the class itself.

The third ground advanced relates to objects of our conscious desire. We strive after a pleasure. This pleasure is in the future—it is yet to be. If all pleasures we know were exactly those that we have previously experienced, we would be altogether ignorant of *the* pleasure which we strive after. But it is absurd to suppose that we may be ignorant of the object of our conscious volition. This difficulty is easily removed when

1 Siddhānta-muktāvali on Kār. 64-65: "Pratyakṣadhūme vahnisambandhasya gṛhītatvāt, anyadhūmasya ca anupasthitatvāt dhūmo vahnivyāpyo na vā iti saṃśayānupapatteḥ"; also Anumāna-cintāmaṇi, pp. 283-284.

we admit that in perceiving particular pleasures in the past we have virtually perceived the whole class of which the future pleasure is one.[1]

These are some of the important arguments advanced in support of the view that a class is perceived *pari passu* with the perception of a member of that class. Let us see now how the Advaitins meet these arguments.

As to the first argument, the Advaitins[2] say that inference is possible even without the perceptual knowledge of all the individuals of a class. Such knowledge would have been necessary had it been a fact that in perceiving a particular we perceived it as a mere particular—had it been the case, for instance, that in perceiving smoke attended with fire in a hearth, we had knowledge of the form "*This* smoke is attended with *that* fire." But as Naiyāyiks also admit, in perceiving a particular we perceive also the universal class characteristic inhering in it. In other words, when we perceive smoke and fire in the hearth, we do not have knowledge of two unique particulars, as such, but two particulars characterized by the two universals "smokeness" and "fireness" respectively. If so, from this perception we know also of a relation between smokeness and fireness; and when subsequently we see smoke on the mountain possessing the class characteristic, "smokeness," we remember its relation with the class characteristic, "fireness," and thereby infer the presence of fire there. What is necessary for inference then, is not the perception of all members of a class, but the knowledge of the universal class characteristic. On seeing smoke on the mountain we can infer the existence of fire there, only if we know that there is some invariable relation between smokeness and firness. And for ascertaining such a general relation it is not at all necessary to *perceive* all smokes and the relation of each instance with an individual fire. The same explanation obviously solves also the question, raised by the Naiyāyikas, as to how by seeing the particular smoke in the hearth attended with fire we can at all have such a problem as "Is there fire on the mountain?" When we happen to see smoke on the mountain. The first argument of the Naiyāyikas for accepting the perception of a class does not, therefore, stand scrutiny.

1 Anumāna-cintāmaṇi, pp. 285-290.
2 Advaita-siddhi, pp. 337-339.

As to the second argument, the Advaitins say that the judgment about the absence of cowness in a horse does not necessarily presuppose the immediate knowledge of all cows. It is sufficient for the purpose to know what the characteristic of cowness is, and that can be known in the perception of any individual cow. We can pass the judgment, "This horse is not a cow," or "There is absence of cowness in this horse," even after perceiving a single cow and knowing thereby the charateristic of a "cow", i.e. "cowness". The contention of the Naiyāyikas on this ground also then breaks down.[1]

As to the third argument, the Advaitins hold that though it is necessary to know the object of our conscious desire, it is important to understand in what sense it has to be known. It is not necessary to have previous knowledge of the identical individual object we desire to attain; it is sufficient if we only know what it is like, i.e. if we only know that it is something possessing the quality which can satisfy our desire—the quality being already known to us in the past perception of some one object of the class possessing the quality.

In desiring a future pleasure and in striving after it, we do not at all require to know that particular pleasure previously; it is sufficient if we know that it is something that possesses the quality of pleasantness, which common characteristic has been perceived in past cases of pleasure. The contention of the Naiyāyikas, therefore, is not so reasonable as it first appears to be.[2]

Thus the Advaitins dismiss all the arguments put forward in support of sāmānya-lakṣaṇa, and maintain that there is no fact of experience, to explain which we may be compelled to admit the theory that in the perception of an object presented to sense we also perceive all other unpresented members of that class. To admit such a theory, the Advaitins think, is to ignore the vast distinction that exists between immediate and mediate knowledge. A further discussion of this theory will be necessary in connection with the question of the possibility of inferential knowledge, and we need not dilate on this topic any more at present. We pass next to the consideration of the second type of extraordinary perception, viz, jñāna-lakṣaṇa.

1 Advaita-siddhi, pp. 341-342.
2 Advaita-siddhi, p. 339.

According to the Naiyāyikas there is a second type of cases which also illustrate the immediate knowledge of objects not presented to sense. On *seeing* a piece of sandalwood at a distance we may say. "Here is some *fragrant* sandalwood", even though we may not actually *smell* the fragrance. How does this *immediate* knowledge of fragrance arise? Evidently there is no ordinary sense-contact to account for its presentation. In such a case, then, we must suppose that the sight of the sandal vividly revives the memory of its fragrance perceived in the past, and the fragrance appears to be immediately felt. We find then that the revived knowledge (Jñāna) officiates here for sense-contact in causing the immediacy of the object.[1]

The perception of illusory objects is also explained with this theory of jñāna-lakṣaṇa by the Naiyāyikas. The sight of a rope in twilight revives vividly, by its similarity, the idea of snakehood perceived in the past in real snakes. This vivid memory causes an apparent immediacy and the illusion of the rope as a snake.

It should be observed that in each of these cases of extraordinary perception—sāmānya-lakṣaṇa and jñāna-lakṣaṇa—the knowledge (jñāna) of some universal does the duty of sense-contact in order to cause perception ; in the former case the agent is the perceptual knowledge of a universal which inheres in the object to be perceived, and in the latter it is the reproduced knowledge of the very object to be perceived. So the difference between these two cases lies in the fact that while in the former the knowledge, that acts as the agent, leads to the perception of the locus (e.g. all individuals like cows) in which the perceived universal (e.g. cowhood) remains, in the latter case the knowledge (e.g. the memory of fragrance), acting as the agent, leads to the perception of its own object (e.g. fragrance).[2]

The Advaitins do not accept the Nyāya theory of jñāna-lakṣaṇa. As we have just seen, the theory of jñāna-lakṣaṇa is advanced by the Naiyā yikas to explain two kinds of facts—one represented by cases like that of the perception of fragrance in a distant sandal, and the other by cases of perceptual error. The Advaitins hold that each of these two types of cases can be explained in a different way which makes the Nyāya theory unnecessary.

1 Bhāṣā-pariccheda. Kār. 65 and Muktāvalī, on the same.

2 Loc. cit. (p. 279. Nirnayasagara ed.).

The first type of cases really comes under inference and not at all under perception.[1] In judging the fragrance of a distant piece of sandal, we really infer the existence of fragrance from the fact of its being sandal. If the perception of the sandal, and the previous knowledge that sandal is fragrant, can be thought of as leading to the perception of the non-sensed fragrance, nothing can prevent us from thinking that even in cases of inference such as the knowledge of fire from the perception of smoke, we do not really infer the smoke, but perceive it. For is there not a similar perception (viz. of the smoke) and a pre-existing knowledge (viz. that smoke is always attended by fire)? It follows therefore that the theory of jñāna-lakṣaṇa removes the distinction between perception and inference—a distinction that the Naiyāyikas try to preserve as much as any other school.

As to the second class of facts (namely cases of false perception) the Advaitins say that the theory of jñāna-lakṣaṇa does not satisfactorily explain the immediacy of the illusory object. The perception of a tortuous length may, on the basis of similarity, revive the memory of a snake. But how this memory (or recollection of snakehood) can amount to the perception of the snake is not explained by the Nyāya theory. There is a vast difference between recollection and perception which cannot be so easily ignored. The presentation of the object in illusion calls for a more adequate explanation. For this purpose we must admit that in illusion the object is somehow presented directly.

On these grounds the Advaitins argue that since the theory of jñāna-lakṣaṇa does not really explain either of the two kinds of facts it seeks to explain, it must be rejected as altogether unjustifiable.

Before we bring this topic to a close, it will be useful to understand critically the real merits of the Nyāya theory and the vedāntic objection. It should be noticed that whereas the existence of the first kind of extraordinary perception (viz. of all members of a class) must be ascertained logically as being necessary for the explanation of the possibility of inference, etc., the existence of the second kind (viz. jñāna-lakṣaṇa) must be ascertained by a direct appeal to experience. In support of his theory that the fragrance of unsmelt sandal is perceived when the sandal itself is seen, the Naiyāyika appeals to direct experience and asks whether we do not pass such a judgment as "Yonder sandal is fragrant," even before we really smell the sandal. If such a judgment is the expression

1 Advaita-siddhi, p. 343.

of an immediate feeling, and if immediacy is regarded as the essence of perception, then we can hardly reject the Naiyāyika's contention that there is perception of the unsmelt fragrance as well.

It may be remarked that what, in Western psychology, is called "assimilation" by writers like Wundt[1] or "complication" by Stout[2] and Ward[3], is virtually the same as the jñāna-lakṣaṇa of the Naiyāyikas. Assimilation, according to Wundt, is a form of simultaneous association taking place between two sets of elements, one of which is derived from "objective impression" and the other from "earlier percepts" or ideas. It is illustrated when, on hearing a word only in part, we seem to think that we have heard the whole of it, or when, on seeing a misprinted word, lacking one or two letters, we read it as if it were printed correctly. In such a case, according to Wundt, we *assimilate* the presented elements to some previous percepts which they most resemble. Illustrations of "complication," according to Stout, are to be found when we say that a thing "*looks* hard" or "soft," "smooth" or "rough," "cold" or "hot," "sharp" or "blunt." In his Article in the *Encyclopaedia Britannica,* Ward illustrates "complication" by the example of the sight of a "suit of polished armour" instantly reinstating "all that we retain of former sensations of its hardness and smoothness and coldness."

What is most important to notice in this connection is that, according to all these writers, we have in these instances of "assimilation" or "complication" not a mere revival of past ideas, as in memory, but a consequent *perception* of the unpresented elements. Wundt explains the correct reading of misprinted words as "due not so much to the fact that we fail to notice the wrong letter which is present, as to the fact that we *see* the right letter for the wrong one."[4] Wundt speaks, therefore, of the "*seeing*" of the right letter that is really absent or unpresented. Similarly, Ward[5] distinguishes the "reinstatement' of "former sensations" of hardness,smoothness and coldness at the sight of "polished armour," from the revival of the "ideas" of "tournaments," "crusades," etc., which also

1 *Outlines of Psychology,* pp. 257-264.
2 *Analytical Psychology,* vol. ii, pp. 26-27.
3 *Encyclopaedia Britannica,* 9th ed., vol. xx, p. 57.
4 *Outlines of Psychology,* p. 261 (my italics).
5 *Encyclopaedia Britannica,* loc. cit.

may accompany that sight. Stout makes the point even clearer when he says, "Yet its cold look is not a suggested *idea*; it is something which is *presented* as if included in the visual appearance, as an integral part of it. It belongs to the *impression* in such a way that any attempt to separate it destroys its sepcific character."[1]

It appears, therefore, that the Nyāya theory of Jñāna-lakṣaṇa would probably be accepted by Western thinkers who also believe in the perception of unpresented elements, the memory of which is vividly revived, through association, by elements presented to some sense.

In the light of these Western views the Nyāya theory would thus appear to be all the more plausible, and the Advaitins' objection considered to be untenable. But a further analysis of this problem reveals some important points which tell against such a conclusion. It is true that we often pass such a judgment as "Yonder sandal is fragrant," or "Cotton *looks* soft," or "This ice *looks* cold," and that each of these judgments seems to imply immediate knowlede of fragrance or softness or coldness. But the question can still be asked :—Does such a judgment really stand criticism? Does it remain unchallenged or uncontradicted when it is further subjected to scrutiny? The reply to this question will certainly be in the negative. When we ask ourselves, on subsequent reflection, whether we really had any immediate feeling of fragrance just as we had while smelling the sandal in the past, or whether we had any immediate feeling of coldness just as we had in tthe past when we touched ice, we find that we lack the memory of any such *feeling*, which alone can enable us to answer the question in the affirmative. In fact, such reflective criticism invariably withdraws from our first judgments the warrant for immediacy. We feel that the sandal was not *really felt* to be fragrant, and the ice not *really felt* to be cold. In other words, we find that the judgment, "Ice *looks* cold" cannot be legitimately upheld, and the judgment "Yonder sandal is fragrant" cannot be maintained to be derived from any immediate perceptual feeling. It must therefore be admitted that a judgment of the type, "Yonder sandal is fragrant," must be derived from some non-immediate, i.e. mediate, source. The justification of the possibility of such a judgment may force us to admit the agency of an implicit inference—an inference of which we are

1 *Analytical Psychology*, vol. ii, p. 26.

not directly conscious, but the existence of which can be logically ascertained through another inference.

If this analysis be satisfactory, the Nyāya view of jñāna-lakṣaṇa can hardly be thought to be tenable. On the contrary, we must admit that the Advaitins who consider jñāna-lakṣaṇa to be a case of inference are nearer the truth.

Of the three kinds of extraodinary perception admitted by the Naiyā yikas we have considered the first two. We have now to notice the third, which is called yogaja-pratyakṣa. The Naiyāyikas and some other thinkers believe that through concentration a yogin can achieve the supernatural faculty of perceiving all things, concealed, distant, and infinitely small. Such a perception obtained without the help of a sense-organ is called yogaja-pratyakṣa or yogi-pratyakṣa.

The Naiyāyikas strengthen their inference about atmost by saying that yogins can perceive them. Bhāṭṭas[1] reject this possibility of extra-sensory perception. The Advaitins also disregard[2] such yogic discipline as harmful to the higher pursuit of Brahman. Moreover, they do not admit the possibility of external perception without sense-activity, as already shown.

6. Internal Perception

We have seen in a previous connection that the Naiyāyikas, as well as many other Indian philosophers, speak of manas as the internal sense-organ (antarindriya). According to them, therefore, an internal perception is one that takes place through the instrumentality (karaṇatva) of this internal sense, manas. The objects of internal perception, according to the Naiyāyikas, are pleasure (sukha), pain (duḥkha), desire (icchā), hatred (dveṣa), knowledge (mati), will or effort (kṛti).

The Advaitins, while generally agreeing with these thinkers as to the direct awarencess of these internal states, differ from them on some essential points. As we have already seen, Advaitins—except those who belong to the school of Vācaspati-miśra—do not regard manas or antaḥkaraṇa as a sense-organ (indriya). According to them, therefore, perception does not take place through the instrumentality of manas *as an organ*. They think that the conditions of perception in these cases are

1 vide Mānameyodaya, p. 70 (Trivandrum, 1912).

2 vide Advaitabrahmasiddhi, pp. 294 and 300 (Calcutta Univ., 1932).

exactly similar to the cases of external perception. The condition of the perception of an object, as we have seen, is that an identity should be established between the object and the antaḥkaraṇa, which assumes the form of the object. Now, while in external perception the object is something other than the antaḥkaraṇa and antaḥkaraṇa has to go out to the object and assume its form, in the case of internal perception the object is identical with the antaḥkaraṇa itself (since pleasure, etc. are but states of antaḥkaraṇa), and consequently the antaḥkaraṇa that is already identical with the object, which is its own self, has not to go out to any foreign object through a sense. It is therefore a limiting case of the ordinary process of perception—a case in which the antaḥkaraṇa-vṛtti and the object are one and the same.[1]

Perceptual consciousness, as we have seen, is not regarded by the Advaitins (as it is by the Naiyāyikas) to be a result of the interaction of a sense and its object. According to the Advaitins immediacy is but the ever-perfect light of the self, as reflected against the inert antaḥkaraṇa. Just as the solar light is only *revealed* by being reflected against a dark background and cannot be said to be generated by that contact, so the light of the self also is only revealed through the antaḥkaraṇa as the background and cannot therefore be said to be generated by any interaction. And just as the particular shape and form that the background possesses become revealed through the solar rays, so the object whose form the antaḥkaraṇa takes is revealed through the light of the cit or the self. This form may be the form of a foreign object, or may be the form of the antaḥkaraṇa itself, according as the object is external or internal—but that makes no difference to the question of immediacy. When the object lighted by the self is a state of antaḥkaraṇa itself (e.g. pleasure, pain, etc.) the object is described by the Advaitins as being kevala-sākṣibhāṣya (i.e. illuminated or revealed by the witnessing self alone). This means that in such a case there is no instrumentality of any foreign source such as a sense-organ, an inference, etc.[2]

Among the objects of internal perception the Naiyāyikas include the self—ātman—as well. But they think that the self as such, i.e. stripped of

1 Vedāntaparibhāṣā, p. 29, Sikhāmaṇi, p. 59, and Maṇiprabhā, p. 60.

2 Vedānta-paribhāṣā : "Na hi vṛttiṃ vinā sākṣi-viṣayatvam kevala-sākṣivedyatvam, kintu indriyānumānādi-pramāṇavyāpāram antareṇa sākṣiviṣayatvam," p. 82.

all predicates or adjectives, cannot be perceived. The ātman is perceived only as the subject of a judgment, the predicate of which is itself preceptible. Such perceptions are found in experiences like "*I am happy*," "*I am sorry*" (where "happiness," "sorrow," etc. are perceptible).[1]

The Advaitins do not believe in such introspection of the self. The self is immediacy itself and it is through its light that other things are revealed. It is self-shining and the idea of its being an *object* of any kind of knowledge—introspection or extrospection—is absurd *ex hypothesi*. The "I" (aham) that is known as "happy" or "sorry" is not the self (ātman) in its purity; it is a fictitious limited self which appears thus to be an object of consciousness.

We have criticized the theory of the objectivity of self in a previous chapter and no fresh comment is necessary on this point in the present connection. But before we close our discussion on internal perception it is necessary to consider one more case, which is much debated by the different schools of Indian Philosophy.

It relates to the question how knowledge is known? According to the Buddhistic idealists knowledge and the object of knowledge are indistinguishable from each other; they are known together. The well-known dictum expressing this position is—"As blue and the consciousness of 'blue' are invariably known simultaneously, 'blue' is not different from the consciousness of 'blue'."[2] If, then, knowledge and its object are identical, knowledge of knowledge is nothing more nor less than the knowledge of the object. Realists, naturally, do not accept such a position. In order to avoid such subjectivism, they attempt to keep the knowledge of an object as distinct from the knowledge of that knowledge as possible. The Naiyāyikas hold therefore that it is not a fact that the knowledge of an object is known simultaneously with the object. We perceive the pot first, and it is only by an act of reflection at a *subsequent* moment (anuvyavasāya) that we become aware of the knowledge of the pot. The Mīmāṃsakas of the Bhāṭṭa school go a step farther. They say that the knowledge of the object, pot, is not perceived even at any subsequent moment. Knowledge is never immediately known, either at the time the

1 Siddhānta-muktāvali on kārikā 49.

2 Sarvadarśana-saṃgraha on Bauddha system. The dictum is "Sahopalambha niyamāt abhedo nīla-taddhiyoḥ."

object is so known or at any subsequent moment of reflection. The dictum runs. "Just as the tip of a finger cannot touch itself, so knowledge cannot know itself by itself." Knowledge is known, however, through inference. In order to explain the quality of knownness (jñātatā) abiding in an object that was known previously, we must suppose, for want of any other explanation, that there was such a thing as the knowledge of the object. Knowledge, therefore, is never known directly; it is inferred from the quality of knownness that is found to exist in the object in such an experience as "The pot is known."[1]

The Advaitins do not accept any of these position.[2] Against the Bhāṭṭas they urge that the Bhāṭṭas seem to think that, as a result of the knowing activity of the self, the object (the pot) comes to acquire the quality of being known which is similar to its other qualities of size, colour, etc., and that the knowledge of the pot is to be inferred from this objective quality (viz. knownness). But this theory is unintelligible, because we cannot understand how the knowing activity of the self should be able to endow the object with a quality of knownness which is to be conceived as objective like the spatial properties of the object—its colour, size, etc. It is contradictory to think, as the Bhāṭṭas do, that knowledge is the activity of the self, and yet the result of this activity (viz. knownness) is an *objective* characteristic on a par with colour, size, etc. The result of the activity of the self must be regarded as being in the self and not in the object; that is, it must be subjective and not objective. The attempt to infer the knowledge of an object from any objective characteristic of the object itself is, therefore, doomed to failure. Consequently the theory of the Bhāṭṭas is untenable.

As against the Naiyāyikas, the Advaitins argue[3] that the theory that knowledge is known in a subsequent reflective knowledge involves a great difficulty. To suppose one knowledge to be the object of another knowledge is to hold that two states of knowledge exist together at the same time, which is inconceivable. But there is also another difficulty. The naiyāyikas hold that the subsequent reflective knowledge, in which the previous knowledge is known as an object, is a self-conscious judgment of the form, "I know the pot (the object)," (ghaṭam aham jānāmi) or what

1 Sāstradīpika, p. 56.

2 Vivaraṇa-prameya-saṃgraha, p. 55.

3 Ibid., p. 55.

is the same, "I am possessed of the knowledge of the pot," (ghaṭa-jñāna-vān aham). In such a case, the knowledge (of the pot) comes to be perceived as a quality inhering in the self. The self is directly perceived, and knowledge is perceived indirectly through the perception of the self. In the Nyāya scheme of relations between the mind and the percept, already explained, the relation between the perceiving mind and this knowledge known falls within the class saṃyukta-samavāya—i.e. inherence in the conjoined. For in this case there is first a direct connection of the mind with the self, and then, through the self, with the knowledge inhering in it. But this account of the naiyāyikas does not satisfactorily explain the knowledge of knowledge. The self, according to the Naiyāyikas, has many qualities inhering in it and all of them are not held to be perceived in the perception of the self. For instance, infinitude, which according to the Naiyāyikas is an attribute inhering in it, is not said to be perceived in the perception of the self. As the attribute of a self is not *necessarily* perceived, therefore, in the perception of the self, it is of little help to say that knowledge is perceived as being an attribute of the perceived self. For even then, to answer the question why the attribute knowledge should be perceivable, whereas some other attributes of the self are not perceivable, the Naiyāyikas must say, "Because knowledge is an attribute the nature of which is to be perceived." If so, the Vedāntin asks, what error is there in supposing that it is the very nature of knowledge to reveal itself, or to be self-manifest?[1] As the Naiyāyikas are ultimately compelled to say that knowledge is perceived, not because it is an attribute of the self but because it is the nature of knowledge to be perceivable, they gain little by resorting to the roundabout way of explaining that knowledge is perceived as an attribute inhering in the self, which is perceived by the mind.

Thus in rejecting the views of the Bhāṭṭas and the Naiyāyikas, the Vedāntins themselves hold that it is the nature of knowledge to be self-manifest. It is unnecessary, therefore, either to infer its existence or to perceive it in subsequent knowledge. When the pot is known, the knowledge of the pot also becomes manifest at that very moment. The self-manifesting nature of knowledge is regarded by the Vedāntins to be a unique subjective characteristic, which therefore cannot be classed under immediacy (pratyakṣatva) as pertaining to objects. As Mādhavācāryya

1 Ibid.

puts it, "Things like pots are peceived (pratyakṣa) as objects. But knowledge (pramiti) being self-manifest (svaprakāśa) cannot be regarded as an object of perception (pratyakṣa)."

But while maintaining that knowledge becomes manifest simultaneously with the perception of the object, the Advaitins hold with the Prābhākaras (who also subscribe to the "self-manifest" view of knowledge) that this position does not necessarily lead, as the Buddhists contend, to the conclusion that knowledge and its object are identical. Knowledge and its object are directly felt to possess diametrically opposite characteristics, neither of which can be reduced to the other. On this point the Advaitins support the Prābhākaras, who criticize the Buddhists by saying that the simultaneity of awareness does not argue identity of existence, and that the very fact that the Buddhists hold knowledge and the known to be identical presupposes that even to them the two are somehow known to be distinct. Were they experienced as wholly identical, they could not even *speak* of the two.[1]

The Advaita theory of the self-manifesting nature (svaprakāśatva) of knowledge, however, calls for a few words of criticism, and explanation. We have shown in a previous context (while discussing jñānagata-pratyakṣa and viṣayagata-pratyakṣa), that the condition of the immediacy of the *knowledge* of a pot, according to the author of the Vedānta-paribhā ṣā, is that the antaḥkaraṇa should go out, through a sense, to the object, pot, to assume its form. Inferential knowledge of a pot does not fulfil this condition, and so it is mediate. If knowledge is self-manifest how can it sometimes be mediate? How would the Advaitins explain this? To answer this question we must point out that he Advaitins primarily start with the theory that every knowledge, whether perceptual or inferential, has a subjective side of pure awareness (cit or saṃvit) which is the life and core of the self itself, so that nothing stands between knowledge and the self (that is to say, no mediation is necessary) and consequently knowledge must necessarily be immediate or self-manifest. But there is another side to knowledge in which reference to the object is all-important. It is from this side that we divide knowledge into two classes, immediate and mediate, though from the former point of view knowledge can be said

1 Prakaraṇa-pañcikā, p. 60 f.

only to be immediate. Now from this latter point of view, knowledge, being about an object, is immediate or mediate according as the object is known immediately or mediately. Knowledge of the pot, from this objective standpoint, can be said to be immediate when the condition, referred to above, is satisfied, and the object is related to the subject thereby. Thus this condition does not conflict with the fundamental Vedāntic position that knowledge in its subjective aspect (chit) is immediate or self-manifest, so long as we remember the two aspects of knowledge, the subjective consciousness which is self-manifest, and the objective mode (vṛtti) which is illumined by the former.

It is necessary to consider another kind of difficulty that may arise in understanding the self-manifesting character of knowledge. In common parlance we sometimes say, "He knows that he knows it," "He does not know that he knows it." If such phrases express our experience faithfully, we must say that knowledge is sometimes known and sometimes not known. How can we reconcile, then, this fact with the theory of the self-manifesting nature of knowledge, according to which knowledge would be always known and could never remain unknown?

In reply to this question, it may be pointed out that these popular usages may be considered to subvert the self-manifestness of knowledge, only if it can be shown that they prove that we may know a thing, and yet may not know that we know the thing *exactly as* it is known. To put it symbolically, it has to be shown that we may know *A* as characterized by *x*, and yet may not know that we know *A* as characterized by *x*. It will not affect the theory of self-manifestness in the least if it be found that the popular usage, when cleared of ambiguity, only means that we may know *A* as characterized by *x*, but may not know *A* as characterized by *y*. Now popular statements about ignorance of knowledge will be found to be reducible to the latter type and will not therefore be found to be subversive of the "self-manifest" theory. To take a concrete instance, we have such statements as "An illiterate Englishman may know English without knowing that he knows English." When the meaning sought to be expressed in this sentence is expressed without any ambiguity, some such expression has to be used : "An illiterate Englishman may know a language for the expression of his thoughts, but he may not know that the language is called English by others." It will readily be seen that in this sentence knowledge, in the first half, concerns one aspect of language (viz. its usability), and in the second half quite another aspect (viz. its nameability). It only shows that a man may know how to speak a language but may not know the name of the language. It would tell against the self-manifest view only if the expression meant that the man knows how to speak the language, but does not know that he knows how to speak the language.

We believe this will be found, on analysis, to be the real nature of the so-called examples of ignorance of knowledge. As we are unable, then, to discover a genuine case of the ignorance of knowledge, criticism of the "self-manifest" theory from this direction falls to the ground. But it may be asked, if knowledge is always self-manifest, why should we not have a judgment like "I know the thing," every time that we know a thing and as soon as we know it? To this question we reply that an explicit judgment, which is but one of the many possible paraphrases or interpretations of an experience, takes place only when it is required to meet a necessity created by any particular situation. A judgment of the kind "I know the thing," takes place when it is thus needed. Such a judgment may take place simultaneously with the knowledge, or at a subsequent moment, or never, according as the necessity for such a judgment may arise simultaneously with the knowledge, at a subsequent moment, or at no time. Such being the case, it does not necessarily follow that if knowledge be self-manifest, it should be attended always with such a simultaneous judgment.

But it may be asked, "How do you even know that knowledge is self-manifest, if along with knowledge you do not have any judgment or experience reporting your awareness of that knowledge?" The reply is that even without any such simultaneous report we can infer the self-awareness of knowledge from the testimony of our memory. At a subsequent moment I can judge not only that " I remembered the table," but also that "I remember to have perceived the table." Both these memory judgments are undoubtedly based on past perceptual knowledge alone. Now if the first judgment shows that I cannot remember the table unless I had a direct awareness of the table, the second judgment shows that I cannot remember to have perceived the table unless I had a direct awareness of the perception also. This *direct* awareness of the perceptual knowledge can but be simultaneous with the knowledge.

Now it remains only to ascertain what the nature of this direct a wareness of knowledge is. Do we become aware of knowledge exactly as we are aware of the objects of our knowledge? To answer this question in the affirmative is to ignore altogether the peculiar nature of knowledge as contrasted with that of its object. The object can be known or can remain unknown, but knowledge remaining unknown is an unthinkable contradiction. The object, by nature, is revealed in knowledge, and knowledge is self-revealing. Knowledge, like a light, reveals the object as well as itself. To say that knowledge, to be known, requires another knowledge is to forget its essential nature; it is like saying that a light, to be seen, requires another light. Thus the direct awareness of knowledge as presupposed by the memory of knowledge, is nothing but the self-revelation of knowledge. Even such phrases as "Knowledge reveals itself" or " Knowledge manifests itself" are misleading, retaining as they do an apparent polarity in the use of the cognate object which, strictly speaking, applies only to the objective world. It would be wrong, therefore, to understand from such phrases that knowledge becomes its own object. In reality, however, knowledge neither needs to be, nor can be, an object either of itself or of any other knowledge. Self-manifestness of knowledge means that knowledge can behave as being immediate without being an object of knowledge. This would be an exact rendering of the explanation of the term svaprakāśatva (self-manifestness) as given by the Advaitins:—avedyatve sati aparokṣa-vyavahāra-yogyatvam svaprakāśatvam.[1] With this we conclude our discussion of internal perception.

1 Citsukhi-, p. 9.

BOOK II

COMPARISON (UPAMĀNA)

BOOK II

COMPARISON (UPAMĀNA)

1. THE PROBLEM

KNOWLEDGE of similarity may be acquired in different ways, one of which, as we have shown in a previous context, is perception. If when a certain object "A" is directly presented to sense and another object "B" is the object of a past perception, we judge that "A" is like "B," the judgment of similarity ("A" is like "B") may be said to be derived from perception. For we can very well say here "A *looks* like B." But if subsequently we pass from this judgment to the judgment "B is like A," we cannot possibly say that the second judgment also is a judgment of perception, because the subject of this latter judgment, namely "B," is not perceived, and we cannot possibly say "B *looks* like A." The question, therefore, arise, "How is such a judgment derived?" This question represents, in short, the problem of upamāna as conceived by the Advaitavedāntins and the Mīmāṃsakas. To understand more clearly the problem and the solution offered to it, we must consider the concrete instances through the investigation of which the Vedāntins try to establish their view.

A certain person who has seen his own cow at home goes to a forest and sees there a gavaya—a wild cow having no dew-lap—and forms the judgment, "This gavaya is like my cow." He passes thence to another judgment, "My cow is like this gavaya." Of these two judgments the first represents knowledge gained through perception, and the second contains knowledge that is derived through the instrumentality of the perceptual knowledge contained in the first.[1] The psychological account of the process is that at first there is a perception of some points of similarity in the gavaya, secondly there is revival, through similarity, of the memory of the cow seen at home, and lastly there is the consequent judgment that the cow seen in the past is like the gavaya presented to sense. The question arises as to what the name and logical status of this psychological process yielding the aforesaid judgment are. It is evident that this judgment—"My cow is like this gavaya"—being derived through the mediation of

1 Cf. Vedānta-paribhāṣā, p. 230 : " . . . gavaya-niṣṭha-go-sādṛsya-jñānam karaṇam, go-niṣṭha-gavaya-sādṛsya-jñānam phalam."

the knowledge— "This gavaya is like my cow"—cannot be classed under immediate knowledge; it must be admitted to be a kind of mediate knowledge. But it is also found that this knowledge cannot be classed under inference (anumāna), which is the chief form of mediate knowledge generally known, because we do not find in the process leading to this knowledge any trace of syllogistic reasoning. We must admit therefore, conclude the Vedāntins, that this kind of knowledge, derived through the perception of similarity, must be given a place distinct from that of perception or inference. In recognition of this unique character the Vedāntins and the Mīmāṃsakas give it an independent name—upamāna—which etymologically means comparison or knowledge of similarity.

2. Is Upamāna an Inference ?

Some thinkers object to this view of the Vedāntins and Mīmāṃsakas, and believe that what is called upamāna by these writers is really a case of inference (anumāna). For they think that it is possible to derive syllogistically the judgment, "My cow is like this gavaya," from the given perceptual judgment, "This gavaya is like my cow." The required syllogism will be :—"If anything is like another thing, then the other thing is also like that thing; this gavaya is like my cow, therefore my cow is like this gavaya."[1]

In reply to this objection the Vedāntins say that though it is true that the conclusion, "My cow is like the gavaya," *can* be derived thus syllogistically from the given premise, it does not necessarily follow that it is always so derived *actually*. It is found, on the contrary, that in most cases the conclusion is reached directly without the help of any major premise—i.e. without the knowledge of an invariable relation (vyāpti) between the middle and the major terms which is essential to syllogistic inference (anumāna).[2] It is quite possible to imagine that even a man who has never *perceived two* similar things together, so as to be able to acquire the general knowledge that if a thing A is similar to another thing B, then B must be similar to A, can judge, while seeing a gavaya in the forest after having seen a cow at home, that the cow at home is like the gavaya

1 Vedānta-paribhāṣā, pp. 232-233. The major premise is put there in the categorical form, which is the practice with Indian logicians. For simplicity of translation we put in the hypothetical form. The sense is not, however, affected thereby.

2 Vedānta-paribhāṣā, p. 233.

before him.[1] The explanation of such cases at least requires us to admit that similarity predicated of a subject that is not presented to sense is at least sometimes known through a unique method of knowledge different from inference (anumāna).

3. Is it a Perception ?

The Sāṃkhya school of thinkers, however, hold that upamāna can be shown to be a case of perception,[2] and does not, therefore, require to be classed apart. Similarity between two things means the existence of some features that are common to both. The features in the gavaya the perception of which enables us to judge that this gavaya is like the cow, are identical with those in the cow, the knowledge of which enables us to think that the cow is like this gavaya.[3] Now these features being identical, they are perceived whether we see a gavaya or a cow. From the perception of the gavaya we can, therefore, know both that the gavaya is like the cow and also that the cow is like the gavaya. It must be admitted, therefore, that the second judgment is derived neither from inference nor from any other unique source, but from perception just as is the first judgment.

In reply to this critcism the Vedāntins say that though the points of similarity between a cow and a gavaya are common to both, these common features as inhering in the two different objects cannot be considered to be identical.[4] If that were so, on perceiving these common features in a gavaya we should have subsequently remembered, not only that we had perceived the similarity to a cow in a gavaya, but also that we had perceived the similarity to a gavaya in a cow.[5]

We can have, as everybody will agree, a memory of the second type, after perceiving only a cow and not a gavaya. This difference clearly shows that the judgment, "My cow is like this gavaya," cannot be derived directly from the perception of a gavaya just as the other judgment, "This gavaya, is like my cow," can be. The attempt to include cases of upamāna in perception must therefore fail.

1 Sāstradīpikā, p. 76.
2 Tattvakaumudī, "Ata eva smaryamāṇāyām gavi gavaya-sādṛsya-jñānam pratyakṣam," (p. 174, Chowkhamba, 1921).
3 Ibid.
4 Ṣikhāmaṇi, p. 232, and Āśubodhinī, p. 137-138.
5 Āśubodhinī, p. 138.

4. Is it Partly a Perception and Partly a Memory ?

Still another type of criticism has been levelled against the theory of upamāna. It has been urged that in the case under consideration we can look upon the judgment, "My cow is like this gavaya," as being derived partly through perception and partly through memory; the subject "cow" is known through memory, while the predicate "like the gavaya" is known through the perception of the points of similarity in the gavaya. If, therefore, instead of giving a sweeping general answer to the question as to whence this judgment is derived, we give the analytic answer, namely that the subject of the judgment is derived from memory and the predicate from perception, there will be nothing left to compel us to hold that the whole is derived through a third source distinct from either of these two.[1]

Forcible as this criticism may appear to be, it is easily met by the supporters of upamāna, who urge that the explanation of the component elements of the judgment by no means explains the judgment completely. For over and above the question as to whence the elements of the judgment are derived, there remains the question as to how these elements came to be related together. And it is this latter question which concerns us most in the present connection. Though we know the cow through memory and know the points of similarity through perception, neither memory nor perception can give us the knowledge of the cow as characterized by the attribute of being similar to the gavaya.[2] And it is for this last knowledge that we are to recognize the existence of an altogether new method of knowledge, upamāna. If the explanation adopted by the critic were to be accepted, we should have no reason to recognize even inference as an independent source of knowledge. For in an inference like "Wherever there is smoke there is fire; there is smoke on that mountain, therefore there is fire on that mountain," we have two terms in the conclusion, one (mountain) of which can be known through perception and the other (fire) through memory. There being no other component left unexplained, the question of inference does not arise at all.[3] It is found, therefore, that the method of explanation pursued by the critic would lead him to an

1 Siddhānta-candrikā, p. 74, and Śloka-vārtika, p. 445, and Nyāyaratnākara thereon.
2 Śloka-vārtika, p. 445: "Viśiṣṭasyānyato siddher upamānapramāṇatā."
3 Ibid.

absurd position, which he himself would be unwilling to accept. Such faulty criticism should not be thought, therefore, to prejudice the case of upamāna, as established by the Vedāntins and the Mīmāṃsakas.

5. The Nyāya View

It is necessary to mention in this connection that the Naiyāyikas, though admitting upamāna to be one of the independent and ultimate sources of knowledge, use the word in a different sense. Upamāna, according to the Naiyāyikas, is the process of knowledge through which we come to know that a certain word denotes a certain class of objects. The illustration they use will make the statement clear. A certain villager is told by a forester that a gavaya is a wild animal that looks like a cow. The villager afterwards goes to a forest and happens to see a wild animal of that description. He perceives in the animal the similarity to a cow, remembers the words of the forester, namely that a gavaya is like a cow, and then comes to the conslusion, "The word gavaya denotes the class of objects similar to the cow."[1] This resulting knowledge is called upamāna. The Naiyāyikas state that this knowledge is attained through the instrumentality of the perception of similarity, which in its turn leads to the recollection of the definition of a gavaya learned from the forester.[2]

But this Nyāya view of upamāna is rejected by the Advaitins on the grounds that if it is to be maintained, we must show that we achieve through this method some knowledge which cannot be obtained through any other accepted method like testimony, inference, etc. But what information do we obtain through this method, according to the Naiyāyikas ? It is the knowledge that the word gavaya denotes the class of objects that are similar to the cow ? Or is it the knowledge that the word gavaya connotes the universal, "gavaya-ness" (gavayatva) ? If it be the first, we find that this information is already obtained from the testimony of the person who tells us what gavaya is like. If it be the second, we find that this knowledge can be derived through an inference like "The word gavaya possesses a connotation (i.e. gavayatva), because it is a word like 'jar,' 'cloth,' etc., which have connotations." It is found, therefore, that the object which

1 Siddhānta-muktāvali on Kārs. 79-80.
2 Ibid.

the Nyāya upamāna seeks to attain is easily obtained either through testimony or through inference.[1]

In this manner the Vedāntins meet the various objections raised against their own theory and try also to refute the parallel theory advanced by the Naiyāyikas. It will now be interesting to judge the merits of the Vedānta view in the light of the logical theories of the West. It will be easily seen that the arguments of the Vedāntins (namely that the conclusion reached through the method of upamāna cannot be said to be reached through inference, because it can be shown to be attained without any syllogistic reasoning, will scarcely convince a student of Western logic.

6. The Evidence of Western Logic : Is Upamānaan Immediate Inference ?

Most Western logicians hold that over and above inference of the mediate or syllogistic type there is a whole class of inferences that are immediate and non-syllogistic. To prove conclusively that upamāna is not a case of inference it is not sufficient, therefore, to prove only that upamāna cannot be a case of syllogistic or mediate inference; it is also necessary to prove that it is not a case of immediate inference. But as soon as we try to prove this second part of the contention, in order to carry conviction to the student of Western philosophy, we are faced with a difficulty before which the Vedāntin's theory seems to give way. For upamāna, in which we pass from knowledge like "A is similar to B" to knowledge like "B is similar to A," seems to be a clear case of immediate inference—a case, namely, of the conversion of a symmetrical relation. It appears, therefore, that the Vedāntin's theory can stand so long as the partial and one-sided Indian view of inference shields it from criticism; but as soon as it is brought out of its original narrow field of dogmatism and called upon to defend itself in the open court of reason, it finds itself hopelessly embarrassed. But weak as the case may appear to be, it is not fair to abandon it do the fate of such a summary trial. We should fully enquire, before we condemn it, if no defence of the Vedānta view is really possible.

It is no defence to point out that Indian logicians do not recognize any inference except of the mediate type, unless sufficient reasons are adduced to show why inferences of the immediate type should be rejected.

1 Śikhāmaṇi, p. 236.

We search in vain for such reasons in Indian philosophy itself. According to the Indian conception, an inference (anumāna) is essentially an argument from at least *two* premises, one expressing an invariable relation (vyāpti) between the middle and the major terms, and the other a relation between the middle and the minor terms. Thus according to this view no inference can be immediate. Indian logicians do not seem to realize the possibility of inferring any conclusion from one premise or one term; hence there is no discussion at all regarding the cases of immediate inference, as found in Western philosophy. We find at times, however, some instances of the so-called immediate inference put in the usual syllogistic form. This fact might indicate that the Indian logicians considered most of these cases to be forms of mediate or syllogistic reasoning. But we have no such view explicitly stated. We cannot, therefore, expect much help from Indian thinkers themselves in our attempt to show that immediate inference should be rejected.

Our next attempt will naturally be to court the support of those Western philosophers like Bain and Bradley, who depart from the general Western theory and reject the existence of so-called immediate inference. But tempting and hopeful as this line of procedure may at first appear to be, it only lands us in fresh difficulties. For though their rejection of immediate inference seems to be favourable to our purpose, the grounds on which these Western thinkers reject this kind of inference prove all the more perplexing to us. They are generally of two kinds :— either that a so-called immediate inference is only a verbal transformation of a known proposition and lacks, therefore, one of the essential characteristics of inference, viz. the attainment of new truth; or that, if it contains any new truth at all, it is a suppressed form of mediate inference. To accept any help from these Western thinkers is to commit ourselves to one of these two alternatives. In other words, we must either hold that upamāna is not an immediate inference because it yields no new truth, or hold that upamāna, though yielding a new truth, cannot be an immediate inference because it is of the mediate type. But both these alternatives would be suicidal, because while the second amounts to the confession that upamāna is an inference, the first puts it altogether out of the bounds of a pramāṇa (which, as we have seen, must yield some new knowledge). We find, therefore, that it is impossible to remove the doubt that upamāna is a kind of immediate inference by showing, with the help of these Western writers, that there is no such thing as immediate inference.

We should recognize, however, that this attempt, though not successful, has revealed one more fundamental doubt, which also has to be satisfied before we can attain any final settlement of the issue. We have learned, in other words, that to establish the case of upamāna we must, in addition to proving that it cannot be inference mediate or immediate, also prove that it is really a case of the acquistion of new knowledge and not a mere verbal transformation of an old piece of knowledge, contained in a proposition of a different form. With these added burdens of proof we must abandon this line of procedure for a more frontal attack on the problem.

We shall take up the last question first. For it is only when we find that upamāna represents a real advance of knowledge, and not a mere verbal change, that the question arises as to whether it is inference or any other kind of knowledge. Otherwise this question does not arise at all. Now in order to be able to do justice to the Vedānta position, we should make the question before us precise and definite by distinguishing it from some other questions with which it may be very easily confused. The two judgments "A is like B" and "B is like A" can be related in at least four different ways. This gives rise to at least four different cases, which we shall consider one by one. In the first case, A and B are both perceived. In the second, they are both remembered. In the third, one of them, A, is perceived and the other, B, remembered. Lastly, in the fourth, the initial premise, "A is like B," is given as a hypothesis or derived from testimony, either or both of the terms being previously unknown. The Vedāntin's enquiry, so far as we understand it, relates only to the third case.

What we have to observe is that in the first two cases, A and B—the subject and the predicate of the premise—are both known in the same way—i.e. either through perception or through memory. And in these cases the passage from "A is like B" to "B is like A" may be thought to be a mere verbal rearrangement of the same fact, because both judgments may here be regarded as having the same ground of assertion. In these cases it may be an abuse of terms to say that "B is like A" *follows* from "A is like B" as a conclusion from a premise; for the very ground that enables us to assert the apparent premise may enable us also to assert the so-called conclusion, and it may be a pure accident that the one is asserted first and the other afterwards; the order might be easily reversed without much difference. The only difference between the two judgments is perhaps (as Hobhouse would put it) that while in the first instance

"A is full in the focus of consciousness as B is rising; in the second B is in the full light, while A is relatively on the outside."[1] Hence it may be thought, after Bradley, that "the alteration which is made is psychological, not logical, and is concerned with nothing but the verbal expression,"[2] and that the passage from the one judgment to the other is apparent, not real.

But a little different from the first two cases is the fourth, in which the ground for the judgment "A is like B" is altogether unknown. Here the only way to obtain the judgment "B is like A" is to *infer* it from the given judgment, "A is like B." B is like A, *because* A is like B. Here the order of the two judgments is not arbitrary; it is externally fixed, and the second judgment cannot be said to be already given in the first. It will be difficult to hold in this case, therefore, that the second judgment is but the first judgment restated in a different form.

But when we come to the third case, which illustrates upamāna as conceived by the Vedāntins, we find it still more difficult to maintain that the second judgment, "B is like A", is a mere verbal transformation of the first judgment, "A is like B." The first judgment represents a perception; A is perceived to be like B; A *looks* like B. The second judgment cannot be considered to be perceptual ; B is absent and cannot, therefore, be said to *look* like A. This difference alone is sufficient to show that in such a case the second judgment cannot be supposed to be derived from the very source from which the first is derived. Consequently it cannot be said that the second judgment only expresses in another form the experience or knowledge which constitutes the first. We may conclude, therefore, that upamāna is a genuine case of new knowledge. Our next task is to prove that it is not a case of inference, mediate or immediate.

That upamāna is not mediate inference has been proved by the Vedāntins themselves, as stated already, and there is scarcely anything to be added to the arguments advanced by them. It will be sufficient to show, therefore, that it is no immediate inference. For this purpose it will be convenient once more to recall the four cases of the knowledge of similarity distinguished above. In either of the first two cases the second judgment, as already shown, does not represent any case of new knowledge; it is

1 *Theory of Knowledge*, p. 259.
2 *Logic, Part* II, p. 416.

derived from the same source as the first and no question of inference arises there at all. In the fourth case, where the judgment "A is like B" is given either as testimony or as hypothesis, it is possible to obtain the second judgment, "B is like A," *only* as an eduction from the first. This eduction may be considered to be a case of immediate inference. But in the third case, which is the case of upamāna, though we pass from the perceptual knowledge contained in the first judgment, "A is like B," to the knowledge contained in the second, there is no eduction here. It will not be a correct representation of our exprience in this case to say that here also we judge B to be like A, *because* A is perceived to be like B. The judgment "B is like A," is derived here from the perception in A of its similarity to B, and the memory of B. The distinction between the process leading to this judgment, and the process yielding the judgment in the fourth case (i.e. the case of inference) noted above, should make it clear that the two cannot be regarded as fundamentally the same, so as to deserve the common name of immediate inference. On the contrary it is felt that the process involved in the third case should be recognized as a distinct method of obtaining knowledge and given a separate name. It is found, in other words, that what is called upamāna cannot be regarded as a case of immediate inference.

But after everything has been said to show that upamāna is not an inference, it is necessary to add a word by way of qualifying our conclusion. In showing that upamāna is not a case of immediate inference we have assumed that an immediate inference is an eduction from a *given term or proposition*. But if it is regarded as a process whereby we derive a conclusion through the mediation of *any* kind of knowledge, upamāna would clearly be a case of immediate inference. It must be added, however, that the distinction between the fourth and the third case is so important that even if they be included in one class, they should be regarded as *two distinct* species under the one genus of immediate inference.

It should be remembered, again, that for the Advaitin, who holds that upamāna is not a case of anumāna, this elaborate defence is partially unnecessary. The word anumāna, as already noticed, stands only for mediate inference, and it is sufficient for him to prove that upamāna is not an inference of this class. The arguments set forth above to show that it is not a case of immediate inference serve, therefore, only to remove the curiosity of a student of Western logic, who may ask the more general question,"Is upamāna a case of inference,mediate or immediate ?" Our answer to this question also, as shown above, should be in the negative, excluding the qualification we have mentioned there.

We should note that upamāna, as described above after the later Mīmāṃsakas and Vedāntins, is very narrow in scope. An earlier view found in Śabara's commentary on Jaimini's sūtras (1. 1. 5) takes it in the wider sense of any analogical "knowledge of an unperceived object as being similar to some known object." Śabara says, "Just as you feel your self, so by upamāna you can believe that others also feel the existence of their selves." This earlier conception would have a very wide scope, though the defence given above of the narrower sense would not wholly apply to it.

Before we conclude this chapter, we shall notice incidentally a question that is allied to that of upamāna. It is : How is the knowledge of dissimilarity obtained ? This question is not dealt with by the chief writers of the Advaita school, and we are compelled to surmise the answer from the general position of the Advaitins. A contemporary commentator[1] of the Vedānta-paribhāṣā seems to subscribe to the view of the Nyāya-siddhānta-mañjarī, that knowledge of dissimilarity also is obtained through upamāna. Let us examine this view.

There are different cases of the knowledge of dissimilarity between A and B, which we shall consider separately in order to arrive at a solution of the question. If A and B are both perceived, or even if A alone is perceived and B is remembered, then the knowledge "A is dissimilar to B" may be regarded from the Advaita standpoint as a case of anupalabdhi (the particular method to which the Vedāntins ascribe the knowledge of the non-existence of the perceptible), because the judgment "A is dissimilar to B" can be interpreted as "There is in A non-existence of similarity to B," and it can be argued that if A were similar to B, the similairty would have been perceived.[2] When again A and B are both remembered and we have the judgment "A is dissimilar to B," the case would be the same as the first. But when A is perceived and B is remembered, and we have the knowledge "B is dissimilar to A," it is difficult to say to what source the Advaitins would ascribe it. As we shall see when we discuss anupalabdhi in Book III, according to the

1 M. M. Ananta Kṛṣṇa Śāstrī, author of Paribhāṣāprakāśikā (vide p. 176 of Vedāntaparibhāṣā edited by him, published by Calcutta University, 1927).

2 For a fuller discussion of this point vide Book III.

representative Advaita works we know a thing through anupalabdhi only when we can argue that if the thing existed it would have been *perceived*. In the above case, we cannot say that if there were similarity in B it would be *perceived*. For as we have seen, similarity in such a case is known not through perception, but through upamāna. Hence it is not an undisputed case of anupalabdhi. It may be regarded as a case of upamāna, because the process of knowledge involved in it is essentially the same that in the knowledge that B is similar to A.

Admitting that dissimilarity is known through upamāna, Ananta kṛṣṇa Śāstrī raises and solves a very pertinent question, viz., what is the use of this source of knowledge for the Advaitin ? He points out that it enables the Advaitins to know the exact phenomenal nature of the world through the knowledge that the world is dissimilar to the Absolute Reality, on the one hand, and, to the utterly unreal, on the other. In the light of the foregoing critical enquiry, this solution would appear to be unacceptable, since the world is a perceived object. In fact, if the narrow sense of upamāna expounded above be accepted it would be hard to find its application in Advaita or even in ordinary life. If, however, it is understood in the earlier and wider sense found in Śabara, then, we can find ample use of upamāna in ordinary life (as illustrated by him), as well as in Vedānta. For example, the Brahman (unknown to the novice) can be understood analogically as being like the material cause of a perceived object, or like the substratum of an illusory object, and so on. The Upaniṣads are full of such uses of upamāna—the attempts of the teachers to convey to the disciples the idea of the suprasensible in terms of its similarity to the sensible.

Book III

NON-COGNITION (ANUPALABDHI)

BOOK III

NON-COGNITION (ANUPALABDHI)

1 THE PROBLEM OF ANUPALABDHI

We pass judgments about the non-existence of things as well as about their existence. Some of these judgments are, of course, based on inference, testimony, etc., as when a judgment about the non-existence of fever is formed from the perception of the low position of the mercury thread in a thermometer, and again when a judgment of the non-existence of headache is passed on the authority of the words of a patient, and so forth. But how (i.e. through what type of knowledge) is the judgement of non-existence derived when, for instance, a person endowed with sight and sitting in a room, sufficiently lighted, says, "There is no jar now on the ground" ? At first sight this judgment of non-existence appears to be one of perception, because the knowledge obtained is evidently immediate. But difficulty arises when we try to understand how sense can possibly grasp non-existence. If the sense-perception of an object presupposes some relation of that sense with that object, we cannot by any stretch of imagination conceive how sense can come into any relation with non-existence, so that it might be perceived. How, then, is non-existence known in such a case? This, in short, is the problem discussed by the Advaita-vedāntins. under anupalabdhi.

2. THE VIEWS OF THE PRABHAKARAS AND THE SAMKHYAS

The solution of this prolem depends chiefly on the conception of non-existence. There are in Indian Philosophy three main conceptions of non-existence (abhāva), and consequently three different ways of solving this problem. The Prābhākaras maintain that non-existence has no reality apart from that of an existent thing. The same existent object is judged to be existent with reference to itself and non-existence with reference to other things.[1] The ground itself on which there is no pot, says the author of the Prābhākara-vijaya, is judged to be existent with reference to itself and non-existence with reference to the pot, and there is no need therefore for assuming that non-existence has a separate reality.[2] The non-existence of

1 Saptapadārthī "Tathāhi prābhākaraḥ bhāvāntaram eva bhāvāntarāpekṣayā abhāva iti vyavahriyate," p.76 (Medical Hall, Benares).

2 Prabhākara-vijaya, p.57 (Sans. Sahitya Parisad. Calcutta,1926).

a jar on the ground is, therefore, nothing over and above the existence of the locus, the ground. It is not, however, identical with *any* state of the existence of the ground; but only with the state of unqualified or pure existence of the ground, i.e. the bare ground (bhūtalamātram), unoccupied by any other thing.[1] The Sāṃkhyas also hold that of the many forms or transformations (pariṇāmas) of the locus, the ground, the one that is devoid of any content is identical with the non-existence of the jar on the ground.[2] In a word, according to both the Prābhākaras and the Sāṃkhyas the non-existence of a thing in a particular locus is nothing but the existence of the bare locus or the *locus per se* (adhiṣṭhāna-mātram or adhiṣṭhāna-svarūpam).

According to this view, therefore, the judgment of non-existence of the type in question can be easily said to be derived through perception. The difficulty as to how non-existence can become the *object* of perception does not at all arise, because perception of the non-existence of the jar on the ground means, according to this view, nothing but the perception of the ground, which as everybody will grant, can be perceived through sense. The non-existence of the jar, therefore, can be known through perception.[3]

3. THE VIEWS OF THE NAIYĀYIKAS

The Naiyāyikas come to the same conclusion by a different line of argument. According to them non-existence of a thing in a particular locus is not identical with the locus but adjectival to it. For we always say that the ground is *characterized* by the non-existence of a jar. The non-existence of a jar on the ground is therefore to be conceived as a character (viśeṣaṇa) of the ground, and it is reasonable to suppose that it is perceived *through* the perception of the ground, just as the attributes of the ground like colour, size, etc., are perceived. Sense cannot of course come into relation with this character, i.e., non-existence in the same way as it can with the attributes of colour, size, etc. The Naiyāyikas admit, therefore, a special kind of relation (sannikarṣa) for this purpose, and call it viśeṣaṇatā or adjectivity. The sense comes into this kind of relation with a character (viśeṣaṇa) like non-existence (and also the relation of samavāya) *through*

1 Śāstradīpikā, p. 84.

2 Tattva-kaumudī, 'na hi bhūtalasya pariṇāmaviśeṣāt kaivalya-lakṣaṇād anyo ghaṭābhāvo nāma,' pp. 179-180 (Chowkhamba).

3 Ibid. : "evam abhāvo pi pratyakṣam eva."

its relation with the locus of that character. They explain in detail how this process takes place specifically in the different cases of the different kinds of *loci,* the particulars of which we need not discuss in the present connection. It is sufficient to mention here that the relation of sense with non-existence varies with the six kinds of relation sense can have with the object, the details of which have been discussed already in the chapter on Perception.[1]

4. THE VIEWS OF THE BHĀṬṬAS AND THE ADVAITINS

The Bhāṭṭa school of Mīmāṃsakas,[2] and with them the Advaitins, hold, however, that non-existence (abhāva) is not identical with its locus but is something additional to it (adhiṣṭhānātiriktam tattvam). The statement of Kumārila Bhaṭṭa in the Ślokavārtika (p. 476) or that of Pārthasārathi Miśra in Sāstradīpikā (p. 83) to the effect that everything has two forms, one of existence and the other of non-existence, above, namely that non-existence is nothing but existence appears to be similar to the view of the Prābhākaras stated of something else, and that the non-existence of the jar is nothing but an aspect of its locus, the ground. A critical study of the texts of the two schools reveals, however, the real distinction underlying this superficial similarity; and it may be summed up thus :—In saying that existence and non-existence are but two aspects of the *same* thing, the Prābhākaras desire to show that the non-existence aspect of a thing cannot be divorced nor abstracted from its existence aspect, but that, on the contrary, the former is reducible ultimately to the latter, which is, therefore, the basic and the only real aspect.[3] The non-existence of a jar is thus nothing but the existence of its bare locus, the ground. But the Bhāṭṭas assert that existence and non-existence are the *two different* aspects of a thing, and as such the one is *not* reducible to the other; that the *two* serve *two different* purposes and possess *two different* meanings. Non-existence therefore is something different from existence. The ground has two *equally real* and fundamental aspects—its own *existence* and the *non-existence* in it of all other things except it; and these two are mutually irreducible. The Advaitins, as the Vivaraṇa-prameya-saṃgraha[4] states,

1 Tattvacintāmaṇi, p. 691, and Siddhānta-muktāvalī on Bhāṣā-pariccheda.

2 Śloka-vārtika and Śāstradīpikā on abhāva.

3 Cf. the Prābhākara dictum :

> "*Bhāvāntaramabhavo hi kayā cit tu vyapekṣayā*
> *Bhāvāntarād abhāvo nyo na kaścid anirūpaṇāt* ":

quoted in Saptapadārthī, p. 76.

4 P. 16—"vyavahāre bhaṭṭanayaḥ."

follow the Bhāṭṭas in these empirical matters, and we do not find any independent elaborate discussion of this point in their works. Let us see how the Bhāṭṭas and, after them, the Advaitins establish their theory by refuting the other two views stated above.

If the non-existence of a pot on the ground were but another name for the bare ground or the ground *per se*, we should perceive the non-existence of the pot, even while it is there on the ground[1] because it cannot be said that the ground, as such, is not perceived while the pot is on it. Again, if perception of the bare locus led to the knowledge of non-existence, there could not arise the knowledge of the non-existence, of a jar on the ground while there was, for instance, a cloth on it.[2] Besides, as there may be simultaneous non-existences of many things in the same locus, we should be aware of all of them every time that we perceive the locus, which is not really the case. However, it happens very often that we become aware of the non-existence of a thing in a locus long after the locus itself is perceived. How could this happen if the perception of non-existence consisted simply in the perception of the locus? These difficulties stand, therefore, in the way of the acceptance of the view that non-existence is identical with its locus, and that knowledge of it means nothing more than the knowledge of the bare locus. If however the statement, "the non-existence of a jar is nothing but the bare ground," be analysed, it is found on the contrary that non-existence has to be understood as something different from its locus. For what does the bare ground mean? It surely cannot mean anything but the ground in which there is nothing else, i.e. in which there is *non-existence* of all other things.[3] If so, this non-existence as being possessed by the ground must be different from the ground, the locus. Perception of the locus cannot, therefore, *by itself* amount to the perception of the non-existence present in it.

Neither is it reasonable to accept the Nyāya view which, while granting that non-existence is different from its locus, lays down that it can be perceived as adjectival to the locus. Since it cannot be understood how *non-existence* can be related either with its locus or with sense.[4] The relation of saṃyoga or samavāya,[5] possible only between two existent entities, cannot relate *non-existence* to either a locus or a sense.

1 Śāstradīpikā, p. 84.
2 Ibid., p. 84.
3 Śāstradīpikā, pp. 84, 86.
4 Vedānta-paribhāṣā, p. 320; Śikhā-maṇi, p. 321, and Śloka-vārtika, p. 479.
5 *Vide ante*, p. 109; and Nyāyaratnākara on Śloka-vārtika, p. 479.

On no grounds, therefore, can it be maintained that non-existence is perceptible through sense. But can it be said, then, that it is inferred? No, because a thing can be inferred from the knowledge of some mark that is invariably related with it, and when the nature of the thing itself is unascertained, as is the case with non-existence, how can the relation of something else with it be ascertained?[1]

Let us explain this remark more fully. The attempt to derive the knowledge of non-existence from inference will take some such plausible form as "The jar does not exist on the ground because it is not perceived there. What is not perceived in a place does not exist there." The major premise of this inference implies a universal relation between non-perception and non-existence. But this presupposes the knowledge of non-existence; and the question would be raised, how is that non-existence again known? As a consequence of this, either a *regressus ad infinitum* or a *petitio principii* would follow.

But if non-existence is known through neither perception nor inference, and the knowledge of it through any other means generally known is inconceivable, how do we at all speak of non-existence? How is it then known? It is known, conclude the Advaitins and the Bhāṭṭas, through a unique means of knowledge (pramāṇa) called non-cognition (anupalabdhi), or rather appropriate non-cognition (Yogyānupalabdhi).

To understand more fully and clearly the conception of this method of non-cognition, it is necessary for us to refer to the account given by the Bhāṭṭas whom the Advaitins, as already said, mostly follow in this matter. Śabarasvāmin (the author of the Jaimini-sūtra-bhāṣya) says that the absence of other means of knowledge is itself a means of the knowledge of non-existence of things not presented to any sense.[2] This meaning is more clearly expressed by Kumārila Bhaṭṭa, who says that if a thing be such that while it exists, its existence is revealed through any of the five means of knowledge, and if still there is no knowledge of the thing, then this non-cognition (anupalabdhi) of the thing is evidence (pramāṇa) for the non-existence (abhāva) of the thing.[3] Pārthasārathi Miśra further explains this view in the following way :—Every object has double aspects, namely existence and non-existence. When an object like a jar has existence in

1 Śāstradīpikā, p. 87.
2 "Abhāvopi pramāṇābhāvo nāstīyasyāsannikṛṣṭasya," sūt. 1. 1. 5. p. 10. (Asiatic Soc. ed., 1873).
3 Śloka-vārtika, p. 473.

some place at some time, it is judged through perception or some other means of knowledge to be existing then and there. But when no such means yields any knowledge of the object, though it is capable of being known under those conditions, the object is judged, through that very absence of knowledge, to be non-existent in that place at that time.[1]

Advaitins (like the authors of Vedānta-paribhāṣā, Śikhāmaṇi, Maṇiprabhā, etc.) define anupalabdhi more precisely and formally in order to obviate possible objections.[2] The pramāṇa of anupalabdhi, says the author of the Vedānta-paribhāṣā, is the specific cause of such immediate knowledge of non-existence as has not been produced by any of the known means of knowledge such as perception, inference, etc. The chief points sought to be brought out in this definition are the following—(1) Knowledge derived through anupalabdhi has for its object non-existence of something; (2) it is immediate and presentative, so that it does not include the memory of past non-existence; (3) it is not produced by any of the ordinary positive means of knowledge, so that inferential knowledge of non-existence also is to be excluded from it. Knowledge of this specified character is then to be regarded as a product of the specific method, i.e. anupalabdhi or non-cognition.

But the question may be asked, "Does non-cognition of a thing always lead to the knowledge of its non-existence? If not, when does it do so?" That non-cognition does not always cause the knowledge of non-existence can be easily seen from the fact that we do not judge the non-existence of a visible thing, say a chair, in a dark room, simply because we do not then have any visual knowledge of it. It is, therefore, necessary to answer the question as to when non-cognition can yield the judgment of non-existence.

The author of the Vedānta-paribhāṣā[3] replies that only an appropriate non-cognition can lead to the knowledge of non-existence. But how is this appropriateness to be ascertained? It may appear at first sight that an appropriate non-cognition is the non-cognition of a perceptible object. This would, of course, hold good of cases like the non-cognition of the pot on the ground ; the absent object, the pot, is perceptible if present ; and hence non-perception of it yields the knowledge of its non-exsitence. But it does not apply to the case of a judgment of non-existence like "There is the difference form a spirit in this pillar" (i.e. This pillar *is not*

1 Śāstradīpikā, p. 83 also Śloka-vārtika, pp. 476-478.
2 Vedānata-paribhāṣā, p. 317. Śikhāmaṇi, p. 317. Maṇiprabhā, pp. 317-318.
3 Vedānata-paribhāṣā, p. 317.

a spirit), or "There is the difference from ether in earth," (i.e. earth *is not* ether) which can be legitimately formed on the visual perception of the locus—the pillar or the earth—though in such a case the absent object (the spirit or the ether) cannot be said to be appropriate because it is not by itself perceptible. These exceptions might tempt one to maintain that appropriateness of a non-cognition depends really on the appropriateness of the locus (adhiṣṭhāna) of absence and not on that of the absent object (abhāvapratiyogī). This will of course hold good in the above cases because there the loci, the pillar, the earth, etc., are all perceptible. But exception to this view also can be taken. For if it were true, the non-existence of virtue and vice (dharma and adharma) in the self (ātman) would be known through non-cognition, because the self is perceptible and therefore an appropriate locus. But the non-existence of virtue or vice can never be so known; it is known through inference. Hence it is easily seen that the appropriateness of a non-cognition cannot be ascertained either from the appropriateness of the object that is absent, or the appropriateness of the locus of absence.[1]

The appropriateness (yogyatā) of a particular non-cognition can, however, be tested, says the Vedāntaparibhāṣā,by ascertaining whether *the object not known would have been known, had it been present there, under those very circumstances.*[2] To take a concrete instance, the absence of the visual knowledge of a jar on the ground in the broad daylight is an appropriate non-cognition, and can therefore lead to the judgment of the absence of the jar, because we can argue, "Had there been a jar under these circumstances, it would have been seen." But the non-perception of a jar in the dark room is not an appropriate non-cognition (and we cannot, therefore, judge that the jar does not exist) because we cannot feel sure that if the jar had been there it would have been seen. Again, though a spirit (or ether) is not perceptible by itself, we can yet argue that if there were a spirit (or ether) as identical with a pillar (or earth), it would have been perceived. Hence the non-existence of the spirit (or ether) as a pillar (or earth) can be said to be known through anupalabdhi. But we cannot similarly argue, had there been dharma in the self it would have been perceived. Hence the absence of dharma in the self cannot be known through anupalabdhi.

1 Vedānta-paribhāṣā and Maṇiprabhā, pp. 318-319.
2 Vedānta-paribhāṣā, pp. 318-319

Mudhusūdana Sarasvatī in his Advaita-siddhi states a similar definition of appropriateness (or yogyatā) though in different words: "The non-exsistence of that thing in a certain place is appropriate, the existence of which in that place is opposed to (not compatible with) its non-perception."[1]

The Maṇiprabhā, a gloss on the Sikhāmaṇi (a commentary of the Vedānta-paribhāṣā), defines the Advaita view more explicitly, including in one long sentence all the conditions and qualifications.[2] It is impossible literally to translate this complicated definition into one sentence in English; but the sense of it can be expressed as follows :—If a particular sense does not yield the knowledge of an object as possessing particular characteristics and as existing in a particular locus, being related to it in a particular way, and if that object be such that it is perceived, if existing, *under those circumstances,* then that absence of knowledge is a means to the knowledge that the object as possessing those characteristics does not exist in that locus in that relation.

The object of mentioning these various conditions will be clear from some concrete instances. If a jar, while perceived from a distance through the visual sense, is not perceived through touch, we cannot, from the absence of the tactual knowledge, judge its non-existence; because it is not capable of being perceived through that sense (i.e. touch) under those circumstances, Again, if a jar is not perceived as existing on the ground, in the relation of identity with it, it cannot be judged that the jar does not exist on the ground, in the relation of conjunction also. If, again, a black jar is not perceived on the ground, it cannot be judged that a red jar also does not exist there, and so forth. It is needless to note here that the qualification mentioned by the Vedānta-paribhāṣā, namely "If the object existed it would have been perceived under those circumstances as such," would, if fully understood, be quite sufficient to remove the various discrepancies sought to be guarded against by the long statement of conditions made by the Maṇiprabhā, which only explicates what is implicitly contained in the universe of discourse.

5. Objections Answered

The Advaitins and the Bhāṭṭas consider some objections that can be raised against their theory, and it is necessary to mention here the more important of these.

1 Advaita-siddhi, p. 810.

2 Maṇiprabhā on Śikhāmaṇi, p. 318

It may be said by the Sāṃkhyas and the Naiyāyikas that since the Advaitins must admit that there can be the cognition of the absence of a jar on the ground only when there is some sense-activity and never without it they should admit also, for simplicity of explanation (lāghava), that the knowledge of the non-existence, like that of its locus, is derived through sense-perception and not through an additional independent source.[1] To this the Advaitins reply that the sense-perception that is invariably present accounts for the perception of the locus and the locus alone.[2] It is inconcivable how sense can come into relation with non-existence, and how the antaḥkaraṇa can assume the form of a non-existent object.[3] It is impossible to argue, therefore, that because the activity of some sense is invariably present in every case of the cognition of non-existence, such cognition must be derived through sense. On the contrary it is reasonable to argue that as sense-activity is present in the immediate cognition of both existence and non-existence, while the *non-cognition* of the absent object is present only in the case of cognition of non-existence, it is this peculiar factor of *non-cognition* which is specially responsible for the cognition of non-existence.

The question how non-cognition—a *non-existent something*—can be the *cause* of some knowledge should not present any difficulty. Just as an existent cognition can yield the knowledge of an existent something, similarly the non-existent cognition or non-cognition can yield the knowledge of a non-existent something. Besides, even in the opponent's view, non-existence has to be credited with causality. For how can non-existence be said to be the object of sense-perception unless it is admitted that this perception is *caused* by *non-existence* as its object?

It is not true that the cognition of non-existence is more simply explained by admitting that it is a case of sense-perception. As the factor of non-cognition (of the absent object) has also to be admitted to be the cause of the knowledge of non-existence (it also being invariably present like sense-activity), the supporters of the view of the perceptibility of non-existence are forced to assume two causes of such knowledge, viz. sense-activity *and* non-Cognition. In view of this, therefore, it is found that the credit for simplicity of explanation is on the side of those who make non-cognition, alone the specific cause of the knowledge of non-existence and not on the side of those who have to accept two causes.[4]

1 Vedānta-paribhāṣā and Śikhāmaṇi, p. 320.
2 Ibid., pp. 320-321.
3 Ibid.
4 Maṇiprabhā , p. 321, and Āśubodhinī, p. 211.

Of the two factors, invariably present, one, non-cognition, alone must be accepted as the special cause since a sense cannot be conceived to grasp non-existence.[1]

By far the most convincing ground for thinking that non-existence is not perceived through sense is, however, the following argument of the Bhāṭṭas.[2] There are cases of the immediate cognition of non-existence relating to past times. One can think, for example, at noon that one did not see a tiger in a particular place in the morning. This knowledge of non-existence cannot be explained as the memory of past perception (of non-existence) that we had in the morning, because the knowledge of the non-existence of the tiger requires at least the recollection of a tiger, and as we may not have thought of a tiger at all that morning, there could not possibly be any knowledge (per-ceptual or non-perceptual) of the absence of a tiger at that time. Such a case of the knowledge of non-existence shows, therefore, the inadequacy of the theory that non-existence can be perceived through sense. On the other hand, it is very easily explained if non-cognition be held to be the means of the knowledge of non-existence. The absence of the memory of a tiger at that place and time is a form of non-cognition, that is a means to the knowledge of non-existence in this particular case. The question may be asked here : Is not anupalabdhi defined by Śabarasvāmin as absence of a means of a right knowledge (pramāṇābhāva), and is not memory excluded from a pramāṇa? How, then, can absence of memory be regarded as a case of the absence of pramāṇa?[3] In reply to this the author of the Nyāya-ratnākara says that though memory is not itself a pramāṇa i.e. an original source of valid knowledge, it is still the result of a pramāṇa (pramāṇa-phala) and consequently the absence of memory implies the absence of pramāṇa as well.[4] According to the Advaita theory, the absence of the tiger can be known through anupalabdhi because even here it can be argued, "Had there been a tiger it would have been perceived." It is not an ordinary case of memory.

From all these considerations it will be sufficiently clear that the knowledge of non-existence in question cannot be regarded as the result of sense-activity, though this latter may be present in every case of such

1 Āśubodhinī, p. 211.
2 Śāstradīpika, p. 84, and Nyāyaratnākara on Śloka-vārika, p. 483.
3 Paribhāṣā-prakāśikā, p. 243 ; a commentary on Vedānta-paribhāṣā by Anantakṛṣṇa Śāstrī.
4 Nyāyaratnākara, p. 484.

knowledge. But an Advaitin may still be asked by a Nayāyika : "In the judgment 'There is no jar here on the ground,' you must admit that non-existence of the jar is as much immediately known as the ground. Why should you not, therefore, admit that the non-existence is known also in the same way as the ground, i.e. that when the antaḥkaraṇa goes out to the ground and sets up a relation between it and the knower, it also thereby establishes a similar relation between the knower and the non-existence that inheres in the ground?[1] If the character of the knowledge produced be the criterion for ascertaining the means through which the knowledge is derived, how can you, in the present case, say that the ground is known through one means and the non-existence through another, notwithstanding the fact that the knowledge of both of them possesses the same character of immediacy?"

In reply to this question the Advaitins say that though the non-existence of the jar is felt to be as immediate as the ground, and though the antaḥkaraṇa goes out to the ground, we cannot say that the antaḥkaraṇa takes the form of the non-existence ; because non-existence, though an attribute of the ground, is such that no sense can be conceived to come into contact with it, and consequently antaḥkaraṇa can be thought to be assuming the form of it.[2] In consideration of this difficulty it canot be believed that the non-existence is known in the same way as the ground. Besides, it is not a universal rule that the character of the resulting knowledge decides the question as to the *means* through which the knowledge is derived. For even knowledge derived through testimony can acquire the character of immediacy. It is the character of the mental function or process (vṛtti) producing knowledge that really decides the question as to its means or method. In the case under discussion, the mental function in the form of the negative judgment, "There is no jar on the ground," cannot be possibly produced by any sense-activity. Hence non-existence cannot be said to be known through sense-perception, even when the knowledge of it is felt to be of an immediate character.[3]

The Advaitins may be asked to solve still another difficulty. Having admitted that the knowlege of the non-existence of the jar is direct or immediate, they must also admit that the illusory cognition of the non-existence of the jar must be of an immediate type. But the Advaitins also

1 Vedānta-paribhāṣā, p. 321.
2 Ibid., p. 322.
3 Vedānta-paribhāṣā, p. 322, and Śikhāmaṇī, pp. 322-323.

lay down the general theory that in every case of immediate illusory cognition the object present is produced by Nescience (Māyā). So they must admit that when we wrongly judge that there is no pot on the ground (though really there is a pot there), the wrongly perceived non-existence, is produced by Māyā. Then the difficulty arises as to how Māyā, which is conceived as a *positive* entity (bhāva-rūpā), can be the material cause of non-existence. But if the present case be said to be an exception, the Advaitins must give up their fundamental theory, namely that Māyā is the material cause of *all* phenomena.

The Advaitins[1] evade this difficulty by saying they do not admit that in all errors of immediate knowledge the object is produced by Māyā. In cases where the wrongly perceived object is really present in a contiguous locus and immediately known, the Advaitins (like the Naiyāyikas) hold that the error is caused not through the fresh production of an illusory object but through the transference of a really perceived object from its own locus to a locus in which it does not really exist (anyathā-khyāti). In the present case also the jar's non-existence in some other contiguous locus is simply transferred to the ground. For example, the absence of a jar perceived in the colour of the ground may be immediately known and this absence, instead of being judged to be in its real locus (e.g. the colour of the ground) is judged to be in another locus, the ground; hence the error.

But even if it be admitted[2] that this illusory non-exsitence also is produced by Māyā, the difficulty pointed out does not really arise. There is no such rule that the effect phenomenon must be in every way like the cause-phenomenon. A cloth is in some respects unlike the yarn out of which it is made. If it be insisted that there must at least be some resemblance between the effect and the cause, it can be pointed out that even between an illusory non-existence and Māyā there is this point of resemblance, namely that both are different from brahman, and therefore false from the transcendental standpoint.

6. The Objects of Non-Perception : The Four Kinds of Non-Existence

There are, according to the author of the Vedānta-paribhāṣā, four kinds of non-existence that can be known through non-cognition (anupalabdhi).

1 Vedānta-paribhāṣā, p. 323.
2 Ibid.

They are respectively called : prāgabhāva, pradhvaṃsābhāva, anyonyā bhāva and atyantābhāva.

Prāgabhāva literally means previous non-existence. It is defined[1] as the non-existence of the effect in its material cause previous to its coming into existence. To illustrate, the non-existence of the jar in its component material earth, prior to the production of the jar, would be called prāgabhāva. It is distinguished from other kinds of non-existence by the fact that it is the basis of the peculiar judgment of futurity like "The jar will exist."[2] The judgment, "The jar does not exist," is common to all kinds of non-existence. But the judgment, "The jar will exist," applies only to the case of previous non-existence. Another distinguishing feature of this kind of non-existence mentioned by the Naiyāyikas is that it has no beginning, but has always an end.[3] The previous non-existence of a particular object cannot be assigned any beginning ; but it is pur an end to as soon as the object comes into existence.

Pradhvaṃsābhāva, or more simply dhvaṃsābhāva, literally means non-existence as represented by annihilation or destruction. The non-existence of the jar in the component parts into which the jar is broken falls within this class.[4] Formally, dhvaṃsābhāva can be defined as the non-existence that is invariably preceded by the object of which it is the non-existence.[5] The destruction of an object is invariably and unconditionally preceded by the existence of the object. Hence the existence of the object is a necessary factor for the production of its non-existence arising out of its destruction. In no other case is non-existence preceded by the object of which it is the non-existence.

Non-existence as annihilation has doubtless a beginning. Whether it has an end is a disputed point. The Naiyāyikas hold that it has none; for they think that the destruction of an object, say a jar, cannot be further destroyed.[6] The Advaitins question the truth of this view.[7] The non-existence of a thing, they argue, must have a locus (adhikaraṇa). That is to say, whenever we say that a jar does not exist we mean that it does not

1 Vedānta-paribhāṣā, p. 524: "Kāraṇe kāryyasya utpatteḥ pūrvam yobhāvah. sa prāgabhā vaḥ."

2 Ibid. : "Sa eva bhaviṣyati iti pratīti-viṣayaḥ."

3 Tarka-saṃgraha, "anādiḥ sāntaḥ prāgabhāvaḥ." (Sec. on Abhāva).

4 Vedānta-paribhāṣā, p. 326.

5 Āśubodhinī, P. 218 : "Pratiyogijanyābhāvatvaṃ dhvaṃsaḥ."

6 Tarkasaṃgraha, "Sādiranantaḥ pradhvaṃsaḥ."

7 "Vedānta-paribhāṣā, p. 326, and Śikhāmaṇi and Maṇiprabhā thereon.

exist in *a certain place*. Now the non-existence of the jar, when destroyed, has for its locus its component parts. When, therefore, these parts are further destroyed, the locus of the non-existence of the jar is destroyed and with it the non-existence of the *jar in those parts* is also destroyed. In other terms, the judgment, "There is non-existence of the jar in these component parts," becomes untenable and false when those parts no longer exist. Hence the Advaitins conclude that when the locus of the non-existence created by destruction is destructible, that non-existence cannot be itself indestructible or endless; but when the locus, in question, is eternal or endless, the non-existence in question is eternal.[1] As the Advaitins hold that nothing except Brahman is endlessly real or eternal, it further follows that according to them only that kind of non-existence is endless which has Brahman for its locus. To illustrate, the non-existence of the world (when negated by the intuition of Brahman) in Brahman is eternal. It need not be supposed that if such non-existence be eternal, there would be another eternal thing except Bahman ; this would tell against the pure monism of the Advaitins. For the Advaitins have shown in other contexts that the negation of an object *illusorily* superimposed on some reality is nothing but the affirmation of that reality, and consequently that non-existence (caused by destruction) of the *illusory* object is nöthing over and above the existence of the real locus. The eternity of the non-existence of the world in Brahman implies, therefore, not another parallel eternal reality but only the eternity of Brahman.

But if the non-existence created by the destruction of the jar the Naiyāyikas[2] might ask, were destructible (and not endless), would not the destroyed jar again spring into existence. For does not the negation of the negation of a thing imply the affirmation of the thing?

In reply to this, the Vedānta-paribhāṣa points out that the annihilation of the destroyed parts of a jar implies as much non-existence of the jar as of those destroyed parts and does not, therefore, amount to the creation of the jar.[3] To explain this statement, when the jar is broken into parts we can pass the judgment, "The jar does not exist now in *these* parts," or "There is non-existence of the jar now in *these* parts." But when these

1 Vedānta-paribhāṣā, pp. 327-328.
2 Gangeśa's Tattvacintāmaṇi, p. 696 : "... ghaṭābhāvā-bhāvasya ghaṭatvāt.
3 Vedānta-paribhāṣā, pp. 326.

parts are again broken into smaller pieces, this judgment, as we have seen, can no longer be maintained; it is no longer valid; for "*these* parts" no longer exist. But falsity of this judgment about the non-existence of the jar in a *particular locus* does not mean that another judgment about the non-existence of the jar in *some other locus* cannot be passed. On the contrary, when the broken parts are further broken we can still pass the judgment "There is non-existence of the jar now in these still further broken parts" which would be quite valid for that time and would prove not the re-emergence but the non-existence of the jar.

But cannot the Naiyāyikas retort to this explanation by saying, "If you admit that there is non-existence of the jar even when its broken parts are further destroyed, how can you say that its non-existence is destroyed when the parts are so destroyed? You have, on the contrary, to confess that non-existence of the jar still continues and virtually admit, with us, that the non-existence created by the destruction of the jar is endless." This objection is quite possible and reasonable and we do not find it answered by the Advaitins in so many words. We can easily conceive, however, the reply that can be given from their standpoint. It can be said that this objection is based on a confusion between unqualified non-existence and non-existence created by destruction. The *jar* can be destroyed only *once*, that is when it is broken into its parts, and consequently non-existence, *created by destruction,* can take place only then. When these broken parts are further broken, there is destruction of the parts of the jar not of the *jar*. So on the completion of the second destruction, though we can say that there is non-existence (general and unqualified) of the jar in the broken pieces, we cannot say that this non-existence in the pieces is such as has been created by destruction of the *jar*. In place of the non-existence created by destruction of the *jar*, there is at that time in those pieces non-existence created by the destruction of the parts of the jar. It cannot be said, therefore, that the former non-existence continues even then as such. On the contrary, the judgment "there is non-existence created by the destruction of the jar," cannot then be formed, as has been already shown. For we fail to answer the question, "Where is it?" The parts of the jar, in which alone it could be said to be, are no more. The fragments that continue till then represent the destruction of the *parts* of the jar and not that of the *jar*, and they cannot therefore be said to contain the non-existence *created by the destruction of the jar*. Such non-existence cannot, therefore, be said to be endless.

The author of the Vedānta-paribhāṣā gives an indeirect proof of the falsity of the statement that the destruction of the non-existence of an object created by its destruction necessarily implies the re-emergence of the object.[1] The existence of a jar, he argues, represents the non-existence created by the destruction of the previous non-existence of the jar. The destruction of the jar is equal, therefore, to the destruction of the non-existence created by the destruction of previous non-existence, and it would as such lead to the re-emergence of the previous non-existence of the jar, had it been true that the destruction of the non-existence created by destruction causes re-emergence. But this is never the case. Hence, he concludes, this statement is not true.

A similar problem in another form has been dealt with by the Advaitins (in the Advaita-siddhi, Gauḍa-brahmānandī, etc.[2]) in another way. The Advaitins say that the world is false and Brahman alone is real. Now the question is raised by their critics : Is the statement, "The world is false," itself true or false? If it be true, then there is another reality in addition to that of Brahman ; this the Advaitins cannot accept. But if this statement be false, then the Advaitins must contradict themselves; for the falsity of the falsity of the world amounts to the reality of it. New it is this last question with which we are concerned at present. Does the falsity of the falsity of an object imply its reality? The Advaitins reply that it does not. For they say that anything that is different from Brahman is, according to them, false. Now both the falsity of the world, and the falsity of the falsity of the world, are different from Brahman. Both are therefore false. The negation of the negation of a thing amounts to its affirmation only when there are two different grounds for the two negations. But when the ground for negation (niṣedhyatāvacchedaka-dharma) is the same in both, the negation of the negation of a thing does not amount to its affirmation.

To clarify this remark for students of Western philosophy we may say that the proposition, "God is not not-black," does not necessarily amount to saying "God is black," if it be admitted that God falls without the universe of colour. For then the ground on which "not-black" is denied of God would be that on which "black" also can be denied.

1 Vedānta-paribhāṣā, p. 327 : "anyatha prāgabhāva-dhvaṃsātmakaghaṭasya nāśe, prāgabhāvonmajjanāpattiḥ."

2 Advaita-siddhi : Mithyātva-mithyātva-prakaraṇam.

The dictum *duplex negatio affirmat* is generally accepted in Western logic as almost a truism. Indian logicians, except the Advaitins, also agree. The Advaitins do not really object to this dictum; they only desire to point out that it is valid within a certain limit or universe of discourse which, they think, should be explicitly mentioned lest it is applied to the few exceptional cases (like those already mentioned) which really fall outside its scope. In is interesting to find that Bradley does not accept the dictum in its popular meaning. He says : "And we must not say that negation presupposes a judgment, which is left in possession when the negative is negated. For we saw before that this positive judgment is not presupposed." "The real reason why denial of denial is affirmation is merely this. In all denial we must have the assertion of a positive ground and the positive ground of the second denial can be nothing but the predicate denied by the first."[1] In a word, according to Bradley, a double negation, like "*A is not B* is false," does not necessarily *yield* the judgment "A is B." But still he thinks that the *ground* for the second denial can be nothing but the judgment "A is B." From the exceptional illustration given by the Vedāntins, it would appear that it is not inconceivable that the ground for the second denial should be something other than "A is B," for it may be "A is C," where C is such that it excludes both not-B and B.

The third kind of non-existence, atyantābhāva, literally means total or absolute non-existence. If a particular thing does not exist in a particular locus at *any* time, then it is said that there is atyantābhāva or absolute non-existence of that thing in that locus.[2] For instance, there is atyantābhāva or total absence of colour in air.

The Naiyāyikas atyantābhāva is eternal. But the Advaitins, following their own theory that Brahman alone is eternal, refuse to accept this view. The author of the Vedānta-paribhāṣā says, therefore, that atyantābhāva (like ākāśa and other things which also the Naiyāyikas hold to be eternal) is perishable.[3] The author of the Maṇiprabhā, explaining this remark, observers that the non-eternity of atyantābhāva is due to the non-eternity of its locus.[4] That is to say, as everything except Brahman is non-eternal,

1 *Logic*, Part I, pp. 158-159.
2 Vedānta-paribhāṣā, p. 328.
3 Ibid.
4 Maṇiprabhā, p. 329 : "adhikaraṇa-nāśa eva atyantābhāva-dhvāṃsa-prayojakah.."

non-existence as existing in any such thing must also be perishable; the judgment that there is non-existence of A in B can be formed, as we have seen, only so long as B, the locus, exists and not after it has perished. But it may be contended, "If that be the ground for the non-eternity of atyantābhāva you must admit that at least the atyantābhāva or total absence of the world in Brahman is eternal, because the locus, Brahman, is here eternal." The same writer meets this objection by saying that though such a case of non-existence may be said to be eternal, yet it can scarcely be distinguished from Brahman itself; the non-existence of an illusory object superimposed on a real substratum, as we have stated above, cannot be proved to be something distinct from the substratum.

Anyonyā-bhāva, the fourth kind of non-existence, is, according to Advaitins, nothing but difference or separateness (bheda or pṛthaktva) owing to which we judge "This is not that." It also has beginning in time, or not, according as its locus has beginning, or not. Thus the difference of a pot from a cloth has a beginning because the pot has a beginning in time. Again the difference of an individual soul (Jīva) from Brahman, or the difference of the latter from the former, is beginningless because Jīva and Brahman are beignningless, according to the Advaitins. But none of these two cases of difference is enternal.[1] The reason for its non-eternity is the same as in the case of the other kinds of non-existence.

It may be mentioned in this connection that some Naiyāyikas[2] classify non-existence into the above four kinds, whereas others[3] recognize only two, anyonyā-bhāva (mutual non-existence or difference) and saṃsargābhāva. They hold that prāgabhāva (previous non-existence), dhvaṃsābhāva (non-existence or destruction) and atyantābhāva (or absolute non-existence), are but three different forms of the second kind, saṃsargābhāva. The *fundamentum divisions* of the two fold classification is the relation of the absent object to its locus. When we say A is different from B, we mean that A is not identical with B. This shows that in the case of anyonyā-bhāva the judgment of non-existence is a negative answer to the question whether A exists as identical with B. But in the case of

1 Vedānta-paribhāṣā, pp. 328-329.
2 Trarakasaṃgraha, loc cit.
3 Bhāṣā-pariccheda and Muktāvalī.

saṃsargābhāva we have a judgment which gives a negative reply to the question whether a certain thing exists *in* another thing in the relation of association (saṃsarga). In brief, the question involved in the former is, "Does A exist *as* B?" or "Is A B?" and that in the latter is, "Does A exist *in* B?" As prāgabhāva dhvaṃsābhāva and atyantābhāva involve the second question, they can be brought within one class—saṃsargābhāva.

We may notice another point in this connection. If a jar is temporarily removed from its locus, the floor, what should we call such non-esistence of the jar on the floor? That it cannot be brought under any of the four kinds of non-existence admitted by the Advaitins can be easily seen. Yet we do not find this question discussed by them. Some Naiyāyikas, who admit the fourfold classification, have however noticed this problem and tried to solve it.[1] According to them the *temporary* absence of a thing from a locus is also to be considered as a form of atyantābhāva. The objection naturally arises as to how this can be so, when atyantābhāva has been defined as an inseparable or perpetual absence of a thing from a locus. To this it is replied that the absence of the jar from the floor does persist even when the jar is brought into contact with the floor, though the absence is not *perceived* at that time. This explanation does not appear to be of all satisfactory. The only way in which it can be interpreted, so as to make it appear somewhat plausible, is to say that the jar never exists on the floor in the relation of Samavāya, inherence (just as it does in its own parts), and such absence exists even when the jar is placed *on* the floor, which involves the relation of Saṃyoga or mere conjunction. Hence there is atyantābhāva or perpetual non-existence of the jar on the floor. But this defence is not of much avail. For it may be asked : If the relation meant be inherence, why should the supporters of this view say that absence of the jar from the floor is not perceived while the jar is there? Surely the existence of the thing in the relation of conjunction with its locus cannot prevent the knowledge of its non-existence there in some other relation. The unsatisfactoriness of this view, therefore, leads another school of thinkers[2] to hold that temporary non-existence, as illustrated above, has to be classed apart to constitute a fourth kind of saṃsargābhāva in addition to the three already mentioned.

1 Siddhāntamuktāvalī on Abhāva (pp. 94-98).

2 Ibid. and Dinakarī thereon (pp. 98-99), Nirnayasagar.

To return to the original discussion of the Advaitins then, it is found that according to them the object of a non-perception (anupalabdhi) can be one of the four kinds of non-existence explained above. There is one more important point to be noticed in this connection. It relates to the question how ajñāna or ignorance is known. According to the view set forth above, ajñāna being the non-existence of knowledge should be known, like other kinds of non-existence, through non-cognition. But the Vivaraṇa does not accept this apparent conclusion.[1] According to it ajñāna can be divided into two classes, namely (1) absence of the knowledge of a particular object (jñāna-viśeṣābhāva) and (2) the general absence of knowledge (jñāna-mātrābhāva). Of these two, the former alone can be known through non-perception. But the latter is directly revealed to the witnessing self (sākṣi-bhāṣya).[2] It is not possible to discuss in this connection the validity of the conception of general ignorance, which we have incidentally noticed previously (p. 49). But if this conception be tenable, the distinction sought to be made by the Vivaraṇa is quite reasonable. The knowledge of the absence of the knowledge of a particular object involves the knowledge (memory or some other kind) of the object at that time, but the general absence of knowledge does not do so.

7. Critical Estimation of Anupalabdhi

We have so far only stated the theory of anupalabdhi (non-cognition) as held by the Advaitins. It is now necessary to estimate critically the validity of this conception. But before we proceed to do so, it is necessary to make the position of the Advaitins more definite. In our treatment we have nowhere distinguished the view of the Advaitins from that of the Bhāṭṭas. On the contrary, we have assumed that there is no distinction between the two. Such a procedure would be supported by the writers of the Advaita school, who closely follow the traditions of the Bhāṭṭas in these matters. As shown in a previous context, the Vivaraṇa explicitly states that the Advaitins follow the Bhāṭṭas as regards the theory of anupalabdhi, and subsequent Advaita writers freely use the phrases and maxims of the Bhāṭṭas as their own. But if we carefully consider the account

1 vivaraṇa-prameya-saṃgraha, p. 16.

2 Ibid., "Asman-mate tu sākṣi-vedyo jñāna-mātrābhāvaḥ."

of anupalabdhi as given by the Vedānta-paribhāṣā and supported by its long line of authoritative commentaries (like Sikhāmaṇi, Maṇiprabhā. As'ubodhinī) we do not feel that these Advaitins have th same conception of anupalabdhi as the Bhāṭṭas.

The point of departure relates to the following question : Does anupalabdhi inform us of the absence of only that thing, the existence of which would be *perceived* if it were present? Or does it inform us also of the absence of a thing the existence of which, if present, could be known through the other non-perceptual methods of knowledge such as inference, testimony, etc? In a word, does anupalabdhi mean only non-perception, or does it mean non-cognition in general? It will be noticed that we have so far used the word non-cognition for anupalabdhi, in order to keep the word vague and general so as to suit any interpretation that may be given. The account of anupalabdhi given in the Vedānta-paribhāṣā, and stated here, would almost clearly show that by anupalabdhi it means non-perception. But what little doubt due to ambiguity might remain is completely removed by the interpretations given by all the commentaries noted above. That this is so is perfectly clear from the long difinition of anupalabdhi given by Maṇiprabhāt and explained by us. It clearly says that when a particular *sense* competent to inform us of a particular thing does not yield any knowledge about it, we can judge that it is absent.

But according to certain interpreters, the Bhāṭṭas do not accept this view, for they are said to mean by anupalabdhi not non-perception alone but non-cognition in general. It is said that the words of S'abarasvāmin, to the effect that the absence of a pramāṇa (pramāṇābhāva) is abhāva (i.e. anupalabdhi), means the absence not only of perception, but also of other valid methods of knowledge. In consequence it is held that there should be five different kinds of anupalabdhi, since it may be the absence of perception or inference, or testimony or upamāna or arthāpatti. In none of the chief works of the Bhāṭṭas school do we find any account of the five kinds of non-congnition, though the general statements made in them may be interpreted as suggestive of the five types of non-cognition. Interpreting the Bhāṭṭa theory in this way, and assuming that the Advaintins *should* not differ from the Bhāṭṭas on this matter, an eminent contemporary commentator, Anantakṛṣṇa S'āstrī, has tried to interpret the Vedānta-paribhāṣā[1] also in the same light, and finds all the authoritative

1 *Vide*. pp. 245-46 of this work edited by him.

commentaries from Sikhāmaṇi down to Āśubodhinī guilty of misinterpretation. But on a close cosideration of the isolated statements and the general drift of the discussion, we feel convinced that the view of the Vedānta-paribhāṣā is faithfully represented by the older commentaries. It is beyond the scope of an epistemological study to enter into the details of textual interpretation; we can present here only the result of our personal enquiry. In any case, if the interpretation of the Bhāṭṭa theory, referred to above, be correct and if our reading of the Advaita view be true, we must say that there is some difference between the Advaitins and the Bhāṭṭas, the while the former understand by anupalabdhi only non-perception, the latter understand by it any form of non-cognition.

But we can turn from the historical aspect of the question to its logical significance. What is the real distinction between non-peception and non-cognition as means of knowledge? What, that is to say, does non-cognition as a source of knowledge really include over and above non-perception? This question seems to be quite easy and we are apt to repeat what the eminent commentator, referred to above, has said, and say, "Why? it includes absence of inference, testimony, etc." But a deeper consideration robs the reply of its apparent simplicity. For though we understand how the non-perception of a thing can directly yield the knowledge of its non-existence, we fail to understand how the absence of inference, testimony, etc., can do so. If there are the necessary data namely the perception of smoke, the knowledge of the invariable connection between smoke and fire, we can infer the existence of fire on the mountain. If these necessary premises are not available, there will be no inference. But the absence of such inference would not give us any knowledge of the non-existence of fire. In fact in the absence of such inference there can only be *doubt* as much about the non-existence of fire as about its existence. Similarly, if the existence of a thing, say a town, can be known through the testimony, say, of a geographer, when such testimony is absent we cannot judge only therefrom that the thing does not exist. We fail, therefore, to understand how the absence of inference, testimony, etc, can, like the absence of perceptual knowledge, yield by itself any information about the non-existence of an object and how consequently there can be five different kinds of non cognition, yielding five kinds of knowledge of non-existence.

From these considerations we must conclude, therefore, that though non-cognition is wider in meaning than non-perception, and though theoretically there can be as many kinds of non-cognition as of cognition, the only kind of non-cognition that can *directly yield any knowledge* about non-existence is non-perception. As a means of knowledge, therefore, non-cognition becomes practically equivalent to non-perception.

But the contention for the five-fold division can be, and is, based also on a different line of argument. Starting from the statement of Kumārila Bhaṭṭa that every thing has two aspects, of which the aspect of existence is known through one of the five pramāṇas, and that of non-existence through anupalabdhi or non-cognition, it is argued that wherever the object of knowledge is the non-existence of a thing, the instrumentality of non-cogniton is involved. Thus the knowledge of non-existence through inference, testimony, etc., would be thought to involve non-cognition, and there would consequently arise five different cases of it. It is from this standpoint that even the case of inferential knowledge of the absence of virtue (dharma), mentioned in the Vedānta-paribhāṣā, is explained by Anantakṛṣṇa Śāstrī as involving anupalabdhi.[1] It is affirmed with the support of a line from Nyāyaratnākara, that even in such a case the absence of the object is *primarily* known through anupalabdhi, though *afterwards*s it may be known through inference *as well*. But it is difficult to understand how in such a case the non-existence of the object (like virtue, vice, etc.) can be ascertained and therefore known, *prior* to and independently of inference, through mere non-cognition, in spite of the fact that even the existence of the object is known only through inference.

The only way, therefore, in which this contention can be maintained is to declare that inference, testimony, etc., can yield *only* affirmative judgments (i.e. judgments about existence) and *never* negative ones (i.e.judgments about non-existence), and that all negative judgments are invariably derived through anupalabdhi. This exactly is what is argued by the eminent scholar to be the theory of the Bhāṭṭas,though the texts quoted in support are not quite clear on the point. This extreme position, viz. that non-existence is known through anupalabdhi *alone*, is not compatible with the above statement of the Nyāyaratnākara (which is called into evidence by him) which grants that non-existence can be known through inference *as well*. Besides, such a position, as already shown, will be hardly acceptable to common sense. But whatever be the view of the Bhāṭṭas, we can state with some certainty that if the Vedānta-paribhāṣā, Śikhāmaṇi, Maṇiprabhā, etc., be faithful representatives of the Advaita school, the Advaitins do not hold that non-existence is known in *all* cases

1 *Op. cit.* p. 240

through non-cognition. On the contrary their view is that it is known in some cases through non-perception and in some cases through other methods of knowledge. For them, anupalabdhi means, therefore, non-perception as a means of the knowledge of non-existence.

Having thus critically ascertained the exact conception of anupalabdhi as maintained by the writers of the Advaita school, we are in a position to estimate the validity and importance of their theory in the light of Western philosophy. The question that we have chiefly to consider is whether non-perception can really be regarded as an independent means of knowledge. To decide it with perfect certainty a student of Westen philosophy would try to ascertain whether anupalabdhi cannot be reduced to perception, memory, inference, etc. These points have been partially discussed, as we have seen, by the Indian thinkers themselves. But they require to be treated further in terms of Western philosophy.

Broadly speaking the problem of anupalabdhi is the problem of the genesis of a *primary* negative judgement. A primary affirmative judgement like "This is green," "There is a jar here," "This is a man," etc., is derived, of course, through perception; the predicate is affirmed on the basis of some positive characteristic directly presented by reality. But is a negative primary judgement like "This is not green," "There is no jar here," "This is not a man," derived exactly in the same way? The apparent answer would naturally be in the affirmative. For it would be said that the negative judgement is as much based on direct experience as the affirmative one, and consequently there can be no distinction between the two as regards their source or origin. It may be further argued : If it be a fact, as Bradley says, that "the basis of negation is really the assertion of a quality that excludes"[1] the predicate, how can we help saying that the negative judgement "This is not green" is also based on the perception of a positive quality, say white, characterizing the subject?

This answer may be compared to that of the Sāṃkhyas, who also, we have seen, hold that the denial of the existence of a jar on the ground is based on nothing more than the perception of a positive form of the ground, i.e. the ground *per se*. Against this it may be urged on behalf of the Advaitins that though the denial of the predicate in such a judgement may start from the perception of some positive object, and though perception may be necessary for negation, it cannot be considered to be

1 *Logic*, vol. i, pp. 116-117.

the all-sufficient factor which can by itself lead to the negative judgement. From the perception of the white colour the only judgement that can directly follow is the affirmative judgement, "This is white." But no such equally simple and direct step can be taken from the perception of the white to the negation of the green. For that we must pass through two peculiar moments of thought, absent in the case of the affirmative judgement; (1) an ideal reproduction of the green, and (2) the feeling of an opposition between the reproduced and the presented. This process has been described by Kumārila Bhaṭṭa as follows : "On the perception of the existing object and recollection of the absent one, there arises the subjective knowledge (mānasam jñānam) of non-existence."[1] This subjective nature of a negative judgement, as contrasted with an affirmative one, has been admitted by Bradley as well. "For logical negation," he says, "cannot be so directly related to fact as logical assertion. We might say that as such and in its own strict character it is simply 'subjective' : it does not hold good outside my thinking."[2] Bosanquet also says, "An affirmation can be, comparatively speaking, *given* as a fact; a negation *cannot*, except in quite another sense, be given. It has to be *made*, and made by setting an *ideal* reality over against real reality and finding them incongruous."[3]

If this distinction between an affirmative and a negative judgement be granted, we cannot say that the primary negative judgement is derived from perception just as is the affirmative. Though based on perception, our belief in the negative judgement, "This is not green," may be immediate like that in the affirmative; the process which culminates in the negative judgement is so unique and so different from that of the affirmative that we cannot reasonably hold that both these judgements are obtained through the same source or method of knowledge. In this light we can better realize the meaning of the Advaitin's statement that though knowledge of non-existence may be felt to be immediate (pratyakṣa), it is to be classed apart from an immediate knowledge obtained through sense-perception, on the strength of the distinction that exists between the two as regards the processess through which they are derived.

Now if the negative judgement involves a process that is not the same as the simple sense-perception through which the affirmative is obtained,

1 Śloka-vārtika, p. 482.
2 *Logic*, Vol. I, p. 120.
3 *Logic*, Vol. I, p. 280 (Ital. ours).

it is reasonable to give this peculiar process a special name that will convey an idea of its unique characteristic. In the process involved in a primary affirmative judgement an ideal content, the predicate, is applied, as Bradley would put it, to the presented reality, the subject, and this application leading to the coalescence of the two is called perception. In the process involved in the corresponding negative judgement, on the other hand, there is the attempt at the application of a suggested ideal content (to follow again the analysis of Bradley) to the presented subject; but the two are immediately felt to repel each other. If the application in the previous case has been called *perception*, the non-application in this latter case should be called *non-perception*. And as this baffled attempt is the very nerve of the process, we may say that the negative judgement is derived through non-perception, just as the affirmative is obtained through perception. In other words, the means by which non-existence is known may be characterized as non-perception. The judgement of the non-existence of the green in the presented subject cannot be said to be due to the perception of the white (which as such can lead only to the judgement of the existence of the white), but to the failure of the *will* to perceive the green, which failure is immediately felt as the opposition that constitutes the very core of the negative judgement, and should be termed the non-perception of the green.

The statement that non-existence can be *known* through non-perception would seem a paradox,[1] being almost equivalent to saying that knowledge can be had through ignorance. But this contradiction appears to exist only so long as we think non-perception to be a blank state of mind. Understood in the sense in which it has been technically used, as just shown, it is not however a blank state, but only a baffled state of the mind that is expressed in a definite judgement like "There is no pot on this ground."

If non-perception be understood in this light it may not be difficult for a student of Western philosophy to understand that it can be regarded, like perception, as a source of knowledge. It may also be clear that the process of knowledge that is involved in it distinguishes it from perception, memory and inference, and consequently that it cannot be reduced to any of these. But a searching critic may not be completely satisfied with the foregoing accounts, which may be considered to hide a

1 Bosanquet feels this paradox : "the paradox consists in this—that in negation the work of positive knowledge appears to be performed by ignorance." *Logic*, Vol. I, p. 277.

difficulty. In the above interpretation, it may be said, it has been implicitly assumed that every non-perception can lead to the knowledge of non-existence, just as every perception can yield the knowledge of the existence of its object. In fact however it is, as the Advaitin himself admits, only an *appropriate* non-perception that can be the source of any knowledge of non-existence. We cannot, therefore, pass directly from a non-perception to the knowledge of non-existence; we have to ascertain, before we can do so, that the particular non-perception is also appropriate. To test this appropriateness we have to ascertain, as the Advaitin tells us, that in that particular case, if the unperceived object were present, it would have been perceived. Is it not legitimate to conclude from the Advaitin's own statements, therefore, that non-existence is known not through non-perception alone, but non-perception, together with the evidence for its appropriateness? If that be so, it follows easily that the knowledge of non-existence is obtained through the synthetic construction of two premises, one expressing the fact of non-perception, the other its appropriateness—which is obviously a process of inference that can be put in the form of the following hypothetical-categorical syllogism : "If A were present it would have been perceived. A is not perceived. Therefore A is not present."

Evidently this is an objection that cannot be lightly passed over; for it is fatal to the view that non-perception is an independent and ultimate source of knowledge. Though we have stated already (pp. 165-6) one reason why anupalabdhī cannot be reduced to inference, it is necessary to see whether it is strong enough to dispel this doubt and whether there are any other grounds to support it.

Before re-examining the reason previously adduced, let us consider what the admission of the Advaitin exactly amounts to. That the appropriateness of a non-perception has to be known before the non-perception can yield any knowledge is explicitly admitted by Bhāṭṭas[1] and Advaitins alike. Thus we find the author of the Vedānta-paribhāṣā saying that the approriateness of a non-perception has to be determined with the help of the hypothetical argument (tarka) : "If the object existed it would have been perceived." But in spite of this, the supporter of the theory of anupalabdhi may try to evade this charge by quoting the opinion of the Naiyāyikas and the Vaiśeṣikas, according to

1 Sāstra-dāpikā, p. 85,

whom a hypothetical argument is not an inference. The employment of the hypothetical argument, "If the object, etc. . .", in order to prove the absurdity of the denial of a desired conclusion, is called by these logicians a tarka[1]; and it is distingushed by them from an anumāna (inference) on the ground that it contains not a categorical proposition but a hypothetical. According to these thinkers, the premises of an anumāna (inference) must be of the categorical type. But a tarka, as containing an "if," shows that the premise does not represent definite knowledge, but a doubt.[2] Only the doubt here is of such a nature that one of the many alternatives which consititute it is strongly emphasized, so that it approaches the nature of a decision.[3] A tarka, therefore, cannot by itself constitute knowledge; it only paves the way for it by helping forward the work of other definite evidenc.[4] In this particular case it helps anupalabdhi (non-perception) to yield the knowledge of non-existence.The admission that the appropriateness of an anupalabdhi has to be ascertained with the help of a hypothetical argument cannot, therefore, force the Advaitin to accept the conclusion that non-existence is known through an inferential process.

This defence, though quite capable of protecting an Advaitin against the attack of an Indian critic, would evidently be of little avail to him in fighting against a Western opponent. For to the latter the defence would appear as nothing but an arbitrary limitation of the scope of inference, based on the rejection of all inferences containing hypothetical premises. In other words, though the Western critic may concede that the process in question cannot be called an anumāna, as conceived by the Indian thinker, he would conclude that there is no reason why it should not be called an *inference* which, as conceived by Western logicians, can very well contain a hypothetical premise.

It can be said, however, on behalf of the Advaitins that the so-called hypothetical syllogism of Western logic is, as Western logicians themselves admit, nothing but a categorical syllogism expressed in another form. It is therefore reducible to a categorical form; and thus the conclusion of a

1 Nyāya-sūtras, 1, 8, 40, and Sapta-padārthī, p. 67: "Aniṣṭa-vyāpaka prasañjanam tarkaḥ."

2 Sapta-padārthī, p.24 : "Tarkas tāvat saṃśaya eva."

3 The Nyāya-sūtras, 1, 1, 40, call tarka an ūha. An ūha is defined by Sapta-padārthī as follows : "Utkaṭaika-koṭikaḥ saṃśaya ūhaḥ."

4 Nyāya-bhāṣya, 1, 1, 1, which states that tarka is "pramāṇānāna anugrāhakaḥ." (p. 32).

hypothetical syllogism has as much force and validity as that of a categorical. There cannot be any categorical conclusion drawn from a really doubtful premise i.e. from a proposition that contains a hypothesis or a tentative supposition and not an established truth, though it is possible to draw one from a hypothetical premise which expresses an accepted truth in the form of conditional relation.

But it may be said[1] against this that if the proposition, "If there were a jar it would have been perceived," presents only a provisional supposition from which no categorical truth can be inferred, it cannot help non-perception to yield the knowledge of non-existence. We do not know how the Advaitin would escape this difficulty. The only course for him is to part company with the general run of thinkers who hold "tarka" to be a form of doubt, and say that a "tarka" is a kind of genuine knowledge. But to admit it is to give up this line of defence altogether. How is it possible to hold, then, that the non-existence in question is not known through inference?

Let us see if the other argument briefly mentioned previously in this chapter can really meet the objection. The argument has been used by the Bhāṭṭas, by Kumārila himself and his followers. According to it the non-existence of a jar on the floor cannot be said to be known through inference for the following reason : The major term, the sādhya (or that which is to be proved to be present in the minor term, the pakṣa, the floor), is here the non-existence of the jar, because the conclusion, in any case, is to be "The floor has non-existence etc." Now for every inference there must be the previous knowledge of an invariable relation between the middle and the major term. So in this particular case we require to know the existence of such a relation between the non-existence (to be inferred) and some thing that would be the middle term. But this requires non-existence and its relation with the middle term (non-perception) to be known previously. This knowledge also cannot be said to be derived through another inference, for ultimately the premises of an inference have to be non-inferentially acquired. So ultimately we are forced to admit that non-existence is known through a non-inferential method.

1 The only apology for introducing this line of defence, which is ultimately shown to be untenable, is that we have really found some Pandits offering it.

Does this argument remove the doubt that the non-existence of the jar on the floor can be known through the hypothetical-categorical syllogism previously spoken of? Obviously the answer should be in the negative. This argument might remove the doubt if the form of inference were "What is not perceived in a locus (where it should be perceived if existing) is non-existent there. The jar is not perceived on the floor (where it should be perceived if existing). Therefore the jar is non-existent there"; which really is the form of the inference the Bhāṭṭas mean to refute. For here the major premise represents the knowledge of a universal relation between non-existence and non-perception. But in the suggested hypothetical-categorical syllogism : "If the jar exists it is perceived. It is not perceived. Therefore it does not exist," the major premise is affirmative, and the universal relation presupposed is not between non-existence and something else, but between two positive contents, existence and perception. How can it be said then, with regard to this form of inference, that the knowledge of non-existence in the conclusion presupposes the knowledge of an invariable relation between non-existence and something else, and therefore a previous knowledge of non-existence itself in the major premise? The Bhāṭṭas' objection to the inferential knowledge of the non-existence in question does not therefore seem to tell against the above form of inference and the doubt is not removed.

But the Bhāṭṭas, and for that matter any other school of Indian thinkers for whom the first figure is the only logical figure, would reduce the above inference (granting for the moment that they do not object to its hypothetical form) to its logical form by taking the contrapositive of the major, "If the jar is not perceived it is non-existent," as the real major of the inference. As a consequence they would argue that the major does really contain a previous knowledge of non-existence (in the form of a knowledge of a univeral relation between non-perception and non-existence).

The validity of this defence would rest chiefly on the question whether the first figure is really the only figure, while every other figure has to be reduced to it for logical demonstration. As is well known, Aristotle, though admitting three figures, conceives the first as the perfect figure, and his *dictum de omni et nullo* and his theory of reduction do suggest that all figures are to be reduced to the first for the sake of clear demonstration. It is impossible for us in the present connection to enter into a thorough and independent enquiry into the merits of this question. But we can say this much, that in this particular case the inference is undoubtedly more evident and more easily acceptable in the first figure than in any of the rest.

But even granting that the affirmative major, "If the jar exists it is perceived," is equally good for the conclusion, it can be said that the attainment of this affirmative premise could scarcely be possible *except through* some knowledge of non-existence, because to establish this premise itself with certainty it is necessary to observe both positive and negative instances. We must know not only that the jar exists whenever it is perceived, but also that it does *not* exist whenever it is not perceived.

But there is a still stronger argument in favour of the Advaitins. If the major be affirmative, the minor at least must be *negative*, otherwise we cannot have the negative conclusion, "the jar does not exist." And as a negatibe proposition connotes some non-existence the old question would still dog us : "How is this non-existence known?" This non-existence cannot be said to have been derived through perception, for it has been already proved that non-existence cannot be perceptually known. Neither can it be said to have been derived through inference, because such inference (again) having a negative conclusion must have a negative premise, and the same question would again arise as to how that premise is derived. So it must ultimately be confessed that non-existence is known through some method other than inference. We have therefore sufficient grounds on which to conclude that non-existence cannot be *primarily* known through inference. Every attempt to derive such knowledge inferentially requires at least one negative premise (i.e. the knowledge of non-existence in some form), and is thus hopelessly entangled in a *petitio principii.*

Considering this result along with what has been shown before, we can say that a negative judgment cannot be *primarily* derived either through perception or through inference. In other words, non-existence cannot be *primarily* known through perception or inference. It is known through a peculiar method of knowledge that is not reducible to any other method ordinarily known. If perception be the name for the method through which existence is primarily known, the method through which non-existence is primarily known can be called non-perception.

But when everything has been proved one doubt still remains unsolved. If non-existence is primarily known not through perception or inference but through non-perception, what is the function of the tarka which the Advaitin employs to ascertain appropriateness? We raised this question previously, but deferred it by showing that its employment raises some difficulties that threaten the Advaita position. What the necessity of tarka really is has not been shown, and it requires therefore to be shown in order that the doubt may be completely removed. We shall conclude, therefore, with some observations of our own on this important point.

Just as we do not believe in the existence of green colour on white paper seen through green glasses, though that colour is perceived, similarly we do not believe in the non-existence of colour on the paper in a dark room though no colour is perceived. Like perception (or inference), non-perception yields a valid judgment only under specific conditions. Like perception and inference, therefore, it must have a canon by which its validity can be ascertained. This canon is supplied by the tarka or hypothetical argument, "If it existed it would have been perceived." Again, as with perception and inference, so here, the canon has not to be explicitly applied in every case. It has to be used only in cases where there are positive reasons for doubt or disbelief and where, therefore, necessity for ascertainment of the truth is positively felt. Our everyday experience would bear out this conclusion. We pass the judgment of the non-existence of a chair or a table in a room only if we do not perceive it there; we do not employ the argument "If it existed it would have been perceived"; this we do only when some doubt is cast on our judgment.

Lastly, the argument, "If it existed it would have been perceived," cannot be considered to be a premise leading to the conclusion, "It does not, therefore, exist"; because this argument is only a canon for testing the validity of the conclusion. What has been said by Western logicians regarding the axiom or canon of an inference applies in this respect to this canon of non-perception as well. They have pointed out that the axiom is "not a premise but principle or cannon of the argument,"[1] and that "The axiom, therefore, is not one of the premises from which we reason when we argue"[2]; so that the cannon or principle might be used only "to stop the mouth of a disputant who denied the conclusion . . . ."[3]

1. Joseph. *Introduction to Logic*, p. 274.

2. Ibid., p. 273.

3. Ibid.

These remarks would also apply *mutatis mutandis* to the canon of non-perception. The non-existence of a jar on the floor is known through its non-perception. But if this knowledge is in any way doubted it is reinstated with the help of the hypothetical argument or tarka referred to above. And even if this validating argument be called an inference, non perception does not cease to be the source of the knowledge of non-existence. The content of the knowledge (viz. non-existence) is even then derived through non-perception, though the validity of this knowledge has to be ascertained through a second source, viz. an inference.[1]

In the light of Western philosophy these arguments enable us to understand and support the conclusion of the Advaitins that non-perception is an independent and ultimate method in being the specific source of the knowledge of non-existence.[2]

1. Vide the author's Article in *Mind*, vol. xxxv, N.S., No. 143.
2. Vide the author's Paper on "The Source of the Primary Negative Judgments," in the *Proceedings of the Indian Philosophical Congress*, 1929.

BOOK IV
INFERENCE (ANUMĀNA)

BOOK IV

INFERENCE (ANUMĀNA)

1. The Meaning of Anumāna

OF all the methods of knowledge none has been discussed more thoroughly and elaborately by Indian thinkers than anumāna or inference. It was the favourite subject of the Nyāya school, which devoted to it centuries of exclusive attention and produced an enormous literature as marvellous in precision and analysis as in the invention of an algebraic type of technical expressions. Suffice it to say that the exact definition of vyāpti (the invariable concomitance between the middle and the major terms) was alone continuously discussed by the Naiyāyikas for some generations. The treatises of the Naiyāyikas naturally influenced the thought and language of other writers also to a considerable extent, and they accepted the Nyāya views in many respects without further discussion. The only systematic account of anumāna according to the Advaita school is to be found in the Vedānta-paribhāṣā and its commentaries. But they mainly deal with points on which the Advaitins differ from the Naiyāyikas, while tacitly signifying their agreement with the latter on other points. To state and discuss in full the Advaita views as regards inference, it is necessary to state in full the general Nyāya views and the deviations of the Advaitins from them. This would however form a vast and independent treatise by itself. The present chapter will therefore be confined, after the Vedānta-paribhāṣā , to the special views of the Advaitins, their general principles being mostly assumed to be already known.

The Sanskrit word "anumāna" is generally translated by the word "inference." But as will appear in the following pages, there are important distinctions in scope and conception between anumāna and inference, and the two terms cannot be considered to be wholly interchangeable. But still we must render "anumāna" by inference for want of a more appropriate term.

Except the Cārvākas, all schools of Indian philosophy accept the validity of anumāna, as a method of knowledge. According to all of them inference proceeds from the previous knowledge of an invariable concomitance (vyāpti) between the middle and the major terms coupled with the knowledge of the minor term as being characterized by the middle.

It should at once appear that thus conceived anumāna can include only the mediate inferences of Western logic. The so-called immediate inferences, as not involving the knowledge of any vyāpti, altogether fall outside the denotation of anumāna. Many eminent logicians of the West have denied the existence of immediate inferences on the ground that most of them are mere verbal transformations, involving no advance of thought and therefore unworthy of being called inferences, whereas the rest are but compressed forms of real mediate inferences. The Indian logician gives no explicit reason for not recognizing immediate inference; for no such problem could at all arise with regard to his conception of an anumāna. But we find him putting into the mediate form some inferences which a Western logician would regard as immediate. For instance, we come across arguments like: "If one thing is similar to another thing, then the other thing also is similar to that thing. The gavaya is similar to the cow. Therefore the cow is also similar to the gavaya." Again, "Earth is different from the four elements air, water, fire, ether, because it is earth. (Of the elements) whatever is not different from these four elements it not earth."[1] (According to Western logic the first will be a case of the conversion of a symmetrical relation, and the second inference from a term.) If any conclusion is possible from such an instance, then according to an Indian logician the so-called immediate inference of Western logic is nothing but a mediate inference.

In any case, if there is really such a thing as immediate inference, the word inference would be on this showing wider than anumāna. Another distinction can be noted. Western logicians generally identify inference with mediate knowledge. But, for an Indian thinker, like an Advaitin or a Mīmāṃsaka, anumāna is not only the form of mediate knowledge; śabda, upamāna, arthāpatti are also of that class. Therefore in this respect also we cannot regard anumāna as synonymous with inference.

2. The Conception of Vyāpti

Though all Indian thinkers who believe in anumāna hold that there can be no anumāna without vyāpti, they are not unanimous as to its formal definition, its function and the means of ascertaining it.

The definitions of vyāpti are many in number and it is neither possible nor useful to notice all of them here. An elaborate account of the many definitions advanced by different writers of the Nyāya school will be found

1 Nyāya-siddhānta-mañjarī, p. 113.

in the *History of Indian Logic* by Dr. S. C. Vidyābhūṣaṇa. It is sufficient for us to state the definition given by the Advaitins. The Vedānta-paribhāṣā defines vyāpti as the co-existence of the major term with the middle term, in all the loci in which the middle term may exist.[1] In the inference, "The mountain is fiery because it has smoke, and wherever there is smoke, there is fire," the last proposition, "wherever there is smoke, there is fire," expresses the vyāpti. The word vyāpti etymologically means pervasion. The cases of fire pervade those of smoke, and therefore fire is called vyāpaka (pervader) and smoke is called vyāpya (pervaded). In such a case the two terms are not equal in extension; hence the relation between the vyāpaka and vyāpya cannot be reversed. Such a case is called viṣama-vyāpti (unequal extension). But in a case like "Wherever there is smoke there is fire fed by wet fuel," there is equipollence or samavyāpti between the two terms, and they can easily interchange their positions. "Wherever there is fire fed by wet fuel there is smoke" will be equally true.

3. How is Vyāpti to be Ascertained

But the question arises : Is it possible to determine such a universal invariable relation as vyāpti? The Cārvākas answer this question in the negative. It is impossible, they say, to ascertain that smoke is invariably and universally attended with fire at all times; for even assuming that a person can know all present and past cases of smoke, the future cases always remain beyond the limits of his knowledge. A universal relation like vyāpti cannot, therefore, be ascertained. The Buddhists, however, think that a universal relation can be ascertained, even without examining all possible cases, if it is known that the two terms are related either by way of causality (tadutpatti) or by way of identity of essence (tādātmya). Thus on the relation of causality can be based such a universal proposition as "Wherever there is smoke there is fire." If fire is ascertained to be the cause of smoke in one case, we can safely lay it down that smoke must be attended with fire in all cases. Similarly if it be ascertained in one case that śiṃṣapā is in essence a tree, and that a śiṃsapā would be no śiṃsapā if it were not a tree, it can be universally affirmed, on the basis of the knowledge of the identity of essence, that all śiṃṣapās are trees.[2]

1 "Vyāptiścāśeṣasādhanāśrayāśritasādhyasāmānādhikaraṇyarūpā," p. 198.
2 Sarva-darśana-saṃgraha, Bauddha-darśanam.

The Naiyāyikas contend that it is neither easy nor necessary for the formation of a universal proposition to ascertain any relation of causality or identity between two phenomena.[1] A universal proposition can be based on the determination of *any* invariable unconditional universal relation. The Advaitins also hold the same view. The relation of vyāpti, says the Śikhāmaṇi, is not necessarily a relation of cause and effect. Had it been so, then we could have a universal proposition like "wherever there is a pot there is the potter's stick," because the stick is admitted to be a cause of the pot; on the contrary a genuine universal proposition like "Wherever there is earth-ness there is thing-ness" could not have been established, there being no causal relation present.[2]

In fact, however, says the Vedānta-paribhāṣā, vyāpti between two phenomena, say smoke and fire, is known when the fire is known to accompany (or co-exist with) smoke and at the same time *it is never known* not to accompany smoke.[3] There is no vyāpti between fire and smoke because though smoke is seen accompanying fire, say, in an oven, it is not found to accompany fire in a red-hot iron ball. Hence though we can have the vyāpti, "wherever there is smoke there is fire," we cannot have a vyāpti, like "wherever there is fire there is smoke."

But the question may be asked : How often is the concomitance between two phenomena to be observed before we can conclude that there is a relation of vyāpti between them? To this the Vedānta-paribhāṣā replies that the number of times the concomitance is to be observed is quite inessential; it may be either one or many.[4] But it may still be asked : "How is it possible to ascerain, by observing once, that one phenomenon found to accompany another at a particular place and time will also do so at other places and times? How, for instance, by seeing, only once, that fire accompanies smoke can we be sure that fire is never absent from a place where smoke is?" If a single observation revealing the concomitance between fire and smoke could be the basis of the knowledge of vyāpti, we should have said both that "wherever there is smoke there is fire" and that "wherever there is fire there is smoke."

1 Seal, *Positive Sciences*, pp. 273-274.
2 Sikhāmaṇi on Vedānta-paribhāṣā, p. 199.
3 "Sā ca vyabhicārājñāne sati sahacāra-darśanena gṛhyate."
4 Vedānta-paribhāṣā, p. 201: "Tacca sahacāra-darśanam bhūyodarśanam sakṛd darśanam vā iti viśeṣo nādaraṇiyaḥ."

In reply to this question the Āśubodhinī[1] says that repeated observation is necessary when there is doubt as to the universal validity of the concomitance known through a single observation. If the relation between fire and smoke observed in one case admits of some doubt, in order to remove this it is necessary to repeat the observation with all available cases of fire (which reveals that all cases of fire are not cases of smoke, though all cases of smoke are cases of fire). But a single observation (or act of contemplation) can yield a vyāpti like "Whatever is possessed of either an attribute or an action is a substance," as no exception to this general proposition can be conceived.

It should be noticed that the canon used by the Advaitins for ascertaining the soundness of a vyāpti or generalization is the method of Agreement in presence (anvaya), together with the non-observation of any exception. But it would be a mistake to think that this is the only method known to the Indian logicians. The Bauddhas and the Naiyāyikas formulated other canons for testing the invariability and unconditionality of concomitance. An excellent account of these canons has been given in his *Positive Sciences of the Ancient Hindus* (chapter on "Hindu Doctrine of Scientific Method") by Dr. B. N. Seal, who has also demonstrated their superiority, in many respects, to the canons of Western logicians. The Advaitins do not, however, discuss these canons, though their silence may be construed by some as a tacit acceptance of them. On some points, however, we find the Advaitins explicitly differing from the Naiyāyikas. The Naiyāyikas say[2] that one of the means for establishing the validity of a vyāpti, say between smoke and fire, is to institute the hypothetical argument (tarka), "If there were no fire there would be no smoke (as fire is the cause of smoke)," so as to ascertain that the rejection of the proposition to be established would lead to a *reductio ad absurdum*. But the Śikhāmaṇi,[3] and following it the Maṇiprabhā,[4] say that it is idle to think of testing the validity of a vyāpti with the help of a tarka, because a tarka itself involves a vyāpti which in its turn has to be proved to be valid.

Again, the naiyāyikas insist that for ascertaining vyāpti the observation of agreement in absence (vyatireka) also should be made wherever possible, and that an inference can be based on a general proposition

1 Āsubodhinī, p. 120.
2 Tattva-cintāmaṇī, Anumāna, p. 214.
3 Śikhāmaṇi on Vedānta-paribhāṣā, p. 202.
4 Maṇiprabhā on the same.

established through this method. But the Advaitins do not accept this view, as we shall see later on in connection with the criticism of vyatireki anumāna.

There is another important point of difference between the Naiyāyikas and the Advaitins as regards the perceptual knowledge of a vyāpti. The question is : How, on perceiving a *limited* number of cases of smoke accompanied by fire, can we conclude—'*All* cases of smoke are cases of fire'? As we have seen in the chapter on Perception, the Naiyāyikas hold that in perceiving a single object, smoke, we perceive, as inhering in it, the universal smokeness, the perception of which again amounts to the perception of all smokes as characterized by the perceived universal. This perception of a class, as we have seen, is technically called Sāmānyalakṣaṇā-pratvāsatti. On this theory the Naiyāyikas explain the possibility of the formulation of a general proposition (or vyāpti) through perception. But the Advaitins, as we have noted, reject this Nyāya theory and offer an alternative explanation. The general proposition, "All cases of smoke are cases of fire," is possible, they say, because by perceiving smoke and fire we can establish a relation between the two universals, smokeness and fireness (dhūmatva and vahnitva), which alone can furnish the basis of a general relation between all smokes and fires, in so far as they are respectively constituted by the universal characters "smokeness" and "fireness."

The views of the Naiyāyikas and the Advaitins on this controversy may be taken as throwing some light on their conception of the universal proposition. The Advaitins, it would appear, take a connotative view of the universal proposition, whereas the Naiyāyikas seem to take a denotative or enumerative view of it : "All cases of smoke=All individuals of the class of smoke." As we have seen already, the Advaitins say that for ascertaining a universal concomitance it is not essential that observation should be repeated several times; even a single observation can yield the knowledge of such concomitance, *only if* no exception to it is known. They mean that under favourable circumstances a connection between the two universals (smokeness and fireness) can be ascertained even by a single observation, and this suffices for inference. It may be asked however: How do the Advaitins use, in inference, the universal proposition : "All cases of smoke are cases of fire"? Does not this proposition state a relation between all individual smokes and individual fires? Does it not, therefore, present a denotative view of the universal proposition? To this the

Advaitins would give the same reply as their friends the Bhāṭṭas, who say that this universal proposition is really inferred deductively from the universal concomitance between smokeness and fireness. After observing this latter kind of concomitance in one case, say in the hearth, the Bhāṭṭas hold that we argue thus : "All other past and future smoke also is accompanied by fire, *because* it possesses the characteristic of smokeness."[1]

4. THE FUNCTION OF VYĀPTI. THE PSYCHOLOGY OF INFERENCE

Having considered the conception of vyāpti and the means of ascertaining it, we may consider next the part that vyāpti plays in inference. The early Naiyāyikas[2] as well as the Advaitins[3] hold that the knowledge of vyāpti is instrumental to inference. But they differ as to the exact function (vyāpāra) that the knowledge of vyāpti as an instrument discharges. Some Naiyāyikas hold that the knowledge of a vyāpti, as that between smoke and fire, generates on being reproduced by the perception of smoke on the mountain, the knowledge : "The mountain contains smoke that is always accompanied by fire" (vahni-vyāpya-dhūmavān ayam parvataḥ)—a knowledge interrelating the three terms S—M—P.[4]. It is through this latter that the conclusion, "Therefore the mountain contains fire," is obtained. This synthesis correlating the three terms is then the function (vyāpāra) by which the knowledge of vyāpti makes an inference possible. The function is technically called by the Naiyāyikas tṛtīya-liṅga-parāmarśa, i.e. contemplation of the mark (the middle term) for the third time. It is so called because according to these thinkers the mark or middle term, smoke, is known for the first time when smoke is observed in the hearth, i.e. when the knowledge of vyāpti is first acquired; it is known for the second time when it is found to be existing on the mountain (the minor term), and it is known for the third time when the smoke is known as correlating the mountain and fire in the way shown above.[5] Another name

1 Sāstra-dīpikā, p. 62, and Siddhānta-candrikā thereon.

2 Bhāṣā-pariccheda, Kār. 66; (Prabhā characterizes this as the view of the early Naiyāyikas).

3 Vedānta-paribhāṣā, pp. 188-189.

4 Bhāṣā-Pariccheda, Kār. 66.

5 Maṇiprabhā, on Vedānta-paribhāṣā, p. 190.

of this function is vyāpti-viśiṣṭa-pakṣa-dharmatā-jñānam, which means knowledge of the character of the minor term, in which that character also is characterized by an invariable, universal relation (vyāpti) of the middle with the major term.

But the Advaitins[1] differ from these Naiyāyikas as to the function (vyāpāra) of the knowledge of vyāpti. According to them, if one knows the vyāpti, "smoke is accompanied by fire," as soon as he afterwards sees smoke on the mountain the impression of this previously acquired knowledge of vyāpti is revived, which at once yields the knowledge. "The mountain is fiery." The function of the knowledge of vyāpti is, therefore, the creation of this impression (saṃskāra), through the revival of which inference takes place. The difference between the Naiyāyikas and the Advaitins as to this psychological analysis of the inferential process may be more clearly understood with the help of symbols. If S is the subject, P the predicate of the conclusion, and M the middle term, the position of the two schools may be indicated through the following steps :—

THE NAIYĀYIKAS

1. M—P, (The knowledge of vyāpti acquired first),
2. S—M, (The minor term found to be characterized by the middle : pakṣa-dharmatā-jñānam),
3. Revival of the memory impression of the vyāpti (which is not yet developed into a conscious judgment),
4. M—P, (The knowledge of vyāpti reproduced in the form of a conscious judgment),
5. S—M—P, (Correlation or synthesis of the three terms :— tṛtīya-liñga-parāmarśa, or vyāpti-viśiṣṭa-pakṣa-dhar-matā-jñānam),
6. S—P. (The conclusion attained).

THE ADVAITINS

1. M—P, (The knowledge of vyāpti acquired first),
2. S—M, (The minor term found to be characterized by the middle : pakṣa dharmatā-jñānam),
3. The impression of vyāpti revived, without any conscious judgment,
4. S—P. (The conclusion attained).

It appears from the above that according to the Naiyāyikas there are five steps necessary for the conclusion, whereas according to the Advaitins there are only three.[2] As regards the fourth step of the Naiyāyikas, the

1 Vedānta-paribhāṣā, p. 189.
2 Āśubodhinī, p. 117.

Advaitns contend that it is not universal, and therefore not essential, though it may sometimes be present when the vyāpti is explicitly recollected (vyāpti-smṛti-sthale)[1]. As regards the fifth step, the Advaitins say that it is altogether redundant. On seeing smoke on the mountain, the impression of our past knowledge that every case of smoke is a case of fire is revived, and we at once come to the conclusion that the mountain is fiery. We have not even to wait for this revival to mature into an explicit judgment of vyāpti, M—P.[2] But even if such a judgment is sometimes formed, the synthetic judgment (S—M—P) correlating three terms is scarcely found to intervene. The Advaitins hold, therefore, that the older Naiyāyikas, who consider this synthesis (tṛtiya-liñga-parāmarśa) to be a function (vyāpārā) of the knowledge of vyāpti, which in its turn is instrumental to inference, and the more recent Naiyāyikas, who consider it to be itself directly instrumental to inference, are equally mistaken, because there is no reason at all for thinking that it is an essential precondition of inference.

As regards the synthetic construction of the three terms, the view of the Naiyāyikas will be found by a student of Western philosophy to resemble that of a logician like Bradley, according to whom the inferential process involves the synthesis of the data into a single whole, and a subsequent discovery of the conclusion from that whole by inspection. As Bradley observes, in the inference: "Man is mortal, and Caesar is man, and therefore Caesar is mortal, there is first a construction as Caesar- man-mortal, and then by inspection we get Caesar-mortal."[3]

But though this analysis by the Naiyāyikas and Bradley may be taken as the *ideal* of an inference as a process of demonstration (as Bradley evidently means it to be), it scarcely represents faithfully what actually takes place in our mind when we infer facts in everyday life. From the latter standpoint the account of the Advaitins would be found to be more accurate. When from the redness of a piece of iron we at once judge that it is very hot, or from the sound of a whistle we judge the arrival of a train, we scarcely explicitly have a major premise in the mind before arriving at the conclusion. It cannot of course be said that since in such

1 Vedānta-paribhāṣā, p. 195.

2 Vedānta-paribhāṣā, p. 196 : ". . . na tu madhye vyāpti-smaraṇam . . .," and Āśubodhinī p. 117: "Vyāpti-saṃskārodbodhānantaram eva anumiti-sambhavena antarā tat-smṛter avasyambhāvitvābhāvāt."

3 *Logic*, vol. i, p. 259.

a case we do not have any explicit major premise, we infer the conclusion from the minor alone—as Dr. Thomas Brown, according to Mill, used to hold.[1] When memory does not exhibit the intervention of any explicit judgment interrelating the major and the middle terms, we must assume, *for an adequate explanation of the conclusion*, that at least the impressions of our past knowledge of such interrelation *must* have been *implicitly* active for the production of the conclusion.

It cannot be denied, however, that when the major premise is used in any inference, it is our past knowledge of the relation between the middle and the major that operates, through its impressions left in the mind. But in no case are we aware of the mediation of the three-termed constructive judgment, S—M—P, as leading to the conclusion S—P.

But apart from our actual procedure in everyday life is the employment of the three-term judgment essential for the purpose of an ideal demonstration ? Does the conclusion of an argument become in any degree more evident in the form :—

M—P
. S—M
. . S — M—P
∴ S—P?

than in the form :—

M—P
S —M
∴ S —P

It is true that the mind cannot move from S to P except through M, and the synthetic judgment, S—M—P, shows exactly how the movement takes place. But the very intuition that enables us to synthesize the two judgments, M—P and S—M, into S—M—P, gives us S—P as well. If so, S—M—P and S—P are co-effects of the same intuition, or better, they are the variant expressions of the same intuition. In that case it is misleading to hold that first we have S—M—P, and then S—P, which would imply that S—P is attained after S—M—P in a subsequently and separate movement of thought; for when S—M—P is attained, S—P is already included in it. Perhaps Bradley, who says that S—P is discovered by "*inspection*" from S—M—P, does not mean anything very different from this; he would perhaps agree that after S—M—P is obtained there is

1 Ibid., p. 227.

no further advance in thought, and the conclusion already contained in S—M—P is simply unravelled and laid bare.

To conclude then, we find that in everyday practice we pass directly from the premises to the conclusion, S—P, without halting at any half-way house, S—M—P. But when the truth of the conclusion is to be demonstrated, it may ensure easier conviction to lead the mind through S—M—P to S—P. But even in that case it is not to be understood, as the Naiyāyikas seem to do, that S—P is obtained by a fresh movement of thought. For S—M—P already contains S—P, just as the judgment x=y=z contains the judgment of identity x=z. We do not *proceed from* S—M—P and *come to* S—P, but we analyse out S—P from S—M—P. When we remember, however, that the Naiyāyikas and the Advaitins have in view here the psychological analysis of the inferential process, and not the determination of the demonstrative form of inference (which they undertake elsewhere in describing the parts of the Syllogism, nyāya), we must agree that the account of the Advaitins is far more accurate than that of the Naiyāyikas.

5. Does Inference Yield any New Knowledge?

It has been seen that according to the Advaitins inference takes place on the revival of the impressions of the previous knowledge of Vyāpti. The question is therefore asked : Does not then inference become indistinguishable from a case of memory, which also is caused by the revival of the impressions of past knowledge ? If this suggestion is sound, inference can no longer be regarded as a pramāṇa, which must be a source of *new* knowledge.

This objection is answered by the Vedānta-paribhāṣā,[1] which says that though the revival of past impressions is a necessary condition of both memory and inference, there is still a marked distinction between the two. Memory is caused by the revival of past impressions *only*, but inference is caused not by that *alone*; it has in addition other causes as well, e.g. the knowledge of the relation of the middle term with the minor, etc.. which must also always co-operate with the revival of impressions in order that inference may take place.

1 Vedānta-paribhāṣā, p. 193.

In explanation of the above, the Śikhāmaṇi[1] and the Āśubodhinī[2] add that the suggestion of inference being memory would hold only if the knowledge obtained through inference, i.e. the conclusion "The mountain is fiery," were the object of the impression revived. In fact, however, the object of the past impression is the major premise, "Wherever there is smoke there is fire," which alone is reproduced from memory. The conclusion, "the mountain is fiery," is not therefore a mere reproduction of past knowledge; it is something new. The suggestion against inference, therefore, fails.

It may be interesting to students of Western philosophy to note that the dilemma of the syllogism being either a *petitio principii* or an inconclusive argument was also felt and explained by Indian logicians. We find the problem formulated in a couplet quoted by the Śāstra-dīpikā as follows : "If the major premise expresses a relation between individuals (e.g. individual smoke and individual fire), then the relation is not universal (and therefore the conclusion does not follow); and if it expresses a universal relation (e.g. between all smokes and fires), then what is already *known* is sought to be proved."[3]

The solution suggested by the Śāstra-dīpikā[4] is that the major indeed expresses a universal relation. But that does not mean that the relations between all individual smokes and fires, as existing in particular times and places, are known. In the major we have knowledge of the relation between smoke and fire in general, i.e. smoke and fire as characterized by the generic properties "smokeness" and "fireness" alone. But through inference we come to acquire the knowledge of a particular fire existing at the particular time at the particular place, which as such was not known before. We have seen previously that the Advaitins also interpret the major premise connotatively. Thus they also would solve the dilemma in the same way as the Bhāṭṭas.

6. THE FORM OF THE SYLLOGISM

It is well known that the Indian logicians generally make a distinction between inference for one's own self (svārthānumāna) and inference for others (parārthānumāna), i.e. inference used for demonstrating a truth to

1 Śikhāmaṇi, p. 194.
2 Āśubodhinī, p. 114.
3 Śāstra-dīpika, p. 63: "Viśeṣe anugamābhavaḥ, sāmānye siddhasādhyatā."
4 Ibid.

other persons. The psychological account of inference we have given already represents, accoding to the Advaitins, the first kind of inference. As to the second kind, the Naiyāyikas, as is well known, are of opinion that it consists of the following five steps :—

1. Pratijñā—Statement of the proposition to be proved; e.g. the mountain is fiery.
2. Hetu—Statement of the reason; e.g. because it has smoke.
3. Udāharaṇa—Statement of the universal proposition along with an instance; e.g. wherever there is smoke there is fire, as in the hearth.
4. Upanaya— Statement of the presence of the mark in the case in question; e.g. there is smoke on the mountain.
5. Nigamana—Conclusion proved; e.g. therefore, this mountain is fiery.

But the Advaitins say that even for the purpose of demonstration the five steps are unnecessary. It is quite sufficient either to state the first three or the last three.[1] This view seems to be quite reasonable. The reduction of steps in no way affects the convincing character of the reasoning, because either of the two groups contains a mojor and a minor premise. In saying that either the first three steps or the last three can be employed, the Advaitins stress a truth the importance of which has been almost ignored in the stereotyped Western syllogism that always places the conclusion last. In inference, it is not always the case that the premise are *given* and the conclusion is to be *found*. It is very often the case that the conclusion is presented first to the mind, and we are required to find the premises that justify it. This latter process is mostly in evidence when we adduce arguments in justification of our instinctive beliefs. The order of reasoning, therefore, may take either form; the premises first and the conclusion last, or the conclusion first and the premises last. In the latter case it is, of course, a misnomer to call the proposition proved a conclusion. It should rather be called a *probandum*, for until the premises are adduced it is not a conclusion but only a proposition to be proved. Hence the Indian logicians call it a pratijñā (*probandum*). But what we wish to point out here is that the Advaitins and other Indian logicians, who think that inferential proof may take both the forms noted above, recognize an important truth which is scarcely realized by Western logicians.[2]

1 Vedānta-paribhāṣā, p. 212.

2 It should be mentioned, however, that Joseph recognizes this truth; vide his *Introduction to Logic*, p. 231.

There is one thing more that is worth notice. Whether we take the first three steps or the last three, the udāharaṇa, that is common to both, is preserved. And the udāharaṇa is the characteristic keystone of the Indian syllogism. As we have seen, it consists of the universal proposition supported by concrete examples. This, as Dr. Seal points out, at once marks off the Indian syllogism from the mere formal and deductive syllogism of Aristotle on the one hand, and the mere material and inductive syllogism of Mill on the other, and makes of it, as Dr. Seal again so aptly says, a "formal-material deductive-inductive" process of reasoning.[1] The Udāharaṇa makes difficult any attmept to affiliate the Indian syllogism to that of Aristotle and furnishes, as Professor Radhakrishnan points out,[2] a strong point against the argument that the Indian syllogism had a Greek origin.

7. The Classification of Inference

The various principles on which Western logicians classify inference are conspicuous by their absence from Indian works on Logic. We have noticed already, in other contexts, that the classification of inference into the mediate and the immediate was never made, owing to the fact that an anumāna *ex hypothesi* involved two premises—the major and the minor.

The necessity of classifying inference into the deductive and the inductive also did not arise, because, as we have seen, for the Indian logician no syllogism was of any value unless based on a universal major established through induction; consequently the processes of induction and deduction blended together to constitute a syllogism. It was no more possible for them to think of classifying inference into inductive and deductive than to think of classifying men into those that have bones and those that have flesh.

This will also explain why the classification of syllogisms into the categorical and the conditional was not made by the Indian logicians. A syllogism with a really conditional major (not a so-called conditional one that is reducible to the categorical type) can claim little more than formal consistency. An Indian logician, as we have seen, demanded of the syllogism, both formal and material, validity; and nothing but a universal major, materially valid, could satisfy him. The hypothetical syllogism

1 *Positive Sciences of the Ancient Hindus*, p. 251.
2 *Indian Philosophy*, vol. ii.

could not, therefore, have any place in his logic. With him therefore, as with Aristotle, every syllogism was necessarily of a categorical nature. It is to be noted, however, that examples of disjunctive syllogisms are not altogether absent. The Sāṃkhyas argue, for instance, "As Devadatta is living he is either at home or out. He is not at home. Therefore he is out." But the disjunctive syllogism was not contrasted with the categorical and was not, therefore, given a separate name.

The reason why in Indian logic we do not find any syllogism with a particular premise may be found to be the same as that which determined its attitude towards the hypothetical syllogism. A particular proposition, like "Some S is P," when stripped of its quantifying mark, is found to be nothing but "S may be P." It was natural, therefore, that this indefinite proposition should be neglected by a logic that would have nothing but concrete and definite facts for the premises of an inference. The neglect of a particular premise was, of course, the principal reason which led to the poverty of moods; but it is difficult to say whether it made the Indian syllogism a less useful instrument for the ascertainment of truth. The only great value that the particular, "Some S is P," may possess, is that it may contain the definite knowledge that may be expressed also as a universal, namely, "S is compatible with P."

With their own conceptions of inference the Indian logicians discuss, however, two chief principles of classification. Of these two we have already discussed one, namely the division of anumāna into the two classes according as it is used *either* for one's own self (svārtha) or for convincing others (parārtha). But the other and the more important classification, recognized by the Naiyāyikas, consists in dividing inference into three different kinds, Kevlānvayi, Kevala-vyatireki and Anvaya-vyatireki. The principle involved here is the nature of the major term[1] (the Sādhya) or rather the major premise. We have seen already that the canons applied by the Indian logicians in inductively establishing the major premise are Agreement in presence (anvaya) and Agreement in absence (vyatireka). In the syllogism, "Wherever there is smoke there is fire, there is smoke in the mountain, therefore the mountain has fire," the validity of the major may be tested both through Agreement in presence (by observing in

1 This is the view of the Cintāmaṇi, Cintāmaṇi-rahasya, Nyāya-siddhānta-mañjari; the Vedānta-paribhāṣā and its commentaries take up this view for criticism. But according to Tarkasamgraha the classification is based on the nature of the mark (liñga), i.e. the middle term.

allows only vyatireka (i.e. observation of agreement only in absence), is called kevalavyatireki. This is the Nyāya[2] classification of inference.

1 Of the five elements earth, water, fire, air, ether, only the first is admitted by these thinkers to have natural smell. If water or air is found to possess smell, it is to be understood that there are particles of earth present in it.

2 It is to be noted that the early Nyāya had another scheme of classification (pūrvavat, śeṣavat and sāmānyatodṛṣṭam), but as the Advaitins do not notice it, it is not necessary to discuss it here.

The Advaitins (such as the author of the Vedānta-paribhāṣā) do not accept this classification. As to the kevalānvayi inference, they say that it is based on a wrong metaphysical presupposition. There can be no term which is all-pervasive, and the absence of which cannot be found anywhere. Brahman, as conceived by them, excludes all predicates and the absence of the so-called all-pervasive major term (like "knowable") can be shown at least in Brahman.

As to kevala-vyatireki, the Advaitins argue that an inference (anumāna) is by conception a process of reasoning based on an invariable concomitance between the middle and the major term. An argument based on an invariable concomitance between the *absence* of the major term and the *absence* of the middle (as we have in a vyatireki induction) cannot, therefore, be called an anumāna, though it may be a quite valid piece of knowledge. It should be given a separate name, viz. arthāpatti.

The rejection of the mixed type anvaya-vyatireki follows directly from the principle on which kevala-vyatireki is rejected. On the whole, therefore, the Advaitins accept only one type of inference—i.e. anvayi—based on an Affirmative Universal Major which is established through the method of Agreement in presence coupled with non-observation of any exception. This is to be distinguished from the kevalānvayi, wherein the testing of the Major through non-perception of any exception is not possible at all.

It is to be noted, however, that Rāmakṛṣṇa, the author of the Śikhāmaṇi, differs from the other Advaitins on this point. He argues that it is not a universal concomitance between the middle and the major term alone that can yield an anumāna. Some other universal concomitance also can lead to an inference, provided that it does not present any opposition to the universal concomitance between the middle and the major terms. It is idle to object, says Rāmakṛṣṇa, that in that case the knowledge of a universal concomitance, like "whatever is produced is non-eternal," might also lead to the inference, "the mountain is fiery," as there is no opposition between this universal and the universal "whatever there is any smoke, there is fire." For we never actually have such an inference in life. The testimony of self-consciousness should be the ultimate judge as to whether any inference actually takes place from a proposition or not.

It need not be apprehended, continues Rāmakṛṣṇa, that by accepting the Nyāya theory of a vyatireki anumāna the Advaitin must necessarily give up his own theory of arthāpatti as a method of knowledge distinct from anumāna. Though the knowledge obtained through arthāpatti *can* be obtained through anumāna also, it does not necessarily follow that it *is* always so known. Here, as elsewhere, the evidence of self-consciousness should decide what *actually* is the source of a particular knowledge. The existence of an object known through perception can also be known through inference. But that neither argues that perception is included in inference, nor shows that everywhere the existence of the object is actually known through inference. It is only self-reflection that can tell us whether in a particular case the object is known perceptually or inferentially. Similarly the distinction between arthāpatti and anumāna also is grounded on the testimony of self-consciousness; the one cannot therefore, be reduced to the other.

Another alternative argument in favour of vyatireki anumāna is advanced by Rāmakṛṣṇa. Even granting that it is only an anvaya-vyāpti, i.e. a universal concomitance between the middle and the major, that can lead to an inference, it may be said that the knowledge of a vyatireka, i.e. Negative Universal (Major), yields an Affirmative Universal, and *through that* leads to an inference.

Thus the Advaitins can, says Rāmakṛṣṇa, accept the Nyāya classification of anumāna quite consistently with their own theory of arthāpatti.

Orthodox commentators of the Vedānta-paribhāṣā urge, however, against Rāmakṛṣṇa that the evidence of self-consciousness does not prove that we ever infer any conclusion from a vyatireki universal. There is no ground, therefore, for accepting a vyatireki anumāna.

We have so far stated only the views of the Advaitins and their critics. It is necessary, however, to understand these statements critically in the light of Western logic. For this purpose it will be convenient to represent symbolically the three kinds of inference discussed above.

Putting P for the major term, S for the minor and M for the middle, they can be represented thus :—

KEVALANVAYI

All M is P,	All nameables are knowable,
All S is M,	A jar is nameable,
∴ All S is P,	∴ A jar is knowable;

(where non-P is unknown and the absence of M in non-P cannot be ascertained).

KEVALA-VYATIREKI

No non-P is M,	No thing that is not different from other elements has smell,
All S is M,	Earth has smell,
∴ All S is P,	∴ Earth is different from other elements;

(where P is such that "All M is P" cannot be ascertained through observation).

ANVAYA-VYATIREKI

All M is P,	All that has smoke has fire,
All S is M,	The mountain has smoke,
∴ All S is P,	∴ The mountain has fire.
	And
No non-P is M,	No thing that has not fire has smoke,
All S is M,	The mountain has smoke,
∴ All S is P,	∴ The mountain has fire;

(where P is such that both "All M is P" and "No non-P is M" can be ascertained through observation).

As to kevalānvayi inference little has to be said. The controversy, as will be readily understood, does not at all concern the validity of the conclusion of a kevalānvayi inference. For the Advaitin questions neither the process nor the conclusion of such an inference. The only point at issue is whether the Major Premise has a unique character which entitles the inference to a separate category and a separate name. As we have seen, if it is admitted that there may be something in the universe the absence of which is unknowable, then the Naiyāyikas are right and kevalānvayi should stand. But if this metaphysical assumption be wrong, the Advaitins are right and kevalānvayi is invalid. In any case this controversy makes it clear that whether the canon of Agreement in presence is universally applicable or not, depends ultimately on the answer to a metaphysical question. It is also found incidentally that we cannot be absolutely sure, as we generally are, that an immediate inference, involving the use of the contradictories of the terms, must be materially valid only if the original proposition be materially valid and the process of inference is consistent with rules. Conclusions like "No S is non-P," "No non-P is S," etc. from "All S is P," can be materially valid only under the condition mentioned above.

The controversy over kevala-vyatireki is of a different kind. As already said, the Advaitins do not object to the inclusion of kevalānvayi within inference, but do so in the case of kevala-vyatireki. They contend, as we have seen, that no inference can take place with a Universal that states a relation between the absence of the major term and that of the middle. Hence there can be no such inference as a vyatireki. The controversy ultimately concerns, therefore, the definition of an anumāna. As we have seen. the Advaitins insist that an inference is a process in which we infer the presence of the major term through a middle term and have to start, therfore, from the knowledge of an invariable concomitance between the middle and the major, and *not* of that between the absence of the major and the absence of the middle. But one commentator of the Advaita school, Rāmakṛṣṇa, is critical of his own master and argues, in favour of the Naiyāyikas, that any universal concomitance can lead to an inference, provide only that it does not oppose the universal concomitance between the middle and the major term. Which of these two contending claims is valid?

Let us try to decide this question by an examination of Rāmakṛṣṇa's arguments. It is obviously ludicrous to hold that *any* Universal, which is not opposed to the Universal expressing a concomitance between the middle and the major term, can be the basis of an inference. For in that case, as the other Advaitins point out, we could have an inference like "Whatever is produced is non-eternal. The mountain has smoke, ∴ the mountain is fiery." Rāmakṛṣṇa of course replies to this objection by saying that we can have no inference in such a case, because self-reflection never reveals that we actually have any such inference. But this defence amounts to the statement that a vyāpti, which is not opposed to the vyāpti between the middle and the major term, and which is actually experienced to be the cause of an inference, can be the cause of an inference. It clearly involves a *petitio principii.*

As to the othe argument of Rāmakṛṣṇa, that the knowledge of the universal concomitance between the absence of the major and the absence of the middle (i.e. vyatireka-vyāpti) yields the knowledge of the universal concomitance between the middle and the major (i.e. anvaya-vyāpti) and generates an inference through the latter, it must be said that it is a more reasonabel suggestion. But it amounts almost to a surrender of the Nyāya position on at least two points. First, a vyatireka-vyāpti can yield an anvaya-vyāpti only when the major term allows it, i.e. when it resides in more loci than one. For instance, "All cases of the absence of fire are cases of the absence of smoke," can yield "All cases of smoke are cases of fire." But as we remember, in a case of kevala-vyatireki inference the major is such that it abides only in one locus and consequently no anvaya-vyāpti is possible. For instance, "All cases of the absence of difference from other elements are cases of the absence of smell," cannot possibly yield, "All cases of the presence of smell are cases of the presence of difference from the other elements"; for there are no *cases* but only *one* case, i.e. that of earth, where the difference from the other four elements fire, water, ari, ether exists. That being so, it is inconsistent with the Nyāya conception of a kevala-vyatireki anumāna to say that in such a case the vyatireka-vyāpti yields an anvaya-vyāpti and thereby yields the inference. Secondly, in saying that the vyatireki universal, "No non-P is M," or "All non-P is non-M," yields an inference *through* an anvayi universal, "All M is P," Rāmakṛṣṇa forsakes the Nyāya contention that a vyatireki universal can by itself yields and inference, and lapses therefore to the Advaita position. In fact the Vedānta blood running in his veins ultimately gets the better of his skin-deep Nyāya sympathies.

The point is that the process of reasoning involved in the vyatireki, "No non-P is M, All S is M, ∴ All S is P," is not at all transparently self-evident, like that of the anvayi, "All M is P, All S is M, ∴ All S is P." Very few can follow the former without reducing it to the latter. But it is after all a question of intellectual ability. And the question whether the vyatireki should be admitted to be an inference must be decided, as Rāmakṛṣṇa rightly asserts, on the authority of self-consciousness. Rāmakṛṣṇa considers that the testimony of self-consciousness is in favour of vyatireki inference, the Advaitins that it is against it. But what is really the case has to be thought out by each for himself. It is important to add that even the great Naiyāyika Gaṃgeśa, after supporting a vyatireki inference, says that it is employed for one's self and cannot be used for convincing others.[1]

We conclude the classification of inference by offering a few remarks about figures and moods.

In Indian philosophy we find no classification of inference according to figures and moods. But some implications regarding these can be gathered from the foregoing discussion. It would appear that the Advaitins,

1 Tattva-cintāmaṇi, Kevalavyatirekyanumānam; "Ayañ ca vyatireki-prakāraḥ svārtha eva," p. 644.

who insist that the major premise must always express a universal concomitance between the middle and the major term, and that the middle term must be present in the minor, virtually hold that both premises should be A propositions. The Advaitins would therefore reduce all inferential reasonings to the first mood, of the first figure, i.e. Barbara.

The Naiyāyikas who believe in vyatireki inference must recognize another mood in addition to Barbara. But it is difficult to say to which of the valid moods of Western logic it would correspond. As we have shown already, the vyatireki, if literally rendered, amounts to the form :—

No non-P is M
All S is M
∴ All S is P.

But this form corresponds to none of the valid forms, since it violates the rule of Western logic according to which the conclusion must be in the negative, if any one of the premises be negative. To change it into a valid form we must therefore make the major premise affirmative or make the conclusion negative. But the first alternative would altogether defeat the underlying object of the vyatireki, which is claimed to have a negative major (representing a relation between the absence of the major term and the absence of the middle term). We must therefore choose the second alternative and state the conclusion in a negative form. The form of the inference would then be :—

No non-P is M
All S is M
No S is Non-P.

If non-P be considered the major term here, the mood would be Cesare, in the second figure. We find, therefore, that if the Naiyāyikas are to reduce their syllogisms to valid Western forms they must admit two figures, the first and the second, and two moods, Barbara and Cesare.

8. The Psychological Conditions of Inference :

The Theory of Paksata

Before we conclude our account of inference, it is important to notice one topic that is commonly discussed by Indian logicians. It relates to the question : Under what conditions does inference take place ?

There are two obvious conditions that suggest themselves to everybody. The first is the absence of positive knowledge about what is to be inferred.

We try to infer something when we are not certain about it. But on closer thinking it is found that though we lack certain knowledge about many things, we do not try to infer the existence or absence of all of them. Another condition should therefore be added to the first, and it should be said that we must not only be ignorant about a thing, but also have a positive *desire* or *will* to infer its presence or absence.

Some Indian logicians[1] go deeper into this question, and by analysing and examining the different combinations of these two obvious conditions discover that the above represents only one of the many situations in which inference really takes place. The different combinations of the presence and the absence of these two factors, namely, want of certainty (niścayābhāva or siddhyabhāva) and the will to infer (anumitsā or siṣādhayiṣā), yield four possible alternatives :— (1) Absence of certainty together with the will to infer. (2) Absence of certainty together with the absence of the will to infer. (3) Presence of certainty together with the will to infer. (4) Presence of certainty together with the absence of the will to infer. Now of these the first, as we have already seen, will certainly lead to an inference. The second appears to be unfavourable for inference. The presence of the will to infer, as already seen, appears to be essential. But the Naiyāyikas point out that when on hearing the sudden roar of thunder we infer the presence of clouds, we can scarcely say that even there we have a previous *will* to infer. Inference takes place as involuntarily as the sudden perception of a thing. Thus inference may take place even in the absence of the will to infer, if there is want of certainty about a thing. This case also proves, points out the Siddhānta-muktāvali,[2] that doubt is not an essential precondition of inference, as many logicians think it to be. We have no previous doubt in the above case as to whether clouds are present or not. The third alternative, namely, the presence of certainty coupled with the presence of the will to infer, also appears to be unfavourable to inference. For, the doubt naturally arises : How can there be inference about a thing when we are certain about its existence or non-existence ? To this it is replied[3] that there are cases when inference takes

1 Bhāṣā-pariccheda and Muktāvali, Kār. 70, and Tattva-cintāmaṇi, on Pakṣṣatā, Anumānakhaṇḍa, pp. 407-432.

2 Siddhānta-muktāvali on Kār. 70.

3 Tattva-cintāmaṇi; Anumāna, p. 424.

place in spite of certainty, only if there is will to infer. A person who has obtained certain knowledge about the self from scriptures may yet try to know it also through inference. It is also found that logicians try to infer the existence of even those things that are immediately known by them through perception. No inference takes place, however, when the last alternative obtains, i.e. when there are both certainty about a thing and the absence of the will to infer it.

On the whole, therefore, it is found, say the Naiyāyikas, that in all cases except the fourth inference can takes place. The condition of inference is, therefore, negatively expressed by them as the absence of the condition in which there are both certainty and want of the will to infer.[1]

Now this condition is described as the characteristic of the minor term of an inference and called, therefore, pakṣatā (the quality of being a pakṣa). The reason is that an inference aims at predicating something of the minor term (pakṣa); and an inference with regard to a particular minor term can take place only when that minor term is such that *with regard to it* there is the absence of the condition in which there are both the certainty that the predicate desired to be ascribed to the minor term is present in it, and also the absence of the will to ascertain through inference the existence of the predicate in that minor term.

The Vedānta-paribhāṣā does not discuss this topic of pakṣatā. But the Advaita-siddhi, and following it the Siddhi-vyākhyā, discuss it incidentally while establishing inferentially the falsity of the world. According to the Advaita-siddhi, pakṣatā (or the condition which should characterize the minor term of a possible inference) is either a doubt that the major term characterizes the minor, or the absence of evidence showing the presence of the major in the minor (Sādhya-sandehavattvam, Sādhya-gocar-pramānā-bhāvavattvam vā).[2] Another alternative definition of pakṣatā given by the Advaita-siddhi is the condition of being the object if some dispute (vipratipatti-viṣayatva).[3] The second alternative has specially in view the case of a parārthānumāna, where the object of an inference is to settle a disputed point.

1 Gaṇgeśa states it as "Siṣādhayiṣā-viraha-sahakṛta-sādhaka-pramāṇābhāvaḥ" Anumāna-cintāmaṇi; , p. 431.

2 Advaita-siddhi, p. 29.

3 Ibid., pp. 30-35.

The gist of all the definitions given by the Advaita-siddhi is that inference must have as its initating condition either doubt, or at least want of knowledge, about the thing to be inferred. In the light of the Nyāya conclusions already considered, this view would appear to be unsatisfactory. For it neither takes into account the factor of the will to infer, nor does it recognize that there can be inference in spite of the presence of certitude about what is to be inferred. Let us try to ascertain the exact shrotcomings, if any, of the Advaita view by considering which of the three cases in which, according to the Naiyāyikas, inference takes place cannot be explained by this view.

The first two cases, namely (1) the absence of certitude accompanied by the will to infer, and (2) the absence of certitude accompanied by an absence of the will to infer, can be easily met by the Advaitins, because in both of these there is absence of certainty, which can only be either a case of doubt or a case of ignorance. So far, therefore, the Advaitins are not at all handicapped by not citing the will to infer as a precondition of inference. In fact, as the will to infer is not common to both these cases, it is seen to be so far only an accidental condition, not an essential one. But when we come to the third case, namely the presence of certitude accompanied by the will to infer, we find that the Advaitin's definition fails to cover it. If there really is any inference in spite of certitude, and if it is initiated only by a will to infer, then the Advaitin is guilty both of making absence of certitude an essential condition, and of omitting the will-factor. But does such a case really exist ? It requires a little consideration.

If in spite of certitude inference takes place, it may either be motiveless, or may have a motive other than the attainment of certitude, or may have the motive of the attainment of greater certitude. The first alternative is ruled out at onec, because the Naiyāyikas explicitly mention the presence of will in this case, and they would not go to the length of holding with modern Western realists (like Russell) that will also is rather a "push" than a "pull." To take the second alternative, if the will to infer has a motive that is something other than certitude, then it is a diseased or a childish will that meddles with the tool of knowledge by putting it to all uses except the one it is intended for; and an account of its abuses should be reserved for the pathology of inference. The third alternative is a plausible one and deserves serious consideration. Even if we are certain about a thing we may, it may be said, want to be more certain about it. The possibility of increasing certainty about a thing is an article of popular faith, on which the poet has put his immortal seal : "To make sure doubly sure and take a bond of fate." But let us see what exactly it means. Enhancement of certainty implies that certainty admits of degrees. It may, of course, be said quite legitimately that even if truth may not admit of degrees, certainty (which is a mental attitude towards truth) may be greater or less, strong or faint. But this raises a question : What constitutes the difference between a lower and a higher degree of certainty ? When we obtain greater certainty, what do we gain that was previously wanting ? The only conceivable reply is that the difference is constituted by the greater certainty possessing a degree of certainty that the less certainty lacks. If that be the case, the inevitable conclusion is that before we employ an inference for obtaining greater certainty there is an amount of certainty that is wanting. It is a case, therefore, as much of the abseance of certainty as of the presence of it. Moreover, it is not the presence but the want of certainty that goads our will to infer, for surely we infer not in so far as we are certain of the thing, but in so far as we want to be certain about the thing by removing the absence of certainty. To take the concrete instances given by the Naiyāyikas, a person who wants to ascertain, through inference, the nature of the self even after obtaining a knowledge about it from the scriptures,wants to be still more certain; and this implies the presence of an element of uncertainty which he wants to remove. Similarly, when a logician infers the existence of things which he immediately perceives to be present, he must be seized with a mood of scepticism, however slight, and his inference aims at nothing but the removal of this oppressive element from his mind. So it is better to say, even in such a case, that there is absence of certainty accompanied by the will to infer, than to say that there is presence of certainty accompanied by the will to infer. Want of certainty, in the form of doubt or ignorance, is therefore found to be the essential condition of inference, and the will to infer a causal factor. The Advaita view of paksata is therefore sounder than the Nyāya one.

This concludes our account of the Advaita views of inference as a method of knowledge. The Advaitins do not discuss fallacies, about which almost all schools accept the views of the Naiyāyikas.

BOOK V

POSTULATION (ARTHĀPATTI)

BOOK V

POSTULATION (ARTHĀPATTI)

1. THE PROBLEM

WHEN a known fact cannot be accounted for without another fact, we have to assume or postulate the existence of that other fact. This process, in which knowledge of the fact to be explained leads to the knowledge of the fact that explains it, is called arthāpatti. The etymological meaning of the word "arthāpatti" is the assumption, supposition, or postulation of a fact (artha = fact, āpatti = kalpanā = supposition).[1] It is claimed by the Mīmāṃsakas and the Advaitins that this process, through which we obtain the knowledge of a fact that explains what is otherwise inexplicable, is a peculiar method of knowledge which cannot be included within any of the other five pramāṇas. Before we are in a position to examine the soundness of this claim, it is necessary for us to consider at some length the various instances of arthāpatti given by these thinkers.

A person who is known to fast by day is still quite stout. This stoutness cannot be accounted for unless we suppose that he eats at night.[2] We find here that the knowledge of the fact to be accounted for (upapādya-jñānam) is instrumental (karaṇa) to the knowledge of the explaining fact (upapādakajñānam) which we obtain.[3] The instances of arthāpatti have been divided into two classes[4] : dṛṣṭārthāpatti and srutārthāpatti. The first literally means supposition of a fact in order to explain perceived facts (dṛṣṭa = perceived). It is illustrated when, for instance, on the negation of the perceptual judgement, "This is silver," by a subsequent perceptual judgement, "This is not silver, but a shell," we assume the falsity of the silver that previously appeared to sight. (Appearance and subsequent non-appearance can be explained only by supposing that the thing must be false or it could not be negated.)

The second, i.e. śrutārthāpatti, literally means the assumption of a fact in order to explain a fact known through testimony (śruta = heard). It admits, again, of two forms, according as it concerns the supposition of a

1 Vedānta-paribhāṣā, p. 310.
2 Ibid., p. 309.
3 Ibid., pp. 308-309.
4 Ibid., p. 310.

verbal expression (abhidhāna) or of a thing meant (abhihita). The first is illustrated when for instance, on being asked "to close" we supply the *word* "door" in order to explain the sense with reference to that context, finding it otherwise inexplicable. The second is illustrated when on being told by the scriptures that by performing the Jyotistom sacrifice one can go to heaven, we assume that the sacrifice must generate some lasting unperceived merit (apūrva) without which a sacrifice which has ceased to be cannot be the cause of a life in heaven.[1]

2. Is not Arthāpatti an Anumāna ?

Now the question can naturally be asked : Cannot all these instances of arthāpatti be taken as cases of anumāna (inference)? The Vedānta-paribhāṣā replies that if we try to reduce any of these to the form of an inference, we shall have for its major premise not a proposition expressing a direct relation of universal concomitance between the middle and the major term (anvaya-vyāpti), but a proposition expressing a universal relation between the absence of the major term and the absence of the middle term (vyatireka-vyāpti). It has been already shown that vyatireka-vyāpti cannot directly lead to an inference. Hence a case of arthāpatti cannot be treated as an anumāna (or inference).[2]

Another argument, advanced by the Vedānta-paribhāṣā in support of this suggestion, is that in none of these cases do we say (on the tetimony of self-consciousness) "I infer" (anuminomi), but on the contary we say "I suppose" or "I assume" (kalpayāmi or arthāpayāmi).[3] On these two grounds the Vedānta-paribhāṣā concludes that arthāpatti is not a case of anumāna. It asserts on the contrary that all cases of vyatirki anumāna can be and should be considered as cases of arthāpatti.[4]

The Śikhāmaṇi, as we have already seen, lays exclusive stress on the second argument, viz. the testimony of self-consciousness, which it considers to be the chief evidence on which to distinguish one process of knowledge from another. In the case of arthāpatti, it says, we always feel "I assume that fact on account of (or to account for) this fact" (anena idem kalpayāmi). But in the case of inference we feel "I infer this from that."

1 Vedānta-paribhāṣā, pp. 311-313.
2 Ibid., p. 314.
3 Ibid.
4 Vedānta-paribhāṣā, p. 315.

Having thus stated the views of the Advaitins, we must now try to ascertain their value. Let us consider first of all the objections against the inclusion of arthāpatti in anumāna. The Advaitins in their criticism assume that arthāpatti, if it be an anumāna at all, must be of the vyatireki type, and argue that as the vyatireki is no anumāna, arthāpatti cannot be one. It is true that the instances of arthāpatti can be rendered in the vyatireki form. To illustrate, the argument that the man who fasts by day and yet remains stout must eat at night, may be put into the form : "No case of absence of eating at night while fasting by day is a case of stoutness. This is a case of stoutness. Therefore, this is not a case of absence of eating at night while fasting by day; i.e. this is a case of night-eating." Again, the argument of the Mīmāṃsakas that as Devadatta is alive and yet at home, he must be out, may be expressed as : "No case of absence of a man outside home, while he is not also at home, is a case of his being alive. Devadatta is alive. Therefore he is not absent outside home while he is not at home i.e. he is outside home."

But it may be asked : Are we in any way constrained to convert a case of arthāpatti into this form of inference alone? To this a student of Western philosophy would surely return an emphatic "No." He would point out, as Vācaspati Miśra[1] did on behalf of the Sāṃkhyas, that the above cases can be put more conveniently in the form of a disjunctive-categorical syllogism. Thus we may argue : "A man who is stout eats either by day or by night. This stout man does not eat by day. Therefore he eats at night." Again : "Devadatta who is alive is either at home or out. Devadatta is not at home. Therefore he is out."

If this be so, the objection against a vyatireki inference does not at all apply against arthāpatti when put in the form of a disjunctive inference. Consequently there is no difficulty, at least on that score, in regarding arthapatti as a case of inference. The Advaitin has nothing left to him, therefore, to stop the month of his opponents except the ineffectual appeal to the testimony of self-reflection.

To avert this obvious defeat the Advaitin has to seek the help of his allies the Mīmāṃsakas,[1] especially the Bhāṭṭas whom he follows in this as in many other respects. Kumārila Bhaṭṭa and his followers have devised

1 Tattvakaumudī, p. 176.

many powerful arguments in defence of arthāpatti, and the Advaitin may very well use them for his own safety. Let us state and examine some of them.

The first thing that the Bhāṭṭas point out is that arthāpatti arises when there is doubt or contradiction[2] in the mind, and we try to free the mind from it by discovering an assumption which dessolves the conflict. For instance, on not finding Devadatta at home while being certain, on some other evidence, that he is alive, we have to assume that he is out. Without this assumption there is a conflict between the knowledge of his absence from home and that of his being alive. It is only when we light upon the alternative idea that he may be out that we can reconcile the two. Again, there is a conflict between the knowledge that a man fasts by day and that he is stout, till the idea strikes us that he may be eating at night. Now the assumption in each of these cases is justified and is a valid piece of knowledge, because the two facts, between which there is the apparent conflict, are known to be certain (so that the conflict cannot be possibly got over by rejecting one of them), and because the fact assumed is the *only* one that can explain away the conflict.

When this analysis of the process of arthāpatti is accurately understood, it is easily found that it cannot be treated as a case of anumāna. It will be admitted by all that in anumāna we know the mark (or the middle term) *first* and ascertain the major term, through that, *afterwards*. But it would be found that this does not hold good if arthāpatti is put in the form of an inference. If arthāpatti were an inference what would be the mark? To go back to one of the instances given above, we cannot say that mere absence from home can serve as the mark for inferring that the man is out, since he may be dead and altogether non-existent; neither can we say that the mere fact of his being alive is a mark of his being out, since he may be at home. We must say, therefore, that the fact of his absence from home related with that of his being alive is the mark from which we can infer the fact of his being out. But we find that the relation of these two facts constituting the mark is not possible without the assumption that he is out; for until that alternative comes to the mind life and absence from home appear incompatible. That is to say, the knowledge of the mark presupposes already the knowledge of the fact to be proved, and nothing remains to be

1 Sloka-vārttika. Nyāyaratnākara, Śastradīpikā, and Prakaraṇa-pañcikā contain many arguments in defence of arthāpatti.

2 Śāstra-dīpikā p. 79.

proved by the inference. Hence the attempt to reduce arthāpatti to inference fails,[1] being vitiated by a *petitio principii.*

A student of Western philosophy would like to understand clearly how this argument of the Mīmāṃsakas affects the disjunctive-categorical syllogism to which, it has been found, arthāpatti can be reduced. It is not easy to understand how the syllogism, "Devadatta, who is alive, is either at home or is out. Devadatta is not at home. Therefore, he is out," can come within the purview of the above criticism. For a disjunctive argument cannot be said to have a middle term, unless it is forcibly converted into the categorical type.[2] But on patient scrutiny we find that though the *letter* of the criticism does not apply here, the *sense* really does.

The major premise, "Devadatta, who is alive, is either at home or is out," here conceals the crux of the whole argument. How could we at all obtain this proposition? We are supposed to know only two facts, namely that Devadatta is alive and that he is not at home, and from these *two* data we are to come to the conclusion that he is out. But we find that in the inference the major premise contains one datum more, namely that if the man is alive and yet not at home, he must be out, for this is what the disjunctive proposition contains as one of its meanings.

But the aim of the inference also is to prove the same thing — namely that the man (who is living and is yet absent from home) must be out. Ultimately we realize, therefore, the truth of the Mīmāṃsaka's argument that the attempt to reduce arthāpatti to inference is vitiated by an unavoidable *petitio principii.*

But it may be thought that this objection applies only when arthāpatti is put into the form of a disjunctive-categorical syllogism. It is necessary, therefore, to consider also the categorical form : "No case of absence of a man outside home, while he is not at home, is a case of his being alive. Devadatta is alive. Therefore, Devadatta is not absent outside home while he is not at home, i.e. he is outside home." We find that here also the major premise presents the same puzzle. For it contains the knowledge that "absence from home" and "absence from all places outside home" are incompatible, except on the supposition that the man is not alive. And how such knowledge is acquired is the very problem of arthāpatti. We have here, therefore, as in the previous case, a *petitio principii.*

1 Śāstra-dīpikā p. 78.

2 Joseph, *Introduction to Logic*, p. 321. He denies that even hypotheticals have really any middle term.

These considerations conclusively show, therefore, that the two data, viz. "the man is living" and "he is not at home," cannot be themselves constitute an inference; for that we require also some major premise which would somehow contain the information, at least in a hypothetical way, that if the man is alive and yet not at home he must be out, or that if the man is neither at home nor out he must be dead. And when we want to know how the major premise was acquired, we are faced with the same original problem, how from home we could know that he is out, etc. And if we pursue this problem further and try to establish the major through another inference, the same difficulty arises. We are thus led to *a regressus ad infinitum*. But if we are to make a start we must stop somewhere, and admit that the major premise need not be known through an inference. In that case that non-inferential method through which we know, without the help of a mojor premise, such propositions as "If a man is living and yet not at home he must be out," requires a name. The name arthāpatti can be given to it. This name, which means "postulation or assumption of a fact," aptly describes the process which consists in assuming or finding out the *only* fact without which a conflict cannot be resolved.

3. Are All Inferences Reducible to Arthāpatti

The opposite question may now be naturally asked : If this line of argument be adopted, is it not possible to show that all cases of inference (and not the Vyatirekins alone) are instances of arthāpatti? It may be argued for example, "the mountain smokes, and smoking cannot be explained except on the supposition that there is fire; therefore the mountain is fiery." Consequently the existence of inference, as a separate method of knowledge, cannot be admitted.

To meet this charge the Advaitin would again use the argument of his ally, the Bhāṭṭa.[1] The latter says that it is quite possible to prove the conclusion of the inference in the arthāpatti way as shown above. But that does not show that inference can be altogether dispensed with. On the contrary, it is found that this arthāpatti can be valid only when it is positively known that all cases of smoke are cases of fire and not otherwise. But as has been shown in connection with the ascertainment of vyāpti, the proposition, "All cases of smoke are cases of fire," is established through inference. So even if we arrive at the conclusion of an inference through an arthāpatti, we have to depend for our data on a previous inference. Inference, therefore, has to be admitted as a separate method of knowledge.

1 Śāstra-dīpikā . p. 79, and Siddhānta-candrikā thereon.

4. Criticism and Conclusion

On all grounds, therefore, we have to admit that arthāpatti is a distinct method of knowledge; that it cannot be reduced to inference and neither can all inferences be reduced to it. But before we conclude, it will be interesting to enquire whether we have any analogue of this process of knowledge in Western philosophy. It may be compared to the hypothesis of Western logic, in so far as both of them are *suppositions* that set out to *explain* given facts. But there are also important points of difference between the two. Like an arthāpatti, a hypothesis may not be always inspired by the motive of solving a conflict or contradiction. What is more important to note is that "hypothesis" is used to connote a tentative supposition that awaits verification, and does not therefore possess absolute certainty. But an arthāpatti, though a supposition, is the supposition of the only possible fact and carries with it absolute certainty. It can claim, therefore, the same place as a method of knowledge as is enjoyed by inference, perception, etc.

We have a closer parallel, however, in the "transcendental proof" which Kant employs throughout his *Critique*. As is well known, this proof consists in arguing from the consequent to its only possible antecedent, without which the consequent cannot be explained.[1] As in arthāpatti, so in this kind of argument, Kant is goaded by an apparent conflict to find out the only possible fact that solves it. The propositions of pure mathematics and pure physics, the truths of which are beyond question, manifest the apparently conflicting characteristics of necessity and novelty. Necessity points to an *a priori* origin, novelty to an *a posteriori* one. To solve this apparent contradiction Kant makes the supposition that there must be such a thing as *a priori intuition* (of space and time). The validity of this supposition rests on the fact that without it the true character of mathematical and physical judgements cannot be explained. Kant's "transcendental proof" can, therefore, be regarded as an instance of arthāpatti.

It may be said, however, that as in the case of Kant's philosophy, so in other instances of suppositions based on arthāpatti, it may be subsequently discovered that the fact that is supposed to offer the only explanation, may be found to be only *one* of the many facts that can explain the contradiction, and may come therefore to be abandoned. Does this not argue, therefore, that arthāpatti cannot be regarded as a valid source of knowledge? To this it is to be said that instances of such failure do not prove that the principle of arthāpatti is defective; it shows only a defect in the principle of arthāpatti is defective; it shows only a defect in the

1 For a discussion of this method *vide* Mahaffy, *Kant's Critical Philosophy*, p. 45.

practical application of the principle. The validity of arthāpatti is not affected, therefore, any more than that of inference, by its misapplications. The validity of the method would suffer if any instance were found where the fact supposed for the explanation of a contradiction were not true, in spite of its being the *only* principle of explanation. In the instance in question the conclusion is invalid, because the supposed fact is *not* t he only fact that can explain away the conflict. The validity of arthāpatti as a method of knowledge remains, therefore, altogether unaffected.

Inference and postulation — anumāna and arthāpatti — are two opposite, and yet complementary processes. The first tries to find out what *follows* from given premises, whereas the second tries to find out what *is presupposed* by the given and explains the given by showing its *grounds*.

The Mīmāṃsaka frequently use arthāpatti for explaining the Vedic texts by supposing missing words and meanings without which the texts cannot be correctly understood. The Advaitins also find this method useful for explaining the Vedā nta texts. For example, the Upaniṣads sometimes speak of the creation of the world by Brahman and out of Brahman; but sometimes they teach that there is no multiplicity. Brahman being the only Reality. This conflict is removed by supposing that creation is not a real transformation (pariṇā ma) of Brahman, it is only an apparent change (vivarta), just like the appearance of a rope as a snake. The supposition of Māyā (as the power of Brahman to create an apparent world) is a kind of postulation.

The Advaitins use this method also in supposing some unperceived facts and principles for explaining experienced facts. For example, they suppose the existence of an objectless blissful consciousness during dreamless sleep, in order to explain the memory we have on rising from such a sleep when we say, 'I had a comfortable sleep; I did not know anything then." We can, again, trace this method of postulation in the supposition (made by the Advaitins for explaining the world and empirical experience) that the six things viz. the individual, God (Īśvara), pure consciousness, Māyā, the difference between the individual and God, and the relation between Māyā and Pure consciousness are all beginningless. In fact, all necessary and indispensable suppositions, such as power or potential energy in things necessary for explaining their effects, the law of Karma necessary for explaining the otherwise inexplicable good and bad lucks of persons, and the existence of God[1] for explaining the distribution of fruits in accordance with an individual's actions, etc., are cases of Arthāpatti. It has thus a very wide scope.

1 Vide Śaṃkara on Br. Sūt. 3. 2. 38. BOOK VI

BOOK VI

TESTIMONY (ŚABDA)

TESTIMONY (ŚABDA)

INTRODUCTION

IN its widest sense, the word śabda means a sound. But in a narrower sense it means a sound used as a symbol for the expression of some meaning. In this sense it stands for a "word." In the present context Śabda means word or words as the source of knowledge; it corresponds, therefore, to "authority" or "testimony." Śabda-pramā means knowledge derived from authority and śabda-pramāṇa means words as the source of knowledge.

With the exception of the Cārvākas, the Bauddhas and the Vaiśeṣikas, almost all Indian thinkers accept śabda or authority as an independent and ultimate source of knowledge.

The chief reason why the Advaitins and many other philosophers tried to establish śabda as an ultimate source of knowledge was to uphold the authority of the scriptures in general, but of the Vedas in particular.

Modern Western philosophy had its birth in the revolt of reason against authority, and the word "authority" has thereby acquired such a repellent association of exploded mediaevalism that when we come across any attempt to justify the infallibility of authority of any kind we can hardly overcome our preliminary reluctance coolly to reconsider the merits of a case on which an adverse judgment was passed long, long ago, which has also been upheld since by the silent assent of the centuries that have followed. So a discussion of the śabda-pramāṇa of Indian philosophy seems to be foredoomed to neglect and ridicule. But no one who can overcome this apathy with a real warmth of philosophical earnestness, will fail to see that hidden in this stupendous mass of unphilosophical and sacerdotal chaff, there are many valuable kernels of real philosophical thought which are worth the attention of all sincere students of philosophy. In their attempt to justify the authority of the Vedas the ancient thinkers raised valuable problems, which can be studied for their own importance, independently of that of the Vedas. The problems of language as the verbal symbol of thought, of words, meanings, and the relation between meaning and its symbols, of the knowledge of meaning, the perception of words and meanings, the worlds of thought, meaning and reality, the import of propositions, the source and ultimacy of the validity of knowledge, etc., and finally of the claim of verbal testimony to be an independent source of knowledge, have been discussed so seriously, thoroughly and logically that their philosophical worth can be ignored only through an unphilosophical prejudice.

A little reflection will show that the belief of the modern man that he has outgrown the age of belief in authority is a complacent delusion. Authority only changes forms from age to age. The modern man is in the grip of authority in the new forms of the endless special sciences and their exponents and specialists whose opinions are implicitly accepted, because no inexpert can possibly understand or verify for himself the ever-increasing technicalities. It is highly interesting to note that even some of the most critical and otherwise sceptical philosophers, the logical positivists, behave towards the sciences today just as the mediaeval ones used to do towards the scriptures. They regard it as their chief, if not sole, duty to analyse, interpret and interrelate the words of their authority, Science. The Indian methodology of the interpretation of authority developed long ago should, therefore, prove instructive to even the modern West.

We shall here deal with the Advaita analysis of verbal testimony and other cognate logical and epistemological problems. We shall first analyse in our own way the whole process from the perception of verbal symbols to the knowledge of facts derived from them, in order to be able to understand clearly for ourselves what issues are really involved therein, and how the various problems and theories had their rise in Indian philosophy.

CHAPTER I

THE PROCESS OF ŚABDA-JÑĀNA

FIVE different stages can be distinguished in the entire porcess of verbal cognition. When any sound is uttered, be it symbolic or non-symbolic, we have (1) the sensation of the sound, (2) the perception or interpretation of the sensation. But when sounds are used as symbols of thought, i.e. when they are words, we have, in addition to the two stages already mentioned, three more : (1) recognition of the meaning signified by each word, (2) a constructive apprehension of the different independent meanings presented by different words (in case a significant sentence or a combination of words is employed), (3) belief in the truth of the meaning of the sentence uttered, or objective reference.

As we are concerned here with symbolic sounds or words alone, we shall deal, one by one, with all these five stages. We shall confine ourselves, at the first stage, to the process of verbal knowledge and shall reserve all considerations about its validity for the last part. A correct analysis of the process itself will serve to dispel much confusion and misconception usually entertained about śabdapramāṇa, and when the real issues are clearly grasped through critical analysis, we shall be in a position to discuss all questions about validity.

SENSATIONS OF SOUND

The sensation of sound, used as a symbol for the expression of thought, is similar to that of any other non-symbolic sound. The only noticeable peculiarity about a symbolic sound is probably that while non-symbolic sounds occur more or less as a jumble of sensations of which the different elements are rarely distinguishable from one another, symbolic sounds are clearly discerned as wholes and also in parts. When a bell is rung or a horn is blown, the sounds produced have duration and therefore elements. But the different elements can be distinguished only to a very small degree. It is difficult to say when one element ends and another begins. In musical sounds, of course, the different notes as well as their order can be distinguished by experts. But the symbolic sounds possess fixity of form and order, and discreteness of different elements to an eminent degree. Thus a slight change in the order of the letters of a word, a shift of accent, a little lengthening of the vowel, etc., are quickly discerned, as can be judged from the corresponding changes in significance. This fixity of a symbolic sound is derived mainly from the fixity of meaning which it represents. While an ordinary sound stands for itself, a symbolic sound stands for some element of thought, and as such it bears on it a definite *impress* of thought which serves also to distinguish it from its fellows. In fact our words are scarcely regarded as physical sounds; they pass for so many phases of thought. The thought-impress of a symbolic sound, say "man," not only distinguishes it sharply from other allied sounds like "men," "mane," etc., which represent different thoughts, but also imparts, within certain limits, a sense of identity to the various sounds produced by the different pronunciations of the word "man," and enables us to think of them all as the same word "man."

The ancient Indians distinguished two kinds of sound, namely the inarticulate, indefinite sounds of, say, a tom-tom and the definite, articulate sounds of human vocal organs. The former were called dhvani and the latter varṇa.[1]

Another noticeable peculiarity about the sensations coming from intelligible speech is that, like other sensations, they are not received passively. They often set up in the hearer an involuntary repetition of a parallel process of speaking, either mental or physical. This is specially noticeable when a successful speaker carries the audience with him and creates an effective impression. The words of the speaker ring through the mind of the hearer, who is apt to repeat them with the tone and emphasis of the speaker himself, almost like a violin that vibrates to the music of another similarly strung. Even in ordinary conversation, especially when the hearer happens to agree with the speaker, the hearer is often found to join the speaker in many places and involuntarily repeat the words of the speaker; and while remembering the words of a speaker whom we heard in the past , we can scarcely perform the process without repeating to ourselves all the words with their original tone and accent. All these facts clearly show the great influence that words exert on the minds of men.

We have been speaking so far about sensations of symbolic sounds or spoken words. But when words are committed to writing and we wish to understand the thoughts of a writer through the written symbols, the sensations we have are no longer auditory but visual. These visual sensations, however, do not directly lead to the process of interpretation and apprehension of meaning; they can perform this function only through the intermediation of sound-images (in case we read mentally without

1 Bhāṣā-pariccheda, Kārs. 164-165, and Śaṃkara-bhāṣya on Brahmasūtras (1, 3, 28).

producing any sound) or auditory sensations (if we read aloud). But as written symbols lack the individual peculiarities of sound symbols, we must read words written by others with *our* peculiar accents and intonations; so that in this case the reader has, in a way, to officiate for the writer by repeating mentally or physically the words of the latter. Generally speaking, therefore, whether communication is held through spoken words or through writing, the sensations received, whether auditory or visual, set up in the mind of the hearer or the reader a parallel process of repetition, in varying degrees, under varying circumstances. With these few remarks about sensations of visual and auditory symbols or words we pass to the consideration of the second stage, namely their perception.

CHAPTER II

THE PERCEPTION OF WORD-SYMBOLS

1. How Sound-series is Perceived

We have already noticed that when a word, say "animal," is uttered, the different elements generally give rise to more or less distinct sensations of sound. They do not fuse together but come one after another, in the exact order in which the different syllables are uttered. But if so, when the sensation arising out of the uttering of the first syllable, "a," is generated, sensations of the other two syllables have not yet come into existence. Similarly, when the sensation of the second syllable "ni" is generated, that of the first has passed out of existence, and that of the last syllable, "mal," is yet to come. Lastly, when the sensation of the last syllable, "mal," has come into existence, those of the preceding syllables have ceased. There is not a single moment, therefore, when all the three sounds are sensed together. Is it then possible to perceive the word "animal" as a whole? If so, how? If not, how is it possible to treat the three syllables a-ni-mal as one word? In reply to this it may be suggested that the unity of the word is based on the unity of its meaning, that the different syllables come to be treated as one word just because they convey one meaning when combined together. But this reply at once raises two difficulties. First of all, the syllables are heard first an the meaning is apprehended afterwards: we must first apprehend the word as a whole, circumscribed by a beginning and an end, in order to understand what it means. Secondly, to say that the different syllables *together* express one meaning is to beg the question. For what must be shown is exactly how and where we apprehend this assumed "togetherness" of the different syllables, which, we have found, cannot be *perceived* together. It might be answered that though the togetherness of the different syllables of a word may not be perceivced, it can be remembered. In other words, when all the three syllables are heard one by one, we may remember the whole word as heard. But even this solution of the difficulty is more apparent than real. For it only lands us between the horns of the dilemma : Are all the syllables of a word present to memory simultaneously, irrespective of their successive order, or do they come into memory one by one according to their fixed order ? If the first alternative is accepted, then we have to explain how we can distinguish between words like pan and nap, or tip and pit, which have exactly the same letters, differing only in their order; for the order cannot be distinguished when the letters are present all together and when, therefore, there is no question of "before" or "after." If however the second alternative is accepted, then we are led back to the old difficulty that if the syllables are remembered in order, they can never be remembered together as a whole.

It will at once be recognized that the problem raised in the above arguments is, at bottom, the same as the problem of the perception of temporal and spatial series, so much discussed at present by psychologists and epistemologists of the West. In India this problem interested some early philosophers who offer various solutions of it.

The Naiyāyikas' solution resembles those of some modern psychologists. They say that since the isolated syllables of a word cannot individually present its meaning,they must do so jointly. Further, since they come one after another into consciousness, they are not perceived together as one whole. But each syllable perceived leaves its impression behind, and when we come to the last syllable the apprehension of it, aided by the accumulated impressions of the past syllables, presents the meaning of the word.[1]

Plausible as this explanation may seem to be, it is not free from all objections.[2] For the impressions of the past syllables must be roused in memory in order that they may be of any use. If so, the syllables must also be remembered in the order in which they are perceived, one by one; and then they are never simultaneously grasped, so that the old difficulty tells against this solution as well.

2. The Theory of Sphota

These difficulties led the grammarian philosophers of India to hold the well-known theory of Sphoṭa.[3] It was hinted at by Patañjali,[4] the great commentator of the Pāṇini -Sūtras, and elaborately discussed and developed by later grammarians.[5]

1 Nyāya-siddhānta-mañjarī, p. 338.

2 Śaṃkara-bhāṣya on I, 3, 28.

3 The word sphoṭa (derived from sphuṭ, to express) is explained either as that which is expressed (or revealed) by letter-sounds or as that which expresses (or reveals) a meaning (*vide* Sarva-darśana-saṃgraha, Pāṇini system, and Vākyapadīya. I. 98).

4 Mahābhāṣya, I, I, I.

5 E.g. Bhartṛhari in Vākyapadīya.

According to this theory, the syllabus of a word do not directly present the meaning of the word, either separately or jointly, as this process has been found to be inexplicable. In reality, however, corresponding to every word perceived, there is an unperceived, partless (niravayava) symbol which directly presents the meaning. This symbol is called sphoṭa (or Śabda — *the* word). The different syllables of a word only serve to reveal this symbol to the mind. The first syllable rouses this latent symbol in the mind only vaguely, and the succeeding syllables, as they are gradually heard, draw it more and more towards the focus of consciousness till finally the last syllable, being heard, fully reveals the symbol to consciousness.[1]

The process of the gradual revelation of sphoṭa by the succeeding syllables of a heard word may be understood more clearly as follows. When a person is about to speak to us, we are quite ignorant of what he will say, and we have only a blank expectancy that allows no room even for a guess. But as soon as we hear him utter the first syllable, "a," imagination begins its work and defines our expectation by ruling out of possibility all words not beginning with "a." As he utters the next syllable, "ni," our expectation is further defined and limited to words that have "ani" as their first two syllables, and the possibility of the utterance of words not having these two syllables at the beginning is removed. When the last syllable "mal" is uttered all the unknowns are solved and the result is completely defined to consciousness, as a meaning fully known. So by analysis we find that meaning is known through a gradually consummated process beginning from complete ignorance, passing through partial knowledge and ending in complete knowledge. Each of these stages of the knowledge of meaning is presented by a corresponding stage of the knowledge of the symbol or sphoṭa of the heard word, which by being gradually perceived defines the sphoṭa from the mere vagueness of the initial stage to the complete certainty of the last stage; so the grammarians speak of the gradual revelation of sphoṭa through the gradual perception of the word-symbol. Thus it will be found that this ingenious hypothesis of a *unitary, indivisible* symbol, which in being revealed express a meaning, solves the difficulty that arises about the apprehension of a sound-series. At the same time it explains the utility of all the different syllables of a word. We may explain the theory graphically and try to make it clearer.

1 *Vide* Sarva-darśana-saṃgraha (Pāṇini system) and Brahmasūtras (1, 3, 28).

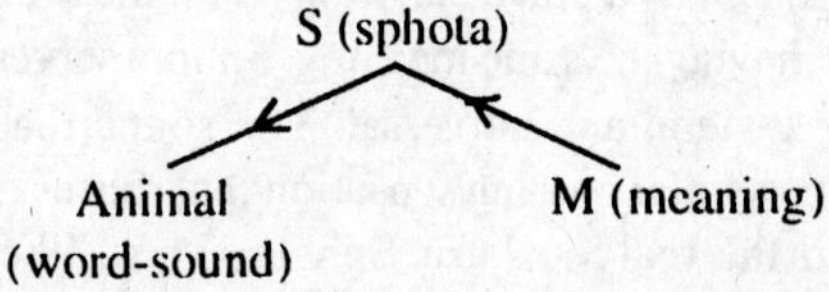

When we hear the word "animal," it cannot directly remind us of the meaning, "M," because neither through memory nor through perception can we grasp the whole word at one moment, as the syllables come into consciousness one after another and not simultaneously. But corresponding to the word "animal" we must have some unitary symbol, S, in which there are no parts and consequently no question of "before" and "after." This S can therefore be grasped by a single act of consciousness, as a whole, which directly presents M, the meaning. The word only serves to arouse the symbol S into consciousness. This symbol or sphoṭa varies according not only to the variation of the component syllables but also to their order, so that the symbol revealed to consciousness by the word "lame" will not be so revealed by the word "male," (having the same sounds in different order), which has quite another sphoṭa corresponding to it. The unity of a word which we generally speak about and which, as we have seen, can be given neither through perception nor through memory, is really derived from the felt unity of the sphoṭa which the different parts of the word serve to reveal to consciousness.[1]

Another consideration is urged to strengthen this hypothesis of sphoṭa. The word "animal" is pronounced differently by different persons. But how is it that these different sounds should lead to the same meaning? We must say that just as there is a general idea of the "cow" that is applicable to all particular cows with varying individual peculiarities, so there must

1 Throughout this discussion we have assumed, for the sake of simplicity, the existence of different sphoṭas as revealed by different words. It is important to remember, however, that according to the upholders of this theory sphoṭa is ultimately *one* and not many; it is in fact the *only* Reality and identical with Brahman (vide Vākyapadīya). But like the Advaitins, these thinkers also admit that though reality is one from the transcendental point of view, it is many from the empirical or practical standpoint. They admit that though sphoṭa is ultimately one, it is not revealed in exactly the same form by every word, but that different forms or aspects of the sphoṭa are revealed by different words, just as different forms of the same face are revealed by different mirrors. There is, therefore, the phenomenal plurality of sphoṭas in spite of its noumenal unity. As the present topic concerns an empirical question (namely how the sound-series is experienced) we have dealt with the empirical aspect of the theory without puzzling readers with its trascendental exposition. We have, therefore, often used the word "sphoṭa" in the plural. For a good discussion of sphoṭa see Eng. Intr. by Ramaswami Sastri in Tattvabindu ed. by him (Annamalai Univ., 1936).

be something, general and universal, to stand for the differently pronounced word "animal" having the same meaning. Sphoṭa serves this very purpose. It is held to be general and universal. The sound that is heard and dies away is only a particular passing sensation that rouses the symbol unheard which is called the real Śabda or Sphoṭa. Thus, like an idea of Plato, Śabda, as sphoṭa, is both universal and eternal. It is this that has a direct and eternal relation to meaning.

3. The Advaita View and Criticism

This theory has been rejected by the Vedāntins. Śaṃkara, in his Brahma-sūtra-bhāṣya,[1] Vacaspati in his Bhāmatī,[2] and Tattva-vindu have shown that the hypothesis of sphoṭa, in order to explain both the felt unity of a word and the possibility of its yielding meaning, is unnecessary and unsatisfactory.

It is unsatisfactory because the problem of the knowledge of a series is not peculiar to words alone. We have many other cases such as the knowledge of a line of ants or a collection of trees or army of soldiers, etc., where the same difficulty arises and where the theory of sphoṭa is not meant to apply. It is unnecessary because what is wanted is a general explanation that will cover all instances of the knowledge of series (spatial and temporal), and not a special hypothesis explaining only a special group of instances, namely the verbal series, since without such a general explanation the fundamental problem remains unsolved. And if a general explanation is possible the special hypothesis becomes altogether redundant.

Śaṃkara, as well as his followers, holds that though a series cannot be apprehended as a whole through perception, we have, after all the members of the series have been perceived one by one, a memory of all the members combined together. We have in experience, in all cases of temporal and spatial series, the knowledge of wholes which preserve the internal relations obtaining among their component members. When we already have such an experience, it is idle to ask how it is possible. We need only admit, on the basis of such experience, that the intellect possesses the power of synthesizing elements which were originally apprehended at

1 Brahma-sūtra-bhāṣya I, 3, 28.
2 Bhāmatī, I, 3, 28

different moments of time. This function of the intellect is called by Śaṃkara, "Samastapratyavamarśinī buddhiḥ"[1] (intellect looking back on past experiences as a whole). The theory of sphoṭa explains only verbal series. What, then, becomes of other temporal series? We must either say that even those have their corresponding sphoṭas, which the grammarians would not admit; or we must say that the knowledge of the unity and internal order of other series is possible without sphoṭa, in which case there is no reason why a verbal series also should not be known in exactly the same way. Consequently we have no ground for making a special case of verbal series, and the hypothesis of sphoṭa becomes unnecessary.

We may add that if the syllables of a word do not present its meaning, but require the intermediate agency of an indivisible sphoṭa, then the syllables become useless to the knowledge of meaning. For why should the word "cow" and not "horse" arouse in the mind the particular sphoṭa which gives the meaning "cow"? As a matter of fact, in order that a particular word should be able to call up its corresponding unitary symbol or sphoṭa, it is necessary to know all the syllables of the word in their fixed order and also as a combined whole. For without such a presupposition, the revelation of sphoṭa itself to consciousness cannot be explained.[2] When the word "animal" is uttered, for instance, the first syllable "a" individually would present to mind all sphotas corresponding to all words having the same sound "a," not necessarily as their first syllable, but as any syllable, because according to the supposition of the sphoṭa-vādin the order, as well as the combination of the syllables, cannot be known. Again the second syllable "ni" will call up all sphoṭas corresponding to words having that sound in any position. Similarly with the rest. Thus even when the whole word-sound is heard, instead of having the definite symbol in our minds, we shall have alternating series of many symbols suggested to consciousness. Nothing but a constructive apprehension of all the syllables, combined together according to their definite order, can locate and define for us the required symbol from amongst an infinity of possible symbols suggested by all other words having any of the syllables of the word heard (or even all of its syllables) in any order different from that one in which the syllables occur in the

1 Brahma-sūtra-bhāṣya on I, 3, 28.

2 Kumārila-bhaṭṭa notices this difficulty, while criticizing sphoṭa-vāda in his Ślokavārtika.

given word. Thus we find that the difficulty which the theory of sphoṭa tries to avoid remains concealed in its very supposition. That we have knowledge of the sounds in their determinate order is the very presupposition which explains sphoṭa-vāda. If that knowledge is possible, then the word itself can present its meaning directly, and the hypothesis of any mediating agency is quite redundant. Again, it is foolish to deny that we have the knowledge of a serial whole, just because it is difficult to say how that knowledge is obtained.

We are concerned, however, with the perception of words in this connecion. Though sphoṭa-vāda has been found to be untenable, the problem raised by this theory is not yet fully explained. Śaṃkara, of course, says that the word as a whole with its peculiar internal order can be grasped in memory through the synthetic activity of the intellect (Samastapratyavamarśinī-buddhi) but he does not think it necessary to explain how simultaneity and succession are compatible in the same act of the mind. The question, how even in memory we can avoid remembering the syllables in their order and therefore avoid failing also to grasp them as a whole, is not further dealt with.

Śaṃkara seems to consider the testimony of consciousness regarding the knowledge of a temporal series to be too strong to be shaken by any doubt, and believes in the existence of a peculiar faculty of the understanding as being the only explanation for the knowledge of such a series. His theory can be compared to Kant's theory of the synthetic unity of apperception and is, therefore, subject to many of the criticisms that his critics have hurled against the theory of Kant. But the more recent Gestalt school of psychologists, whose experimental researches have come to be generally accepted, would support Śaṃkara regarding the possibility of the perception of wholes.

CHAPTER III

WORDS AND MEANINGS

1. WORDS AS SYMBOLS

WE come now to a more important part of our discussion, namely the "meanings" of words. The aspects of words so long discussed are not peculiar to words or symbolic sounds alone; they are common to both symbolic and non-symbolic sounds. What distinguishes a word from other sounds is its possession of meaning. And we shall deal with this special property of words in this connection.

A word is a symbol of some idea. Three different aspects of a word can be distinguished : its existence, its content and its meaning. The existence of a word is physical, when uttered or written. It is composed, as we have seen, of some sounds, or of some lines on paper or any other writing material. But when we neither utter words nor write them out, but speak within ourselves, we have word-images whose existence may be said to be psychical. The content of the word consists of the order, the loudness or softness of sounds and peculiarity of tone, accents, etc., with which the word may be uttered, or the length, size and colour of the lines, the order of the letters, etc., with which the word may be written, or again the order, vividness, intensity, etc., with which the word may be imaged to mind. In short, whatever constitutes the unique characteristics which define the existence of a word and distinguish it from other words may be said also to constitute its content. The meaning of the word, however, is something quite distinct from its content and existence. It is the idea of which the word is a symbol.

The meaning aspect of a word is the most important, since a word is such only because of the meaning it symbolizes. In becoming a symbol, the word has to fuse its other two aspects, namely its existence and its content, into the third aspect, its meaning; the former two exist only to subserve the purpose of symbolizing meaning. Thus a word, as existence and as content, loses its independence and becomes merely adjectival. It is only because it can pay such a great price that it gains admittance into a world, to which otherwise it would have no access. The story is the same with every symbol. The gift of a dear friend acquires so much value not because of its intrinsic worth, but because of the love for which it is a symbol. A blade of grass, a petal or a scrap of paper, thus comes to command inestimable value. Again, a piece of stone, installed as the symbol of a deity, comes to inspire love, fear or reverence that knows no bounds. It is by sacrificing their individual independence that such insignificant objects can acquire so much importance and can discharge such novel functions. "A symbol," says Bradley, "is a fact which stands for something else, and by this we may say it both loses and gains, is degraded and exalted. In its use as a symbol it forgoes individuality and self-existence."[1] "A fact, taken as a symbol, ceases so far to be a fact. It no longer can be said to exist for its own sake, its individuality is lost in its universal meaning."[2]

This remark is seen to be specially true of word-symbols. Whenever we read a book or listen to a speech, the ink and paper, or the sound and accent, behave exactly like a transparent medium which demands absolutely no attention for its own private existence. In fact the moment we turn our attention to the individual characteristics of the medium, to the ink, the paper or the type, or to the accent or intonation of the sounds, we fail to catch the meaning they sought to express. Grant existence to the symbol, the meaning is lost; grant importance to the meaning, the individuality of the symbol is completely submerged. "The word dies as it is spoken, but the particular sound of the mere pulsation was nothing to our minds. Its existence was lost in the speech and the significance. The paper and the ink are facts unique and with definite qualities. They are the same in all points with none other in the world. But in reading we apprehend not paper or ink, but what they represent; and so long as only they stand for this, their private existence is a matter of indifference."[3]

The degree to which a symbol sacrifices its "private existence" varies, however, from case to case. An important distinction was based by some Indian philosophers on this fact. They distinguished between a symbol which is bodhaka or merely indicative, and a symbol which is vāchaka or expressive or connotative. Natural signs and gestures, and many other rudimentary specimens of language, can vaguely *indicate* the mental disposition of the person who uses them. But they cannot definitely *express* any meaning, whereas the verbal symbols we use can *express* a precise meaning with a remarkable degree of accuracy. It is only with the help of

1 The Principles of Logic, p. 3.
2 Ibid., p. 4.
3 Ibid., pp. 3-4.

such symbols that we can both think logically and communicate our ideas without any ambiguity. The symbols of the former class have not permanently effaced their private existence. It is only occasionally that they put away their individuality to accept a temporary rôle; so when removed from a particular universe of discourse or set of circumstances an indicative sign might mean a quite different thing or might cease to mean at all. The gnashing of the teeth may indicate anger while quarrelling, but it means nothing if exactly the same sound is produced while cracking a nut. A finger on the lips indicates "silence" in certain circumstances, whereas at other times it means nothing. The symbols of the other class, on the contrary, have sacrificed their individual existence and content for good. They have exchanged their substantive character for an adjectival one; so in all connections and at all times they must have meanings. A word without a meaning is a contradiction. This unconditional and implicit sacrifice on the part of a word is rewarded by the inseparable intimacy that it acquires with the meaning. Consummation of this intimate relation leads to the mutual interchangeability of words and meanings.[1] When this ideal stage is reached a word as much defines its meaning, as meaning or an idea defines the symbolic word. Thus connotation becomes entirely fixed, and chances of confusion and ambiguity are completely removed.

But it should be noted that this ideal is fully reached by very few words of a language. Indeed the very life of a spoken language depends on its adaptability to changing situations, and consequently the change in meaning as well as in form is the inevitable lot of every word in a living language. Hence arises the necessity of developing technical words for scientific purposes, which demand logical precision. But even such terms come to acquire many senses.

In India, the intimacy of relation between words and meanings led to many cosmological speculations and metaphysical theories; we do not wish to discuss them in this connection, because they fall outside the scope of our investigation, which is mainly logical and epistomological, and also because Advaita Vedānta, with which we are concerned here, attaches little importance to these views. We shall discuss, however, some important logical problems that were raised in Indian philosophy with regard to the meanings of words.

1 Cf. "Yoyaṃ śabdaḥ soyamarthaḥ, yorthaḥ sa śabdaḥ"—Nyāyakośa under Saṃketa.

2. Is Primary Meaning Particular or Universal ? Five Views

One of the important problems discussed almost by every school of philosophy is : Does a word primarily mean a particular (Vyakti) or a universal (Jāti)?

Different answers are given to this question by different logicians.[1] According to the Sāṃkhyas a word signifies a particular, since they hold that in speaking we have to deal with particulars alone. When we say, "The cow is red," we mean a particular cow, and not the whole class of cows. To say that the cow, as a class, is red, is meaningless. To state this in the words of a modern eminent thinker, "Nothing that can be said significantly about things, i.e., particulars, can be said significantly (i.e., either truly or falsely) about classes of things."[2] "An attribute can be predicated of a substance alone, not of a universal."[3] Besides, there are terms which are singular or proper, such as sun, moon, Ganges, etc., which can never refer to any class, as there is no other object to which the same term can be applied. Consequently we must admit that a word signifies a particular and not a universal. This view, it may be mentioned here, is supported by some Neo-Naiyāyikas also.[4]

The Jaina philisophers and some others,[5] however, hold that a word cannot mean a particular. For the word "cow" does not apply to a particular cow, but to all animals having the general form of cow. It is the knowledge of the generic form, or ākṛti, which guides us in determining the particular animals to which the term is to be applied. Therefore a word primarily means this ākṛti or generic form. As the form cannot be understood without the particular object or objects having the form, knowledge of the form necessarily leads to the knowledge of particulars. Hence a word, though it primarily and directly means a universal, comes indirectly to mean particulars as well.

This theory, we may add, does not fail to explain singular terms, since knowledge of form is essential there also. To-day we are told that a

1 Vivaraṇa-prameya-saṃgraha, p. 181.

2 Russell, *Our Knowledge of the External World*, p. 206.

3 Vātsyāyana's Nyāyabhāṣya, 2, 2, 62.

4 Nyāya-siddhānta-mañjarī, p. 178.

5 Vivaraṇa-prameya, p. 181, and Nyāya-sūtra, 2, 2, 63-5.

particular man who is sitting by us is called John. Ten days hence the man is seen walking in the street. How can we then apply the term "John" to him who is no longer the sitting man we saw, and who has possibly put on new clothes also, without knowing that the appellation has to be applied to the man who preserves a universal or general form through all his changing postures? If the particular, the man sitting to-day, is signified by the word John, then surely the same name cannot be applied to him in all his postures and at all times. Besides, as we shall show afterwards, a particular can be known only once, and even memory cannot reproduce it for us a second time ; so it is doubly impossible that a particular should be meant by a word that is to be used more than once and in more than one connection. Hence it is a universal, namely the generic form, which is the meaning of a word.

This theory is criticized, however, by some thinkers who point out that though this theory is an improvement on the first one, as it recognizes that *only* a universal (and *never* a particular) can be meant by a word, yet it is not altogether free from objections. For the universal which is the import of a word is not simply the universal form or figure, but the universal or common character in virtue of which different individuals can be known to belong to a particular class, and one individual in varying states can be known to be the same identical individual. For there are cases where,in spite of a mere similarity in form or shape, we never think of applying a name which would have been applied, had there been found some identical common class character. As Gautama[1] illustrates this, a clay cow may possess all the formal similarities of a cow, and still we never seriously call it a cow. We must qualify it with the adjective "clay," just to show that it is not a real cow. On the contrary a substance like gold is always called gold, whether it is a bracelet or a ring or a necklace, none of which possesses any formal similarity to the rest. Thus it is found, argue these philosophers, that the universal that is the import of a word, and on the strength of which we apply a term, is not the mere universal form or shape but the universal class character. It is not the ākṛti, but the jāti, which is the primary meaning of a term.

This view is held by a majority of Indian thinkers, the Mīmāṃsakas the Vedāntins and the grammarians of the older school.[2] We shall have to consider this view in full detail later. In the meantime we shall refer to some other views on this point.

1 Nyāya-sūtra, 2. 2, 66.

2 "Sarva-darśana-saṃgraha" Pāṇini system.

The Naiyāyikas of the old school,[1] Gautama and Vātsyāyana, for instance, held that all these three views are partial and do not contain the whole truth. For a word means all three—vyakti, jāti and ākṛti.[2] Only in some particular context some meaning is predominant and the rest subordinate. When emphasis is laid on a peculiar individual aspect, the word means mainly a particular, though its universal import either as regards form or essence is not altogether absent. Similarly, when the object of the speaker is to emphasize the formal similarity, then that is the meaning predominating in that context. Again, when essential similarity is the main object, that meaning is predominant.

This theory tries to reconcile all the contending views by giving each a share of the importance otherwise claimed by each as its exclusive monopoly. But a compromise in philosophy is almost always the outcome of a reluctance to pursue a perplexing problem with close reasoning through all logical mazes. This general truth applies to this particular case as well. Let us see how.

As we have already seen, the mere shape or form of a thing cannot be considered to be the meaning of a word. If it were so, mental phenomena lacking physical shape would have all remained unnamed. But we must consider here whether there are not *at least some* cases where the ground for the application of a name is the form. The names of geometrical figures may be easily suggested as affording such instances. We call both a scalence and an equilateral figure "triangle" because they have a common shape. While we cannot altogether deny this, we can yet say that if we take essential generic character (jāti) to be the meaning of a word, the cases of formless mental phenomena and those of geometrical figures are all equally explained, and no special theory of form being the meaning in some cases is required. In other words the form of a thing, in so far as it enters also into the essential generic character of the thing, is included in the jāti and does not require separate mention. It is altogether unnecessary therefore to say that in certain cases the "form" alone is meant by the word. It should rather be said that in certain cases the form is the most prominent (or even the sole) factor that constitutes the generic

1 Nyāya-siddhāntamañjarī, pp. 178-179, and Nyāya-sūtras and Vātsyāyanabhāṣya, 2, 2, 68.

2 Vyakti = individual, particular, jāti = class-characteristics; ākṛti (= niyataavayava-vyūha) = abiding-component-structure.

properties expressed by a word. When one hypothesis can cover all cases it is illogical to advance another hypothesis to explain a part of such cases.

We find then that whatever be the context, form should not be considered to be the meaning, far less the important meaning, of a term. That the particular cannot be the import of a word we have already observed, and we shall have occasion to adduce additional grounds to prove this point. We conclude then that there are no grounds for saying that vyakti and ākrti, i.e. the particular or the form, can be the meaning of a word.

Besides, the contention that some meaning is important in some connections and others in other context does not touch the real problem. The problem, as we stated at the beginning, is : What is the *primary* meaning of a term? A word which deserves the name must primarily symbolize one meaning, and that meaning must be a universal, or the word cannot be used more than once and of more than one particular. It is true that every language falls short of the ideal of logical accuracy, and many words happen to possess several meanings. But even in those cases, none of the primary meanings can fail to be universal for the reason already stated. To say that, in a certain context, a word may signify a particular does not amount to saying that the primary meaning has changed. We shall find, on the contrary, that even those who hold that a word means a universal primarily (when it is isolated), hold that it means also a particular secondarily (when used in a sentence, in a particular context). Thus, the answer given by this theory is not at all relevant to the problem raised. To say that one meaning is perdominant in one context and others in others is to remain silent as to which is the primary meaning. If however this theory is understood to mean that all the three meanings are primary, then our previous objections tell equally against such an interpretation. For we have shown that of the three factors, vyakti, ākṛti and jāti, only the last can be the primary meaning of a word while the other two cannot. We find therefore that the theory which tries to reconcile the three views is wholly untenable.

A fifth solution, however, has been offered to this problem. Let us state and examine it. It is argued by some Naiyayikas[1] that a pure particular as well as a pure universal is not really the meaning of a word. What we have in experience, and consequently what we have to name, is a particular

1 Nyāya-siddhāntamañjarī pp. 177-178. and Dinakarī on Kārikā 81.

characterized by a universal. The cow which has become the object of our knowledge is no longer an unrelated individual, a pure particular, or kevala vyakti ; but it is the individual that has been integrated to the universal concept, viz., cowhood. The meaning of a word is, therefore, a universalized particular (jātiviśiṣṭa-vyakti). This view has been upheld by the renowned Naiyāyikas, Jagadīśa, in his Śabda-śakti-prakāśikā,[1] and also, in a slightly modified way, by Viśvanātha, in his Siddhānta-muktāvalī.[2]

As against this view the Advaitins hold that the primary and explicit meaning symbolized by a word is the universal alone and not the universalized particular. When we say, for instance, that the word "cow" means an individual possessed of cowness (gotva-viśiṣṭa-vyakti), we already assume the knowledge of the universal "cowness." For here the individual is the substantive (viśiṣṭa) which is qualified by the universal as the adjective, and it is a well-known dictum that the knowledge of the qualified (viśiṣṭa) presupposes the knowledge of the adjective (viśeṣaṇa) that qualifies it. If so, then it is in virtue of the knowledge of the universal, connoted by the word "cow," that we can apply the word to the particular individual. It follows, therefore, that the meaning that is logically primary is nothing but the universal pure and simple. Moreover, if we say that the universalized particular is the primary meaning of a word, then it has to be made clear whether the meaning of a word implies the knowledge of all such particulars or only one of them. The first alternative is impossible, because all particulars, past, present and future, cannot be always known. The second also is incorrect, because the knowledge of one particular implied by the meaning cannot help us in determining other particulars which also are signified by the word possessing that meaning.

This is the criticism advanced by Rāmakṛṣṇa, the author of the Śikhāmaṇi.[3] We may make this criticism clearer by a few more observations. It is true that what we usually know, being a universalized particular, a word which is used to signify objects of knowledge alone, is applied to universalized particulars only. But we should not forget that the point at issue is not to what thing a word is actually applied in a

1 Śabda-śakti-prakāśikā; cf. Jagadīśa's, Comment. on Kārikā 19.

2 Siddhānta-muktāvalī on Kār. 81. (He says that a word means a particular qualified by both jāti and ākṛti.), pp. 377-81.

3 Sikhāmaṇi on Vedānta-paribhāsā, p. 269.

particular sentence and in a particular context, but what is the *primary* meaning of an isolated word by itself, by virtue of which it can be applied to different particulars. This being the real issue, the primary meaning of a word, by knowing which we are able to apply the word to different particulars, cannot be itself a particular, be it unique or universalized. By knowing a red animal to be a cow we are able to call another black animal of that class cow, not because the latter also possesses the same particularizing colour red, but because it possesses the essential common character, cowness. On knowing that a certain word is applicable to a certain universalized particular, what enables us to apply it to a fresh universalized partiucular is not the particularity of either of them, which is unique, but the universal element which is common to both. And the primary and explicit meaning of a word is that by knowing which we are able to apply the word to different objects. Hence the meaning consists of the universal essential character alone and not of any other particularizing element. Hence the fifth view, according to which the meaning of a word is a universalized particular, is also untenable.

3. The Advaita View Critically Considered

We have stated and criticized five different theories which came to be held as answers to the question : Is the primary meaning of a word a particular or a universal? To recapitulate them one by one : the word means (1) a particular; (2) a universal as the mere generic form; (3) a universal as the essential generic character; (4) all these three; (5) lastly, the universalized particular. We have also tried to show that all are untenable except the third view, namely that the meaning is a universal as generic essence or character. The Advaitins, the Mimāṃsakas and the early grammarians support the third view. We have already stated the general grounds on which this view is based. But there are certain objections against this theory which must be considered here.

It may be asked if a word means a universal, how does it come to denote a particular? If the word "cow" means "cowness," how can we at all apply the word to an individual cow? As we actually apply the word "cow" to an individual or particular, does it not argue that the word means also an individual? The meaning of a word has surely to be inferred from its application.

This objection has already been partially answered. Here we have to make these answere more explicit. The knowledge of the universal or the concept which constitutes the meaning of a word necessarily leads to the knowledge of a particular which *is subsumed* under that concept, since in experience we have always the universal and the particular synthesized together, as the universalized particular which becomes the object of the same knowledge. As we perceive a cow always as an individual possessed of the universal character "cowness," given the universal "cowness," we can in the light of the knowledge of this universal find out in experience the particular or particulars to which the universal is applicable. The universal, as the Vedānta-paribhāṣā remarks, is known in the same knowledge that reveals the particular.[1] It may be interesting to note in this connection that the question : What is the relation of the universal to the particular proved a serious puzzle to Plato also. But thinking as he did that universals had an existence independently of the particulars of experience, away in the eternal transcendental land of the reals, Plato failed to bridge the widening gulf that, according to his own imagination, separated the universal from the particular. The same difficulty presented itself to Kant when he had to face the question in the Transcendental Analytic : "How, then, can a perception be subsumed under a pure conception? How can a category be applied in determination of an object of sense?"[2] Kant, as we know, answered this question by assuming a third thing, a "mediating idea" which he called the "transcendental schema," as to the exact nature of which he said, "This schematism of our understanding in its application to phenomena and to their pure form, is an art hidden away in the depths of the human soul, the secret of which we need not hope to drag forth to the light of day." In Indian philosophy, the Naiyāyikas were similarly perplexed. So we find the great logician Jagadīśa saying in his Śabda-śakti-prakāśikā,[3] "If jāti or the universal alone be signified by a word, the knowledge of the particular would be very difficult."

The underlying reason why the Naiyāyikas also felt puzzled as to how, if meaning was universal, a word could be applicable to particulars, is to be sought for in their conception of jāti, which, like the Platonic idea, made passage from universal to particular so difficult. For according to them also, the universal or jāti was real and eternal (nityatve sati

1 Vedānta-paribhāsā, p.269, and Sikhāmaṇi thereon.

2 Transcendental Analytic, the Schematism of the Categories.

3 Śabda-śakti, Kār. 19.

anekasamavetatvam jātitvam). But the Vedāntins, who were definitely empirical in these matters, held, as against the Naiyāyikas, that a jāti or a universal was not a mysterious eternal entity but consisted of the common essential characteristics actually existing in a group of particulars (dravya-guṇa-karma-vṛttiḥ sāmānya-dharmaḥ).[1]

In virtue of this common-sense conception of the universal, therefore, the Vedantins easily solved the puzzle raised by the Naiyāyikas. They replied, as already observed, that it was a fact of experience that the particular was also characterized by the universal, and consequently both were known together in the same process of knowledge.[2] Thus, although a word meant only the universal aspect of the universalized particular, there could be no difficulty in the application of the word to a particular which invariably possessed the universal characteristics signified by the word. We may note, in passing, that the word used for the universal by Kumārilabhaṭṭa in his Ślokavārtika,[3] is ākṛti, though he says at the same time explicitly that by ākṛti he means a jāti. Śaṃkara also follows the same usage, and in his Brahma sūtra-bhāṣya[4] he says that the relation of a word is not with a vyakti but the ākṛti, which has been interpreted by his followers as jāti, in the sense we have just indicated. The later Vedāntins, of course, use the word jāti to indicate the universal.

Another solution[5] given by the Vedāntins is that, though a word primarily and explicity means a universal, it does not follow that it does not mean the individual at all. But reference to the individual is latent (Svarūpa-satī), whereas reference to the universal is explicit (jñātā). The meaning which must be explicitly known by a person so that he may be able to use the word is, as we have already seen, the universal and not the particular. When the universal meant by a word is known, the particulars possessing that universal character become, by their very nature (svarūpa), denotable by the word. But it may be asked: If so, why should the particular not be included in the meaning? The reply is : because the knowledge of the universal alone is logically *presupposed* in the use of the word, and if this alone is sufficient for its application it is needless,

1 Āśubodhinī, p. 157

2 Śikhāmaṇi on Vedānta-paribhāṣa, p. 269.

3 Ślokavārtika, ākṛtivāda, 1,3. "Jātim eva ākṛtim prāhuḥ ..."

4 Brahma-sūtras, 1, 3, 28.

5 *Vide* Vedānta-paribhāṣā, p. 270, and Paribhāṣāprakāśikā, p. 198.

on the principle of the simplicity of hypothesis, to hold that the particulars also must form a part of the meaning. Moreover, to know *all* the particulars possessing the same universal would be impossible, while to know only a few would not be enough.

We shall understand the foregoing remarks better if we refer to the psychological origin of language. Language is essentially the result of conceptual analysis and synthesis. The percepts that are directly presented to us require names to signify them. When different percepts are analysed and compared and similarities are detected, we begin to classify the previously unrelated percepts on the grounds of similarity. It is thus that we arrive at a single concept subsuming different percepts under it. Consequently, a mark or a name has to be given to the concept. As Stout says : "Conceptual analysis and correlative synthesis would seem from this account of the matter to be a prior condition of the existence of language." Again : "Each word stands for some general aspect of the concrete detail of actual perception—in other words, it stands for what is called a *universal or concept*."[1] It is found, therefore, that from the psychological standpoint also the origin of language rests on the classification of particulars on the basis of the universal characters common to all of them. Consequently it is only natural that isolated words should primarily mean not particulars of experience but the universals present in them.

It is clear therefore why the word "cow" primarily stands for the universal concept, "cowness," though *prima facie* this seems ludicrous. But the theory will not appear to be at all ludicrous or absurd if we only remember that what is meant here is not that "cow" is "cowness," but that the meaning of the word "cow" is cowness, or, in other words, it connotes cowness. And the meaning of the word "cow" being the concept that defines and determines the use of the word, can on no score be the particular animal, it must be the essential common attributes which bring all such animals under the same category.

It seems at first sight absurd that a universal which is a mere abstraction can possibly stand for particulars which are concrete; that is to say, for instance, that cowness can signify all cows. But nothing will be more convincing than a direct appeal to some cases even in English where we have been actually perpetrating this absurdity without question. To illustrate, we use the word "aristocracy," an abstract term, for the

1 Manual of Psychology, pp. 597-598.

concrete persons, namely the aristocrats. Similarly, we use populace or population for the people, labour for labourers, ministry for ministers. Majesty, Highness, Honour, Excellency are freely used with pronominal adjectives, to denote particular concrete persons. When these instances are remembered the apparent absurdity of the theory, that the universal abstract concepts can signify concrete individuals, should at once disappear.

As to the possible objection that, as the meaning is to be inferred from the particulars to which a word is applied, the meaning must be also particular, we may say that inference from such application proves the contrary view. On seeing that a black, a white and a red animal are all called by the common name "cow" what we necessarily infer is that in spite of their differences there must be some common characteristic which is signified by the term "cow". Thus not the particular, but the universal concept, "cowness," which is common to all kinds of cows, comes to be known as the meaning of the word "cow," even as the result of inference from application.

We find, then, that the objections against a universal being the meaning of a word do not stand sifting. We shall conclude this discussion by adducing a few more arguments to show why a particular has no place in the primary meaning of a word, though in virtue of this meaning the word is actually used to signify the particular.

We have remarked elsewhere that a particular can occur only once, and consequently if a word denoted a particular, it also could be used only once. Let us devote a little attention to it.

Supposing that a word can signify a particular, this particular can either be a thing or an idea. The thing that can be named must be a thing known. But the particular thing as known at this moment cannot persist to be the same particular the next moment also, just because the whole environment, physical and mental, which particularizes the thing in a unique way to us this moment, is not the same the next moment: If then a word stood for a particular thing, it could be used only once, as such a thing is known only once. Even in memory we cannot call back the particular to mind, just because the mental environment which particularized the first impression of the thing into that particular is constantly changing and cannot repeat the same process, except by a miracle. Even if the thing-in-itself was signified by a word, it would not follow that the word signified a particular, since the thing-in-itself, which remains the same through all the changing aspects, is more a universal than a particular. What we really mean by the word "thing," when we commonly say that such a word stands for such a thing, is not the particular thing but the ideal synthesis of the particular thing known.

When a word signifies a mental state, there also it is not the particular mental state, but a synthesis of such similar states that is symbolized.

Bradley has severely criticized and exposed our ordinary illusory notion that we have the same idea again and again in our minds. "It is a mere mythology," he says, "to talk of the copy, which the impression has sloughed off, persisting in the world and preserving its identity through the flux of change."[1] Again, "The idea, like the impression, exists only for a moment. Then how can it 'recur' unless it is the same, and how can it be the same unless it has remained. The word 'recur' must be struck out of the formula."[2] And if a particular cannot recur, and if the meaning of a term is to remain the same every time it is used, then clearly the term cannot mean a particular.

There is another important point to be noticed. We have already said that the so-called particulars of which we ordinarily speak are not pure particulars, but universalized particulars, or better still particularized universals. We call a particular object before us a table only when we apprehend in it some similarities or some universal elements that are common to all objects of that name. Before the particular is known as containing these universals, it is of course a pure particular, but it is then an undifferentiated sensum, which is the content of sensation or intuition. It can scarcely be an object of knowledge, and far less can it be named or spoken of. So the author or Śikhāmaṇi says that those who hold that a word can mean a pure particular must necessarily accept the absurd position that a word means something which is not yet an object of knowledge, i.e. of differentiated consciousness.[3] Russell also speaks in the same strain in his *Analysis of Mind* : "but as language was invented for practical ends, particulars have remained one and all without a name."[4]

We find thus that the case of the particular is hopelessly doomed. But a question may be legitimately asked here : You hold that the word stands

1 *Logic*, vol. i. p. 313.

2 Ibid.

3 Śikhāmaṇi, p. 269.

4 Analysis of Mind, p. 193.

for a concept. But is not a concept also an idea, and consequently a particular as well, according to your own confession? We admit that this question calls for an explanation, as there is a common confusion regarding the various uses of the word "idea."

As Bradley has so clearly shown in his *Logic*,[1] three aspects can be distinguished in an "idea" : (1) idea as a psychical existent, (2) idea as content and (3) idea as meaning. It is for the third aspect that a word stands. The first two aspects are but the symbols of the last one. While the first two are particular, the last is universal. Let us see how.

Suppose I hear the word "fish." I have at once an idea in my mind which as an *existent* is but a particular mental state, while its *content* is the particular image, say of a big white fish, which comes to my mind and also the feelings and desires the image creates in my mind. If I am a vegetarian I have possibly only the image of a nauseating fishy smell that creates in me a strong feeling of disgust and aversion, or if I am a fish-eater the image might call up the images of sweet savour and nice flavour which directly create a strong desire for a dish of fish. All these images, feelings, desires and aversions constitute the particular content of the idea. But the particular existence and content do not exhaust the whole idea. For, while having these particular images, I am all along aware that "fish" means not these particulars, but something more which includes as much a big white fish as a red small fish, a salmon as much as a cod. I also know that these particulars are there only by sufferance, and as soon as it is necessary they may be turned out to make room for any other image which a particular context might demand. If immediately after this "a small red fish" is presented to me and I am asked, "Is this a fish?" my former image of a "big white fish" does not prevent me from saying "Yes." so the particular existence and particular content of the idea are but symbols, which stand for the meaning-part of the idea by denying their private independent existence. As I hear the word "fish," in many other connections, while the existence and the content vary from case to case, the meaning symbolized by them remains constant. Schiller says : "And anyhow the imagery is *logically irrelevant*. It is never the particular fluctuating imagery we have in judging that we mean." So idea as meaning, for which a word stands, cannot but be universal. The doubt that the meaning of a word in being a concept which in its turn is an idea must be particular, is thus removed.

1 P. 3 et seq.

It is interesting to note in this connection that in Western philosophy Locke discussed[1] the problem of language in a similar manner and came to hold, like the Advaitins, that a word always denotes something universal. But Berkeley[2] subsequently opposed this view, on the grounds that an abstract universal is a pure fiction, because the mind does not possess the power of conceiving it. According to him, a word presents to the mind the idea of a particular individual which stands as a proxy or representative for the whole class of individuals. In the light of the elaborate discussions we have already had, this view would be found to be based on an imperfect apprehension of the nature of an idea, As we have already seen, the idea called up by a word has three aspects. The meaning aspect of the idea which is symbolized by a word is universal, though the other two aspects may be particular. In fact it is on account of this universal meaning-aspect that a particular can be made the representative of a class.

We come thus to the end of a somewhat lengthy discussion regarding the problem, whether the primary meaning of a word is a particular or a universal; and we see also that the Advaitin's answer that the universal or jāti is the meaning of a word, is highly reasonable.

4. Is any Word Non-Connotative?

A student of Western logic is likely to be troubled by at least one doubt which will not allow him readily to accept this Advaita conculsion. It is necessary to state and remove it.

If you say, he may ask, that every word has a concept, a universal, for its meaning, the inevitable conclusion is that all words are connotative and that there are no non-connotative words. We realize that to those who are so much habituated to the observation of the time-honoured distinction between connotative and non-connotative terms, this doubt is too radical to be easily removed. But we shall show reasons which may serve at least to unsettle the prejudice to a certain degree. We may first observe that the whole problem discussed in the foregoing pages turns ultimately on the problem of connotation and denotation also. But we have purposely excluded these terms in order to avoid the many associations which they possess in Western logic, and which would have served to confuse the understanding of the problem as it arose in Indian logic. In terms of Western

1 *An Essay Concerning Human Understanding*, Book 3.

2 "Introduction" to *The Principles of Human Knowledge*.

logical concepts the problem might be put in two forms, namely : Has every word a connotation? Is connotation, or denotation, primary? We have just answered the second question. Let us consider the first.

The answer to the first question, from the Advaita standpoint, as may be easily seen, can only be in the affirmative. But we have to show how, in that case, the so-called non-connotative words of Western logic are to be explained.

In European logic, two classes of terms are held to be non-connotative, (1) proper names and (2) certain abstract names. Illustrations of the former, given by Mill, are "John," "London," "England," etc., and of the latter are "whiteness," "length," "virtue," etc.[1]

A proper name, it is said, has only denotation but no connotation. Connotation or Intension is defined by Johnson[2] as a set of adjectives, and denotation or extension as a set of substantives. A proper name stands for a substantive alone, without signifying any adjective or attribute possessed by the substantive. Mill also distinguishes connotative and non-connotative words thus : "A non-connotative term is one which signifies a subject only or an attribute only. A connotative term is one which denotes a subject and implies an attribute."[3]

We apply the word "judge" to a man because he judges, or the word "fool" to him because he has no intelligence. But we apply the word "John" to him neither because he does or does not do anything, nor because he has or has no attribute; we use the word simply to denote the substantive, the man. So far the distinction is intelligible.

But the question may be asked here : Do we ever have, in knowledge, a bare subtantive without any adjective, a bare man without an attribute or characteristic? If not, how can such a thing be spoken of as being signified by a proper name? Is the man signified by the word "John" devoid of all characteristics? It will be answered readily that though the man signified by "John" is not devoid of attributes or characteristics, the word "John" has no connection with the characteristics of the man. But this reply is of little help. For if the characteristics of the man have no connection with the name "John," what leads me to call the man, in different states and contexts, "John," and what prevents me from applying

1 *Logic*, Part I, p. 31.

2 *Logic*, Part I, p. 100.

3 *Logic*, Part I, p. 31.

the same term to another man? Evidently, it is wrong to say that the word "John" has no connection with the attributes of the man. On the contrary, the appearance, the voice, the character of the man are so intimately connected with the name "John," that these determine the use of the term, as much as the attributes "animality" and "rationality" determine the use of the term "man."

The first use of the word "John," it will then be said, is arbitrary; but not so the first use of the word "judge." This reply rests on the philological assumption that all connotative words are derived from roots, meanings of which are already known, and the words have some pre-established connection with those meanings. But this assumption is not at all easy to prove. Take, for instance, the connotative word "man." It is little known what the word radically means, and still less is it known what connection that radical meaning has with "rationality" and "animality" for which the word has come to stand. If so, is not this name, in spite of its being connotative, as arbitrary as the name "John"? When pushed to its logical conclusion, the theory that all connotative words are radically significant and not arbitrary must either fall back on the theory of the eternal and internal relation between words and meanings, or be rejected. For if we can show that at any time there was a single connotative term, which was used to signify something, though there was no previous relation of the word with the meaning signified, then the distinction between a connotative name and a proper name, on the basis of their first use, vanishes altogether. In fact when my attention is first directed to an object and I am told that it is a Zebra, and when again my attention is drawn to another object and I am told that it is John, to me both words are equally devoid of previous significance. But the very moment I learn the names, both of them become connected with the characteristics of the animal and the man, and it is on the strength of this connection that I can repeat the use of the words in other connections and gradually gain better acquaintance, which also modifies and enriches the significance of the words.

To this it will be replied that the logical connotation of a word is not subjective, not even objective, but conventional. The connotation of the word "Zebra" has been conventionally fixed, on the basis of the knowledge acquired about it by different persons. It can be applied only to objects possessing the characteristics which constitute that fixed connotation. But the word "John," though it also has a fixed significance in so far as the same man is denoted by it, can be applied to another person having altogether different characteristics. If that be so the difference between a connotative name and a proper name comes to this : whereas the former has only one fixed significance, the latter can have more than one. Let us see how far this distinction is tenable. First of all we may ask : If it be so, what becomes of connotative words like "bar," "bench," "flag," etc., which have different meanings? Though of "bar" and "bench" it may be said that the different meanings are internally connected, it cannot be so said about "flag." which is traced to altogether different etymological sources, as it carries the different meanings : a "banner," "a stone," "a plant," and "to grow languid." It may be said that, though we have different meanings of connotative terms in our actual lauguages, in a logically ideal language there would be only one significance to one word and *vice versa*, in order to avoid ambiguity. To this the reply would be : Surely this applies to the case of proper names as well. There would only be one proper name for one object in an ideal language, exactly for the same reason of avoiding ambiguity, from which we suffer so often even in cases of proper names.

It is often said that logic, as an exact science, can deal only with words whose significances are fixed, and that a proper name with its unfixed connotation cannot be of any use in logic. Though we ourselves have supported, in another context,[1] the principle that uncertain meaning (e.g. suggested meaning) cannot be recognized by logicians, yet we do not think that the significance of a proper name is of such an uncertain character. For otherwise logic could not recognize any inference the premises of which contain a proper name. The very fact that we have such recognized inferences as "The King of England is the Emperor of India. George V is the King of England. Therefore he is the Emperor of India," shows that logic has valuable use for proper names.

It has been held by the eminent Western logicians like Johnson and Keynes that the denotation of a term is determined by its connotation. But if proper names have no connotation, what is it that determines its denotation? As Johnson himself asks, "But if we allow of any name that it contains an element of non-significance, how is it possible that this name should be understood as applying to the same object when used at different times or by different persons or in different and varying

1 *Vide*, Sec. 5 of this chap.

connections?"[1] This leads Johnson to say that a proper name has meaning or significance but no connotation. As he puts it : " When, then, finally we agree with the general position of the best logicians that the proper name (as Mill says) in non-connotative, this does not amount to saying that the proper name is non-significant or has no meaning, etc."[2]

But we must confess that we fail to understand the distinction between "significance" and "connotation," between "non-significant" and "non-connotative". But we are relieved of the pain of ignorance when we find that the eminent writer himself forgets his own distinction overleaf when he solemnly pronounces, "I propose, therefore, to define the word proper as equivalent to non-connotative, non-descriptive or non-significant (since these three terms are themselves synonymous), and the only debatable point which remains is as to whether any names can properly be called proper."[3] We are forced to believe then that the great writer fights shy of his "best logicians." and while verbally agreeing with them has grave doubts which make him vacillate between conflicting views. Applying logic to his own confessions, we might as well say that as a proper name, according to him, has significance, and as significance and connotation are also synonymous according to him, it follows that a proper name has connotation. But the qualification he adds at the end of the statement quoted above renders this task of applying logic unnecessary. For he expresses his doubts as to whether there is any proper name at all, as understood by his definition. Of modern Western logicians, Bradley[4] and Bosanquet[5] and some others agree in holding that a proper noun has a universal meaning as its connotation.

We may on our part conclude, on the grounds already adduced and without carrying the discussion any further, that it is wrong to suppose that a proper name has no connotation. A proper name stands for the ideal synthesis of the various stages and phases of the substantive. As such it connotes a universal concept, namely the essential characteristics common to the various states of the substantive. In the words of the great author of the Sarvadarśana-saṃgraha, "The universal (jāti) connoted by

1 *Logic*, Part I, p. 82
2 Logic, Part I, p. 96.
3 Ibid, p. 99.
4 *Logic*. p. 59.
5 *Essentials of Logic*, pp. 91-93.

a proper name (saṃjñā) like Devadatta is proved on the basis of the knowledge of his identity (as, 'it is he'), from his birth till his death, through all the changing stages of childhood, boyhood and youth."[1] And it is due to this fact that a proper name can at all be used sometimes as a common name (e.g. He is a Hercules) or can yield an adjective (e.g. Herculean).

To come to the second class of the so-called non-connotative terms, namely singular abstract terms. Most of what has been said about proper nouns applies here as well. According to Mill, whose view is still accepted by many on these matters, "white," "long," "virtuous," are connotative, whereas "whiteness," "length," "virtuousness" are non-connotative. The reason assigned is that "the word white denotes all white things, as snow, paper, the foam of the sea, etc.," and "connotes the attribute whiteness." But "whiteness signifies an attribute only." Two shortcomings then disqualify a word like "whiteness" from taking its place in the aristocracy of connotative terms. First, it has no other attribute to qualify it as its connotation; secondly, it is singular, that is, it has no other subjects of which it can be predicated (just as white can be predicated of various subjects).

As ragards the first disqualification, we believe that it is absolutely wrong to hold that "whiteness" has no further attribute or "adjective" (as Johnson would say) to stand for its connotation. On the contrary, without such an attribute or adjective it would have been simply impossible for us to distinguish whiteness from redness, yellowness and blackness, and also to know exactly what it is. Just as the quality of being "white" distinguishes "white" from "red" and "yellow," etc., and makes it what it is, so the quality of being whiteness is the quality or attribute or adjective that distinguishes "whiteness" from "redness," "blackness," etc., and makes it what it is. And this is the connotation of the term whiteness. If the quality of being white is denoted by whiteness, logical conformity demands that the quality of being whiteness should be denoted by the word "whiteness-ness." But in English, where logicians have to depend for their terminology on the step-motherly provision of non-philosophical grammarians, such a direct and logical use of double suffixes will be at once tabooed as hypercritical, though in their utter ignorance they would neither discern nor object if the same thought were smuggled into usage through a long cumbrous phrase.

1 Sarvadarśana-saṃgraha, Pāṇini system.

Consequently, since language is the greatest help in the analysis and accurate grasp of thought, these abstract conceptions are bound to be, and have been, relegated to the sphere of confusion. In India however, where grammar was constantly enlightened by logic, the language was left plastic enough to receive any and every mould of thought, and where meaning necessitated a fresh coinage, the intelligent grammarians did not grudge this. Consequently Indian logic could attain great accuracy and precision. And whereas in English logic a word like "whiteness-ness" will be looked upon as a horrible monster, even a beginner in Indian logic will readily receive a word like "gotva-tva" (cowness-ness) with intelligent appreciation.

But to return to our discussion proper, we find that even whiteness is not devoid of an attribute as its connotation. Its connotation is, with apologies to the grammarian, "whiteness-ness". The same line of argument will show that even whiteness-ness has the connotation whitenessness-ness and so on *ad infinitum*. Where meaning requires it, there should be no parsimony of expression. And if we could take the first step in abstraction by separating white from white things, and a second by isolating whiteness from white colours, why should we stop here and not proceed further in the process of abstraction, if the same purpose, namely the clarification of meaning, has to be served? We are agreeably relieved to find, however, that Johnson has come to realize that "adjectives can properly be predicated of adjectives as such," though he is shy enough to qualify his remarks with "ifs" and "seems". The illustrations[1] he gives of primary, secondary and tertiary adjectives will be instructive to students of Western logic, and will corroborate the views of Indian logic given above.

As regards the second disqualification, that a word like whiteness or justice is singular and cannot therefore stand as a class concept or as a universal, it is best to refer to the words of Mill himself. In another context[2] he says that some abstract names such as colour are "certainly general," and that "such is even the word whiteness, in respect of the different shades of whiteness to which it is applied in common." But he still thinks

1 *Logic*, Part I, p. 103. The illustrations are : "A is moving," "The movement of A is rapid." "The rapidity of the movement of A is surprising."

2 *Logic*, Part I, p. 30.

that there is a residual class of attributes which are "neither variable in degree nor in kind," such as milk-whiteness, etc., and these attributes refer to themselves alone and to no other subjects. Does this statement stand scrutiny? The very fact that a term is called abstract signifies that it has been abstracted from some subject or subjects. If so, it can always be referred to or predicated of that or those subject or subjects, so that there can be no attribute, however abstract, which lacks a subject for reference. But it may be asked, if the attribute is abstracted from a singular object, how can it be general? To this we reply, because what is metaphysically or even psychologically a single subject or is identical can, for logic, be many, as each of its states or aspects can serve the purpose of a separate logical subject. Hence it would seem that no abstract term can be singular. Milk-whiteness can be referred to various subjects, viz., the milk-whiteness as in cow's milk, goat's milk, buffalo's milk, etc., or even as in Indian cow's milk, Australian cow's milk, or even as in to-day's cow's milk, yesterday's cow's milk. All these being logically different subjects, the term milk-whiteness is not singular but general.[1]

It is interesting to note that even Mill himself, after making these distinctions, feels puzzled and breaks down by saying, "To avoid needless logomachies, the best course would probably be to consider these names as neither general nor individual and to place them in a class apart."[2] If so, our purpose is served. The ban on some abstract attributes on the score of their being singular vanishes.

To conclude, then, the double objection against the inclusion of abstract terms among connotative terms is found to be groundless, as they have both attributes for connotation and subjects for reference. That proper names are connotative has already been shown. And these being the two kinds of terms which are spoken of as non-connotative, it is also found that all words are connotative. It need only be remembered that by "words" we mean, as we said at the very beginning, the vāchakas or expressive or meaningful words, not the bodhakas, or merely indicative signs. Then, we believe, the doubts entertained about the Advaita view will all be removed. With these remarks we pass on to another problem about the meaning of a word.

1 *Vide* Johnson's *Logic* Part I, p. 181, Art. 4.

2 *Logic*, Part I, p. 30.

5. Primary, Secondary and Tertiary Meanings

We have hitherto been dealing with the primary meanings of words. But in addition to these primary meanings there are also secondary ones. In Indian logic, the primary meaning of a word is called vācyārtha or śakyārtha, or mukhyārtha or even abhidheyārtha. The secondary meaning of a word is called lakṣyārtha. The Indian rhetoricians,[1] however, hold that in addition to the primary and secondary meanings of a word there can be a tertiary meaning as well, which they call vyaṅgyārtha and which can be roughly rendered into suggested meaning.

The primary meaning of a word has already been discussed. When in a certain context the primary meaning of a word is not suitable, we must understand the word in a secondary sense. For instance, when a dog is spoken of as being a "lion in the field and a lamb at home," we at once understand that really a dog cannot possibly be a lion or even a lamb. Hence the primary meanings of the terms must be abandoned and some secondary figurative meanings sought out. The primary meaning of a word is known by adults mostly through memory. On hearing the word "lion" or lamb" we remember the primary meaning which it stands for. The primary meaning, constituted as it is of all the common essential attributes found in all the particulars, is not a simple thing; it is something complex. The secondary meaning is generally obtained by selecting a part of the original meaning and rejecting the rest. For instance in the above case, the word lion stands only for a part of the original meaning of the word "lion," namely the surpassing strength and prowess of the animal; the physical appearance, etc., are abandoned. So also of the word "lamb." Again, when a weight-lifter is called a "crane," it is the physical appearance of a crane, to the exclusion of other aspects, that is aimed at. In some cases, however, the original meaning is entirely preserved and a change occurs only in the grammatical part of speech. For instance, when the word "original," primarily an adjective, is used as a substantive, the meaning is neither narrowed nor widened. But in some cases, e.g. the "three R's," the special meaning is not directly connected with the primary general meaning, but is only indirectly connected with it through a special case of the use of the sound "R" as initials in the three words, Reading and Writing and Rithmetic. Here we have really the case of a symbol of a symbol. "Rs" stand for some other words and the words stand for the

1 Mammaṭa's Kāvya-prakāśa, 2, 6, and 2, 19; Ekāvalī, 2, 3, and Sāhitya-darpaṇa, 2, 13.

meanings. In such a case, then, the original meaning is altogether forsaken. We have thus three types of secondary meanings : First, where a part of the original meaning is preserved and a part is rejected. This is called in Sanskrit, jahad-ajahallakṣaṇā. Secondly, where the original meaning is preserved *in toto*, which is called ajahallakṣaṇā. Thirdly, where the original meaning is altogether given up and a quite new meaning is acquired, which is called jahal-lakṣaṇā.

So long as the primary meaning of a word serves a particular context, no recourse to a secondary meaning is at all necessary. It is only when the primary meaning is found in any way incompatible that the necessity arises for seeking a new meaning. The primary meaning of a word is known *at first* either through some authority, e.g. a person or a dictionary, or through the inductive method, i.e. inferring the meaning from the many contexts where the word occurs. But the surest way of knowing the exact meaning of a word as fixed by usage is to learn it from authority. When the meaning is once learned, in all subsequently uses of the word the meaning, of course, is remembered. But in cases where doubt arises as to the meaning of the word in a particular context, owing either to the fact that the word possesses more than one meaning (as the word "dear"), or to the fact that the word, though primarily possessing only one meaning, is used there in some secondary figurative sense, memory fails as the only guide to the knowledge of meaning. The motive of the speaker or the writer, as judged from that particular context or universe of discourse (parkaraṇa), is a second help to the ascertainment of meaning. The secondary meaning of a word, therefore, is known through arthāpatti, the data of which are the remembered primary meaning, and the inferred motive of the writer. When a dog is spoken of as a lion, the primary meaning is found to be impossible and the secondary meaning is found, through arthāpatti, to be the only meaning which can remove the conflict between the primary meaning and the motive of the speaker as inferred from the context.

As precision and accuracy are the chief objects of logic, it should always demand the use of a word in its plain, primary, unambiguous sense. But change of meaning is such a vital factor in the existence and development of a language that this demand, if strictly enforced, would reduce speaking and writing almost to an impossibility. Hence logic must recognize, though against its will, the secondary changed meanings as well, provided these meanings are ascertained tolerably accurately through the primary meanings and the particular universes of discourse.

We said previously that Indian rhetoricians pleaded for the recognition of a tertiary meaning of words, namely for suggested meaning or, as it was called, vyaṇgyārtha. Logicians, however, systematically rejected their contention, for the simple reason that though suggested meaning possessed great literary beauty and merit, it was too vague, fleeting and subjective to have any place among logical meanings, the recognition of which is based purely on their objective certainty and accuracy. An illustration of such a meaning will show the propriety of the attitude assumed by logicians. When it is said, "The house is on the Ganges," the primary meaning, namely a house being actually on water, is unreasonable. So the secondary meaning, "the house being on the bank of the Ganges," is to be understood here. But it may be asked, when the meaning could have been quite clearly and accurately expressed by saying that "the house is on the bank of the Ganges," what motive led the speaker to the indirect way of expressing his idea? To this the rhetoricians reply that this indirect and figurative form of expression has an inward motive of suggesting that the house must be cool and sacred, as though it was in actual contact with the sacred and cool water of the river. So in addition to the primary and secondary meanings, hold the rhetoricians, a tertiary suggested meaning must be recognized. Similarly when it is said, "You are the descendant of the great Rama," the meaning indirectly suggested is that "You must be noble and courageous, etc."

Such suggested meaning, as we have said, has an important place in common parlance and also in poetry, where the appeal is more to the emotions and sentiments than to reason. But to logic, whose only appeal is to reason, accuracy and precision are indispensable. So primary, direct and fixed meanings alone can be recognized by logic. It is only a concession to the imperfection of current languages that even secondary meanings are recognized. But a secondary meaning is recognized because it can be fixed with tolerable certainty from the context. Indeed some secondary meanings have become almost as fixed as primary ones.[1]

1 The Indian rhetoricians distinguish secondary meanings into those that have been fixed by usage (rūḍhi-lakṣaṇā) and those that are occasionally and purposively conferred (prayojanamūlā lakṣaṇā). To the former class would belong words like "spinster," originally meaning "a spinning woman," but now always meaning "an unmarried female," and to the latter class "lion," "lamb," etc., as figuratively used. *Vide* Sāhitya-darpaṇa, 2, 5.

It takes a little time to realize that the English expression, "The house is on the river," is at all a figurative use. Similarly secondary figurative meanings in the expressions, "the bench and the bar," "right-hand man," "the crown versus the people," "the head of the department," etc., are almost as unambiguous and constant as primary meanings.

But the meanings indirectly suggested and insinuated are so uncertain that they cannot be recognized in logic. In a previous discussion we saw that the logical significance of a word has nothing to do with the changing existence and contents of the idea called up by the word, but rests on the universal meaning part of the idea. And it is the confusion of the meanings of an idea with its existence and contents (which includes images, emotions, desires, etc., roused in the mind by the particular word differently in different contexts) that is responsible for the unreasonable demand for the inclusion of the suggested sense in the logical meaning of the word. "A house on the Ganges" may call up the holy sentiments of a reverent Hindoo, but to others it may serve only to call up associations of smoke, dirt, filth and blind superstition. The expression "you are the descendant of Rama" may be flattering to some and indifferent to others. The expression, "you are a fish-eater," invariably means a reproach for a Madrasee Brahmin, but none to a Bengali, who may be reminded, on the contrary, of the savour and relish of a dish of fish. Thus it is only natural and reasonable that such fleeting and subjective suggestions should not be accepted by logicians as the logical meanings of words. In Vedāntic literature no mention even is made of this contention, and so it would seem that this view of the rhetoricians is not considered by the Vedāntins even worth criticism. We mention this view in this connection because its consideration would serve to dispel some possible confusion and would bring into bold relief the logical meaning as contrasted with the subjective and suggested meaning of poetry and common parlance.

We may summarize the main results of this somewhat lengthy chapter before we conclude. A word is the symbol of thought. As a symbol, it negates its private existence and content for the meaning it symbolizes. The meaning is neither a particular psychical state nor the imagery called forth by the word; it is a universal. A word means a particular not primarily but secondarily. In addition to its primary meaning, a word can have a secondary meaning also. The so-called suggested meaning is too fleeting and subjective to be regarded as a logical meaning.

The primary meaning of a word is at first known either directly from authority, or by induction from its particular uses by authoritative persons in different contexts. But subsequently the meaning is remembered when the word is heard. The secondary meaning is resorted to only when the primary meaning is found to be incompatible in a particular context; but it is somehow connected with the primary meaning. The secondary meaning therefore must be known through arthāpatti based on the primary meaning and the context. But if the secondary meaning is not occasional, but permanently fixed by usage to the complete loss of the primary meaning, as in "spinster," "beef,"[1] etc., it is known also like primary meaning through memory in all subsequent uses.

1 Originally an "ox".

CHAPTER IV

THE SENTENCE AND ITS MEANING

1. The Nature of a Sentence

We have hitherto been speaking about the meaning of isolated words. The meaning of an isolated word is, as we have seen, a universal. As universal, it is necessarily indeterminate for knowledge. The universal symbolized by the word "cow" is based on the abstraction of common essential attributes from all particular cows, white and not-white, milch and dry, present and past. But if it is based on the one hand on abstraction, it is also based on the other hand on subsumptive classification. Consequently the universal potentially contains all particulars as well. And it is on the strength of this potency that the indeterminate universal can once more be determined into a particular, with the help of suitable determinants.

When the two words "red" and "horse" are combined together into the expression "red horse," we have two universals which limit each other to yield a synthetic meaning. "Red" by itself has the potency of being applied to all subjects, horse and not-horse, having the quality of redness; and "horse" also potentially includes all subjects red and not-red, having "horseness" as their essential attribute. But when combined together, "red horse" means horse having the attribute of redness, so that the universal, "red," becomes relatively limited and particularized through the elimination of all subjects that are not horses; and the universal, "horse," becomes similarly particularized through the elimination of all subjects that are not red. The combination of two universals resulting in a synthetic meaning is a new grade of knowledge, that is quite distinct from the knowledge of the isolated universals. It is termed śābda-bodhah. We shall speak about the exact nature of this knowledge afterwards. What we have to notice now is that, according to Indian logicians, this new meaning marks the beginning of a vākya or sentence. The ordinary idea of grammarians, Indian as well as Western, is that without a verb there cannot be a sentence. The reason advanced by them is either that without a verb the thought sought to be expressed by the speaker is not complete, or that without it the expectancy of the hearer is not fully satisfied. But these reasons, if rigorously considered, cannot stand criticism, since very often we find that the use of a verb is neither a means to the complete expression of a thought, nor a means to the satisfaction of curiosity. On the contrary, expressions like "good morning," "alas," "hurrah," etc., are found sufficient to relieve the speaker of the full burden of his thought and the listener of his expectancy even without the help of verbs (whether spoken or understood). Thus if satisfaction of the speaker or of the listener be the test of a sentence, then even an interjection has to be called a sentence. Consequently the grounds on which a verb is thought to be indispensable to a sentence are not justifiable. Jagadīśa remarks, therefore, in his Śabda-śakti-prākaśikā, "The old traditional view that there can be no sentence without a verb is to be rejected as it has no grounds."[1]

The only way, then, in which a sentence can be distinguished from an isolated word is, as we have already said, that while a word presents only a single isolated meaning, a sentence conveys a meaning that presents a synthesis (anvaya) of the meaning of more than one word. Thus according to this view, the expression "red horse" is as much a vākya or sentence as the expression, "the red horse is grazing in the field, in front of the King's palace."

2. Does Construction Precede Expression? Two Views

The distinguishing characteristic of a sentence, then, is the construction (anvaya) of different meanings into a single meaning. But a question necessarily arises here as regards the relation of the words of sentence to the construed meaning of the sentence : Do the words of a sentence possess the double function of presenting their individual meanings and also the construed meaning of the sentence? Or do they only present their isolated meanings, while these meanings subsequently combine again to produce the single meaning of the sentence?

This question was seriously debated by the two opposing schools of Mīmāṃsā philosophy. The Prābhākaras maintained the first position, which was called anvitābhidhāna-vāda, whereas the Bhāṭṭas held the second view termed abhihitānvaya-vāda.

The Prābhākaras, who resemble in many ways the modern pragmatists or instrumentalists in according primacy to the will, held that all words spoken must directly or indirectly enjoin some duty or practice on the

1 Śabda-śakti-prakāśika, Kār. 13, commentary "Kriyārahitaṃ na vākyam asti iti prācām pravādo niryuktikatvāt aśraddheyaḥ."

listeners. Even the apparent existential propositions must be ultimately inspired by some practical interest. On hearing the word 'cow,' we must necessarily expect that something has to be done with the cow. It is either to be brought or driven away or fastened or let loose. Thus we get the verb expressing the action to be performed. In order to perform the action some agent and some *modus operandi*, some locus, etc., are required. Hence the nominative, the instrumental, the locative and the various adverbial expressions are all acquired. It is held, therefore, that the verb expressing an action is the nucleus of a sentence, and around it the agent, the object, the instrumental, etc., cluster and are held together through their relationships with the verb. In learning a language we learn the meanings of words from the different particular contexts in which they occur. And in all contexts words occur as invariably related to some verb in the various ways mentioned above. Though afterwards through generalization we get the universal meanings of words, these universals are not altogether purged of their relations to the verbs. On the contrary they always retain a general reference to verbs. Words, while explicitly and primarily expressing their universal meanings, contain therefore implicit and indirect general reference to verbs also; and it is in virtue of this second function that they readily combine together to yield the meaning of the sentence. Consequently, it is found that words themselves can discharge the double function of presenting their own individual meanings and the meaning of the sentence. It is not true that words present only their own isolated and unrelated meanings, while these meanings afterwards combine together to yield the construed meaning of the sentence. This assumption is gratuitous and far-fetched, because it is only related and construed (anvita) meanings that are expressed by words. Construction is not therefore a subsequent function; it is already presupposed in the very uttering of the words of a sentence (anvitānām eva abhidhānam, na tu abhihitānām anvayaḥ).[1]

As against this view the Bhāṭṭas hold that words cannot discharge both the functions ascribed to them by the Prābhākaras. They can only present their own isolated meanings, and construction takes place afterwards. It is not true that all words in a sentence are related to the verb. In the sentence, "Bring the white cow," the adjective "white" is connected with the noun "cow," and not with the verb "bring."[2]

1 For a discussion of the Prābhākara view, *vide* Prakaraṇa-pañcikā, p. 93 et seq.

2 Vivaraṇa-prameya-saṃgraha, p. 258.

This difficulty may induce the supporter of the above theory to modify the original position and hold that a word has reference to some word, not necessarily a verb. In the above illustration, the noun has reference to the verb and the adjective to the noun. The meaning of no word, therefore, is primarily presented to us as an isolated universal.

But the theory is not free from difficulties even in this modified form. If meanings of isolated words had the construed relations already embedded in them, all words would have been synonymous.[1] For according to this view, in an expressing like "red horse," "red" would mean, even before the whole expression is uttered, "red as related to horse," and "horse" also would mean "horse as related to red." Both would thus virtually mean the same thing. But if it be replied that "red" does not possess any reference to any particular noun (e.g. horse) but that (as an adjective) it has a general reference to all nouns, two objections can still press against this reply.

First, it may be asked : If it were so, why should we fail to make any meaning out of "square circle," where both the words possess meanings and where there is also a noun to be qualified by the adjective, "square"? If construction always preceded expression, then such phrases could never be uttered even in jest; for nothing unconstrued could be uttered. To obviate this objection an attempt may be made to modify the original statement further. It may be said that the words of a sentence, in expressing related and construed meaning, contain previous reference neither to the particular meanings actually presented by the particular words used in the sentence, nor to all general meanings that can bear grammatical relationship with them, but only to meanings that are compatible. So in the expression "square circle," the word "square" presents originally a meaning that has reference only to words that are not only grammatically suitable, but are also logically compatible. Hence "square" excludes even originally all reference to circles, triangles, etc., which are not compatible with its own meaning.

A second objection would still press against the view that construction precedes expression. Even granting that the meaning of a word is already related to other general compatible meanings, one must have to admit that the particular construction or relation is something new, and arises after all the words of the sentence are uttered. For instance, the word

1 Ibid., p. 279.

"red" might originally have a general reference to those things alone that can be red; that is to say, "red" may and does mean a colour that is attributed to a suitable thing, a cow, a dog, a horse, a bird, etc., and not darkness, virtue, etc. But until the particular word "horse" is uttered, the general construed meaning of red cannot be particularized to yield the meaning "the red colour as attributed to a horse." If so, we must come back to the view that the particular construed meaning of the sentence is known only after the whole sentence has been uttered. If so, construction is not prior to expression but subsequent to it. We must, therefore, ultimately accept the view of abhihitānvaya (which literally means construction of the uttered, abhihitānām eva anvayaḥ).

According to this second view, the words of a sentence present only their primary isolated meanings. Those meanings afterwards combine to produce the particular synthesized or construed meaning. So the construed meaning is obtained not directly from words themselves, but indirectly through the meaning of the words.

An objection may, however, be raised against this theory also. If the words of a sentence do not present its meaning, how is it that a change of word affects the meaning of a sentence? And why are words uttered at all to convey thought? To this it is replied that, to say that words do not present the meaning of a sentence is not to say that the component words have no relation whatsoever to its meaning. Words are really spoken to express the meaning contained in the sentence. They are the invariable antecedent condition for the understanding of the meaning of a sentence; only they are not the *immediate* antecedent condition. As Kumārila says[1]: "Just as fuel is the indispensable condition of cooking, but cooking is performed not directly by fuel, but through the flame generated by it, so are words indispensable to the understanding of meaning of a sentence; but this understanding is not immediately caused by the words, but by the meanings they present to the mind." If words themselves could give rise to the knowledge of meaning, then the meaning of a sentence, composed of words, the meaning of which are known, would invariably be known. But as a matter of fact, we often find cases where the component words are understood, but not the meaning of the sentence. This would suggest that some other condition is to be satisfied. And this condition, as we shall see, is the construction of the meanings of the words into the synthetic meaning of the sentence.

1 Śloka-vārtīka, p. 943.

Now the Advaitins are divided among themselves on the question : Which of these two views is correct? On empirical questions the Advaitins as a rule follow the Bhāṭṭas.[1] But on this point some Advaitins deviate from that custom. The authors of the Vivaraṇa and of the Vivaraṇa-prameya-saṃgraha[2] regard both these views as equally good for their purpose. The author of the Vedānta-paribhāṣa,[3] while discussing the problem of the relation of the universal (as the meaning of a word) to the particular, offers as one of the solutions the view of the Prābhākaras, that the particular is also implicity meant by a word, though explicitly it means a universal. But almost all the great authorities on Advaita, namely Vacāspati,[4] Citsukhācāryya,[5] Madhūsudan Sarasvatī,[6] hold that abhihitānvaya-vāda alone is tenable. The author of the Citsukhī goes to the length of saying that this is the only view that Śaṃkara himself favours in his commentary on the Samanvaya-sūtra. But Śaṃkara does not really explicitly mention there any of these two theories in so many words.

What affects the Advaitins vitally in this matter is the interpretation of the Vedic texts which assert truths about God and self, and which have no reference to any practice or injunction. The Prābhākaras hold that Vedic texts without exception directly or indirectly refer to some injunctions, and that even those texts which apparently contain statements of facts are to be understood as *incidental* expressions calculated to actuate persons to follow the Vedic injunctions or avoid their violation. With this definite purpose they advanced the theory of anvitābhidhānam, which made the verb (or action) the very nerve of a sentence, making all other words subsidiary to it. The essential motive of this theory, therefore, was antagonistic to the Advaitins, who laid the greatest emphasis on the texts that speak of the reality that can be attained not through action but through knowledge. But Śaṃkara, while refuting the original proposition that all texts are for some ritual practice, says that even if that were conceded, yet one must admit that there are texts which state the existence of materials

1 Cf. the Vedāntic maxim, "Vyavahāre Bhāṭṭanayaḥ."

2 Cf. Vivaraṇa-prameya-saṃgraha, pp. 257-262.

3 Paribhāṣa, chap. iv, also commentary of Ananta Kṛṣṇa Śāstri (pub. by Calcutta University), Paribhāṣāprakāśikā.

4 Bhāmati on Brahma-sūtra, 1, 1, 4.

5 Citsukhī, and Nayanaprasādinī, chap. i, p. 155.

6 Advaita-siddhi, chap. ii, p. 687.

necessary for practice. The texts themselves do, therefore, state the existence of things, as preconditions to commandments themselves. The fundamental position of the Prābhākaras, that the texts are never statements of facts but always express some injunctions, therefore, falls through. Śaṃkara thus refutes the Prābhākaras by assuming their own dictum; and as this served his purpose he did not raise the questions about anvitā bhidhāna or abhihitānvaya.

The author of Vivaraṇa raises this question and says that while abhihitānvaya-vāda is in perfect agreement with Vedāntic interpretation of the texts about self, Brahman, etc., even the theory of anvitābhidhāna is not opposed to it.[1] In order to prove this contention the author interprets anvitābhidhāna-vāda in a new light. He says that it is absurd that this theory should mean that the meanings of all words are connected with action alone. What it should mean is that all words have meanings that are originally construed or have reference to all suitable things like attributes, substance, action.[2] Interpreted in this way, this theory can explain the texts in question, because the theory would no longer demand that every word must have a reference to some *verb* (or action): and then even according to this theory the Advaitin's object would be obtained.

In explaining the theory of anvitābhidhāna we have already considered this modification suggested by the author of Vivaraṇa. This modification may be sufficient to save the Vedāntic texts from the particular objection raised by the Mīmāṃsakas. But considered from other points of view this theory, as we have already shown, cannot stand even in the modified form. The author of Vivaraṇa and some others look at the question only from that limited point of view, and they think, therefore, that both the theories are tenable as serving their purpose. But the authors of the Citsukhī, the Bhamātī and the Advaita-siddhi consider the question from other points also, and declare that abhihitānvaya-vāda alone can be supported.

We have already shown that anvitābhidhāna-vāda is not acceptable even in any modified form. Indeed, if universals be the meanings of words, the meaning of a sentence cannot be directly obtained from words. The meanings obtained from words have to be synthesized in order that we may be able to know the constructive meaning of the particular sentence; and the primary meaning of a word being a universal according to the

1 Vivaraṇa-prameya-saṃgraha, p. 260.

2 Ibid., p. 258.

Advaitins, abhihitānvaya-vāda is the only possible logical conclusion. In connection with the meanings of words, however, we have given as one of the Vedāntic views the theory that though the *explicit* meaning of a word is a universal, the particular also is *implicitly* meant. This view is originally held by the Prābhākara School, and the author of the Vedānta-paribhāṣā adopted it.

This theory, if analysed, can be understood to mean two things, only one of which is compatible, to a certain extent, with the theory of anvitābhidhāna, while the other is definitely against that theory. The theory (that the particular is implicitly meant by a word) may either mean that the universal which is the primary meaning of a word implicitly contains all the individuals as such (i.e. with their individual peculiarities within it), or that the universal contains implicitly all individuals *as characterized only by the universal*. If the first be the meaning, namely if "horse" means explicitly "horseness" and implicitly "red horse," "black horse," etc., it may then be somehow held that the word when used in a sentence could, without any subsequent construction, signify the particular as meant in that sentence. This interpretation may lend some support to the anvitābhidhāna-vāda of the Prābhākara school. But we have seen already that even if the word "horse" could really mean the particular horses, with their individual peculiarities, some construction would still be necessary to select the particular horse meant in a particular context by eliminating the other possible particulars. And this constructive function, taking place as it would after expression of the sentence, would undermine the theory of anvitābhidhāna. But even apart from this consideration the theory, in its first meaning, is not itself tenable. For, as we have seen in a previous chapter, the word "horse" as meaning "horseness" cannot include in it individual peculiarities that fall outside the essential generic attributes. Hence, the theory can be accepted by the Vedāntist only in the second sense, according to which a horse would mean implicitly a red horse or a black horse, in so far as it possesses the essential generic attributes "horseness" connoted by the word, and not in so far as it is red or black. The theory in this form is really useful as an explanation of the Vedāntic view, which does not consider the universal to be a pure abstraction purged from all reference to particulars. But if the theory is to be understood in this second sense, anvitābhidhāna-vāda becomes far less acceptable. According to the Advaitin then, whether he holds that a word means a pure universal, or that it means a universal having implicit reference to particulars, abhihitānvaya-vāda can be the only consistent conclusion. It is natural, therefore, that some of the greatest Vedāntic authorities should reject anvitābhidhāna-vāda and support the other theory.

Though anvitābhidhāna-vāda cannot be accepted in any of the forms in which it is advanced by its supporters, there is some important truth in it, which should not be overlooked. First, in holding that words have implicit reference to particulars, it represents a reasonable reaction against the extreme view which holds that words mean abstract isolated unrelated universals. Secondly, in holding that construction or synthesis of meaning is prior to the expression of a sentence, it contains some truth from the *speaker's point of view*, though not from that of the listener. Though in Indian philosophy we do not find any explicit distinction between these two points of view, we believe some distinction was implied. As the problems about Sabda arose, with all sections of Indian philosophy, on the interpretation of texts, it was the standpoint of the hearer that must naturally have been implied. As the primary function of speech is the communication of ideas to other persons, the principal standpoint in the interpretation of language must also necessarily be the *standpoint of the hearer*, for whom words are spoken. And so far as the hearer is concerned, it is of course true that words are first heard by him and their meanings are afterwards integrated into a constructive whole. But from the standpoint of the speaker himself, it is perhaps true that the meaning of the sentence is already present to his mind, however vaguely, even before he utters the sentence. So anvitābhidhāna-vāda contains some truth from this point of view also. It should be added, however, that the Prābhākaras never pressed their theory on this ground.

The most important difference that follows from the two different theories, however, is as regards the knowledge of the meaning of a sentence. According to anvitābhidhāna-vāda the meaning of a sentence can be known through *memory*, since the meaning is presented by words themselves, which are *remembered* to possess certain meanings. But according to abhihitānvaya-vāda the knowledge of the meaning of a sentence, being *constructed* out of the meanings presented by the words, is not mere remembering. It is a new kind of knowledge, though usually built on the materials supplied by memory. This is generally called śābda-bodha or constructive knowledge of the meanings of words.

Let us consider the relative merit of these two views on this important point. Take the sentence, "Black cows give profuse milk." We have here five words that possess five universals as their meanings. These meanings are, of course, remembered as soon as these words are heard. But how is the whole meaning of the sentence known? Can it be also legitimately spoken of as being remembered, supposing of course that this sentence is heard for the first time? We do not see any reason why it can be. Even if we must think that the remembered meanings of the words are simply put together through what is called memory-synthesis, the resultant meaning cannot be called an object of memory. Memory is essentially a reproduction of past experience, and in the past the five words were learned separately in different contexts. They were not originally together in experience. So in putting together their meanings, we do not simply have a reproduction of past experience. The remembered contents are arranged in an order and relation that were absent in the past experiences, where the meanings of the individual words were learned. Consequently even in memory-synthesis the result itself cannot be memory. As Hobhouse says, "we must recognize in it (memory-synthesis) a new factor of knowledge"[1] not reducible to perception or memory. He calls it construction.

But as a matter of fact, it is not even by simply putting together the meanings of the five words that we can obtain the resultant meaning of the given sentence. Memories of sense-percepts, say of "black colour," "a cow" and "milk," received at different moments, can afterwards be placed side by side perhaps as they were first perceived. We may image to ourselves a cow with black colour and with milk flowing. But meanings remembered on hearing the words "black," "cow," "give," "profuse," "milk," are not memories of sense-percepts, but of universal ideas. And the universals do not become combined *in toto* just as sense-percepts do. The universal represented by the word "cow" is neither a red cow nor a black cow nor a white cow. It is all and none of them. So the universal, the meaning of the word "cow," as such, cannot be combined with the meaning of the word "black" which also refers to the colour of neither cows nor horses nor elephants, but to all and none of them. Consequently the universals as such cannot combine together to yield the meaning of the sentence. We find, therefore, that the materials supplied by memory in the case of universal meanings cannot, as such, produce any knowledge.

1 *Theory of Knowledge*, p. 83.

The meaning of a sentence cannot be obtained, therefore, through memory alone. The supporters of the theory of abhihitānvaya are right, therefore, in holding, as against those who support the theory of anvitābhidhāna, that the meaning of a sentence cannot be known through memory, but that it has to be known through a new method of knowledge.

3. Conditions of Significant Combination

A combination of universals such as leads to śābda-bodha (or knowledge of the meaning of a sentence) is a construction that can take place only under specific conditions, which distinguish it from other kinds of constructions such as memory-synthesis, on the one hand, and inference on the other. And it is because of this fact that any and every combination of significant words, such as "cold fire," or "hot ice," is not itself significant. Let us examine the conditions under which a significant combination or śābda-bodha takes place.

A combination between any two elements can take place only when there is a mutual affinity between them. In the physical world we come across two kinds of collocation called mechanical mixture and chemical combination. In mechanical mixture, the two constituent substances lie side by side (as sand and sugar) without the interpenetration of the one element by the other, and consequently the mixture acquires no new properties. But in chemical combination the elements interpenetrate to produce a new substance possessing properties that were not present in the constituents. The cause of a chemical combination lies however in the mutual affinity between the two combining atoms. Hydrogen and oxygen combine because of this chemical affinity, and sand and sugar do not because they lack it. This analogy holds good in the mental world as well. Two ideas can combine when there is mutual affinity between them. But this mutual affinity consists of two factors. First, there must be a want, a feeling of incompleteness—a fellow-seeking—so to say, on the part of each constituent member, and secondly there must also be a potency and compatibility on the part of its fellow to satisfy its want. The first has been called ākāṃkṣā (hankering, desire), and the second yogyatā (fitness, compatibility) by Indian thinkers.

The universal, as represented by the meaning of a word, is an abstraction. An abstraction, by itself, is not a fact but a wandering adjective[1] that constantly gravitates along innumerable lines of attraction towards

1 Bradley, *Logic*, p. 10.

the numberless subjects from which it was abstracted. Like a homeless disembodied spirit it seeks its way back to the concrete which was once its body and home.

When any word is uttered, we are aware of a meaning that is universal and , as such, too abstract, too indeterminate and too incomplete to be a self-sufficient mental state. So a sense of incompleteness (ākāṃkṣā) is invariably felt, and expectancy for factors that can make the idea more complete and determinate is aroused. In a significant sentence the meaning of every word is made more determinate and complete to consciousness by the meaning of every other word in the sentence. The more the meanings of the words of a sentence can mutually help to determine each other, the more is the tension of indeterminate expectancy relieved.

But apart from the universality of meanings, which applies to all words alike, there are some other special causes which make some words more indefinite and incomplete in meaning than others. The meaning of a noun-word, for example, is more complete and self-subsistent than that of an adjective or a verb. The reason is that while a noun can denote a relatively self-sufficient entity, an adjective or a verb denotes only a particular abstract aspect, quality or action of the substantive, and as an aspect can never exist in thought apart from the thing of which it is the aspect, an adjective or a verb invariable requires a noun-word and is comparatively less complete to thought than a noun. Again, among noun-words, those expressing the explicitly related, as "son," "father," "friend," carry a sense of greater incompleteness than the rest, the absolute terms; as the related always require the other side of the relation without which they are unintelligible, they are so to say *half-thoughts*. Again, words expressing mere relations (as, in, on, before, and , etc.), are still more incomplete, since they present to thought relation without the related, a middle without the beginning and the end. So they fail to present even half a thought.

In these special cases, the incompleteness of meaning and consequent striving after completion (ākāṃkṣā) are always felt without exception. But in other cases, the incompleteness though existing may not always be felt. For instance, on hearing the sentence, "James is going," one may feel quite satisfied, and may have no further questions to ask; though all the same, numberless questions like "which James?" "Going wherefrom?" "Whereto?" "How?" etc., might still be asked. But on hearing the sentence "The son is going", we have an invariable feeling of incompleteness, and can hardly help asking the question "Whose son?"

We have thus to distinguish between the logical and psychological aspects of ākāṃkṣā, according to the distinction between objective incompleteness and felt or subjective incompleteness. According to this distinction, ākāṃkṣā has been differentiated into *utthita and utthāpya*, i.e. expectation that has been actually aroused and expectation that can be aroused. The psychological always presupposes the logical; that is to say, expectancy can be felt only where it can be aroused. But the logical does not always imply the psychological, because expectation may not be actually aroused wherever it is possible. Psychologically then there is a limit to expectancy, but logically there is none. For the process of determination being infinite, a meaning, however determined, cannot yet be made too determinate to be determined further. There would be no end, therefore, to possible questions and no end to logical incompletenss of thought. When reading or listening to a long, complex but significant sentence, with many qualifying clauses, we are often ready to be satisfied at many stages before the end; but when dragged on to further lengths by the speaker or the writer, we may afterwards appreciate the possibility of questions to which his added clauses supply the answers. It is ākāṃkṣā in the logical sense which is at work in such a case, though in the psychological sense it is absent.

But ākāṃkṣā is only one of the conditions of combination of meanings. Another condition is, as we have said, yogyatā or compatibility. Every word, as we have seen, can raise an expectancy and a desire for the completion of thought, so that the meaning of a word requires something else in combination with which it may become more complete to thought. This fellow-seeking of a meaning is not and cannot be satisfied by any and every other fellow. In the combination "square circle" for instance, we have two members, each of which presents a meaning that requires combination for self-perfection. But notwithstanding this longing, the two members stand repelled from each other. This shows that the desire for completion exhibited by the meaning of a word is not blind. The meaning itself guides the choice of its fellow. Thus when two meanings are combined, their combination is not a mere external relation, but is internally determined by both. As Hobhouse has shown so elaborately, two ideas, like two physical objects, require common points of contact between them. "On the side of construction," he says, "it is limited by the necessity that the elements which it combines should be applicable to one another. Each brick in the building determines in some degree the next, even if in the form of the bed in which the new brick is to lie. Combinations of ideas, in short, are limited by the points of contact between them."[1] This common point determines the compatibility or yogyatā which must obtain between the two meanings that are to be combined. The common point is not, however, always very evident. In simple cases like "red horse" it is easily found out. The word "red" always implies a surface that is red, and "horse" implies an animal that has a surface that requires some colour. But in the case of "human food," no physical point of contact is possible, neither can food possess any characteristic in common with "man." But "food" implies an eater and man may be one of the eaters, so the common point or point of contact is the relation between the eater and eaten. But in some cases the connecting bond or bonds may be still more indirect and complicated, and the relation between the two may be established through a series of intermediate links. "A silent wish," for instance, is the wish of a man whose voice is silent while entertaining the wish. The adjective primarily applies to the voice, then through the voice to the man, and through the man to his wish. Thus "warm reception," "cold comfort," "dumb agony," "breathless haste" and even "tall talk" come to be significant combinations. It will be evident from these examples that the common point may at times yield place to a long, complicated, varied and indirect process, and the passage from one idea to the other may be through a chain of causal connections. Through this process the meaning of a word may gradually undergo much transformation, acquiring many new associations and losing many old ones. But the transformation in meaning, that a word may undergo to suit a new combination, is always limited by its original meaning. There may be something in the meaning of one word that may make any association with another meaning altogether impossible, so that the two cannot be related (except by opposition or negation) by any length of mediating links. For instance, in "circular square" no amount of indirect linkage can trace the connection between a circle and a square. Not that a circle and a square have no common points between them; indeed a circle resembles a square more than an argument, with which it is, however, easily related in the phrase "circular argument." Both a circle and a square are material forms, are bounded geometrical figures and so forth. But these common points cannot help the establishment of the *desired* adjectival relation between them,

1 *Theory of Knowledge*, p. 208.

and there is something in the meaning of each of them which positively prevents such a relation being set up. Yet other relations such as "circle and square," "circle in a square," "circle outside a square," are quite possible, whereas combinations like "circle with an argument," "circle outside an argument," etc., may fail.

Hence the author of the Vedānta-paribhāṣā defines compatibility as non-contradiction of the *relation desired* to be set up in a combination of ideas (Yogyatā ca tātparyya-viṣaya-saṃsargābādhaḥ).[1] This definition will suit all cases which we have hitherto considered and the manner in which we have considered them. But if we desire to go more thoroughly into the question, we shall find the definition somewhat narrow, so that it must be further widened to cover all cases of combination. We have considered so far only *relational* combinations and not non-relational ones. But there are cases, though very rare, where the motive for placing two ideas together is not to establish a *relation* at all, but is, on the contrary, to show the want of relation or a mere identity, e.g. "This is Devadatta," "Thou art Brahman."[2] Madhūsudana Sarasvatī, the author of Advaita-siddhi, defines yogyatā, therefore, as merely the non-contradiction of the desired object of combination (yogyatāpi tātparyyaviṣayabādha eva),[3] and omits the word "relation" (saṃsarga).

We have discussed hitherto only two conditions, ākāṃkṣā and yogyatā, under which śābda-bodha, or the knowledge of the meaning of a combination of words, can arise. But in addition to these two material conditions there is also a third, a formal condition which must be fulfilled. It is āsatti, or contiguity or proximity (which will be *spatial* in the case of written words and *temporal* in the case of spoken words) between the two words presented for combination. It is not sufficient that the meanings of two words should be individually incomplete and should possess also the potency for satisfying their mutual wants, but they should also be presented in close proximity, just to show that it is these two meanings that are also meant to be combined or construed together. Non-fulfilment of this condition may give rise to doubt as to which words are meant to be construed together. It is a great syntactical fault that often prevents the accurate knowledge of the meaning of a sentence.

1 Vedānta-paribhāṣā, chap. iv.

2 For a fuller discussion of such cases refer to end of this chapter.

3 Advaita-siddhi, p. 689.

To illustrate : the *son* of Edward VII, *who* is the present king of England, is the Emperor of India. In poetry and even sometimes in prose this rule is not observed. In these cases it has to be inferred from external data (if such data are available) as to which words are to be construed together; and it is by putting these words together in thought that the meaning is obtained.

When these three conditions are satisfied, the meaning of a sentence can be known. But even this is not all. So long as a sentence is considered by itself, these three conditions are indeed sufficient. But a sentence is not really an isolated, abstract entity. It is organically related to a speaker, a context or a universe of discourse which determine, out of the many possible meanings of a sentence, the particular meaning relevant to a particular case. It is also necessary therefore to know the intention of the speaker or the drift of the context (where the speaker is not known). So, a fourth condition, namely tātparyya-jñana, or the knowledge of what is intended or relevant, must be taken into consideration. The actual meaning can be gathered from the universe of discourse, the introduction, the conclusion, etc.[1] This condition is especially active when there is some ambiguity or when the ordinary or primary meaning does not suit and a secondary figurative meaning has to be found, e.g. in 'The crane is moving', 'The die is cast' etc. Similarly when we are told in the Bible, that a camel can pass through the eye of a needle, but a rich man cannot enter heaven, we must understand the first sentence just in the opposite sense, only in deference to the intention of the speaker, or it would have been altogether unintelligible. In ordinary cases, however, when there is no occasion for doubt or ambiguity, this condition may remain in the background as a negative factor. In other words, in such cases a vague assurance that the speaker does not mean anything else than what the words by themselves mean, may be thought responsible for the non-existence of doubts that might otherwise handicap the knowledge of the meaning of a sentence.

We see, therefore, that the knowledge of the meaning of a sentence or a combination of words arises under the four conditions, ākāṃkṣā, yogyatā, āsatti and tātparyya jñāna.

1 *Vide* Vedāntasāra (ed. Hiriyanna, Oriental Book Agency, 1929), pp. 12, 35 and 59, for the six marks with which tātparyya can be ascertained. Cf. F. C. S. Schiller's distinction between potential and personal meanings in *Logic for use*, Chap. IV

Śābda-bodha is, therefore a peculiar kind of knowledge. It can, of course, be brought under the general category of construction under which are included memory-synthesis on the one hand and inference on the other. But the special condition of śābda-bodha, mentioned above, distinguish it even as construction from both memory-synthesis and inference, in which these conditions are absent.

4. The Conception of a Proposition

We have dwelt thus far on the structure and meaning of a vākya, which we have rendered by the term "sentence." It will be interesting to discuss in this connection the relation between a vākya and a proposition and consider the Vedāntic theory of a proposition. It will be evident from the foregoing discussion that the understanding of a vākya is not a mere consideration of its grammatical relation. On the contrary, it involves an apprehension of thought relations which constitute a sentence. And even "the understanding of the grammatical structure of a sentence, which includes such relations as those of the subject to the predicate and of subordinate to co-ordinate clauses, requires us to penetrate below the mere verbal construction and to consider the formal structure of thought."[1] Although Indian logicians had no special name[2] for what is called a proposition in Western logic, they virtually discussed certain points relating to a proposition in course of discussing the nature of a vākya, and in so far as the general view of a declaratory vākya in Indian logic is that it must contain a subject (uddeśya) and a predicate (vidheya), we may almost identify such a vākya with a proposition, which is also generally understood in that sense in Western logic.

The Mīmāṃsakas discussed elaborately the logical aspects of a vākya in the course of their investigation into the methodology of Vedic interpretation. But they were primarily interested in the Vedic injunctions regarding rituals, that is, in the imperative sentences rather than the indicative or assertory ones (i.e. logical propositions). But Vedantins were primarily interested in the latter kind of sentences asserting the nature of Self, God, Reality, etc. All Indian logicians generally analysed an assertory sentence into two parts, uddeśya and vidheya, which may be rendered as subject and predicate. It is interesting to note that as

1 Johnson, *Logic*, Part I, p. 8.

2 The word "pratijñā," often translated by proposition, is the name of a special proposition, which represents the thesis to be proved by an inference.

the Sanskrit idiom did not require the use of the verb "to be" as the connection between subject and predicate, the problem concerning the copula, which has vexed many modern and ancient Western logicians who thought it to be an independent entity constituting a third component part of a proposition, did not trouble Indian logicians at all. That the two parts, subject and predicate, exhaust the proposition, and that the copula is no component part of it, have been realized by some Western thinkers also.[1] Referring to the copula, Johnson observes, "that in some cases the word may be omitted is further evidence that the *tie* is not an additional component in the construct, but a mere formal element."

As regards the general relation between the two parts of a proposition and their respective functions, it is held that a subject must have three characteristics, uddeśyatva, anuvādyatva and viśeṣyatva, and that a predicate also must possess three corresponding characteristics, vidheyyatva, upādeyatva an viśeṣaṇatva. To explain these terms, uddeśyatva means the characteristic of being referred to, anuvādyatva that of being already known, and viśeṣyatva that of being a substantive. Further, vidheyatva means the quality of being referred, upādeyatva means that of being newly acquired or known, and viśeṣaṇatva that of being an adjective. In other words, in a vākya or proposition the subject is the object of reference, and the predicate is referred to it. The subject, being the starting-point, is *already known*, and the predicate represents some *new information* concerning the subject. Again, while the subject is the substantive or the determinandum (viśeṣya) the predicate is the *adjective* or the determinans (viśeṣaṇa).

It should be noted that while the subject is spoken of as anuvādya or already known, the statement should be understood in a qualified sense. The subject is not wholly known. Indeed, if it were so, there would have been no need for predication or further determination of it at all. It has been said, therefore, that the subject is already known only in some ways, and has yet to be known in other ways (prāptasya dharmāntara-prāptaye kathanam uddeśaḥ).

Regarding the function of a proposition, then, the general view in Indian logic is that it expresses a relation (saṃsarga) between a substantive and in adjective.[2] The import of the proposition, "The cow exists"

1 Cf. Bosanquet. *Logic*. vol. i, pp. 75 f., and Johnson, *Logic*, Part I, p. 11

2 Śabda-śakti-prakāśikā.

(gauḥ asti), is "the cow characterized by existence" (astitvavān gauḥ). Similarly the import of the proposition, "The pot is blue" (ghaṭaḥ-nīlaḥ), is "the pot characterized by blueness" (nīlatva-viśiṣṭaḥ ghaṭaḥ), and that of the negative proposition, "the pot is not blue," is "the pot characterized by the non-existence of blueness" (nīlatvābhāva-viśiṣṭo ghaṭaḥ).

We may incidentally compare the above views of the subject, predicate and import of a proposition with those of some eminent Western logicians. It is interesting to note that Johnson[1] considers the subject to be the substantive and the predicate to be its adjective, just as Indian logicians consider the subject as the viśeṣya and the predicate as its viśeṣaṇa. According to Bradley,[2] a proposition *expresses* the reference of an "ideal content" to Reality. Bosanquet similarly holds that in a proposition an ideal content is referred to Reality [3]; and Hobhouse[4] thinks that "of the total content of the judgment, one element at least is ideal," and "this element the judgment connects with some further content, real or imaginary, ideal or perceptual." We find that these authorities are almost unanimous so far as the predication of an ideal content is concerned, though they differ on the nature of the subject of which it is predicated. From the manner in which the import of a proposition is expressed (e.g. that "The pot is blue" means "The pot is characterized by *blueness*") by Indian thinkers, it may be supposed that according to them also the predicate (as being expressed as a concept) is ideal. As regards the question of reference to reality, we reserve our remarks for the present, as the whole matter will be considered in the next chapter.

5. Do All Propositions Contain Substantive-Adjective Relation?

The Advaitins accept in general the view of a Vākya set forth in the preceding pages. But they contend that though most sentences can be considered as propositions, in which an adjective is predicated of a substantive, there are a few vākyas which cannot be taken as expressing this general subject-predicate or substantive-adjective relation (uddeśya-vidheya-sambandha or viśeṣya-viśeṣaṇa-sambandha).

1 *Logic*, Part I, pp. 9-17.

2 *Logic*, vol. i, p.10.

3 *Logic*, vol. i, p. 73.

4 *Theory of Knowledge*, p. 157.

In recent times, Russell[1] has vehemently criticized the traditional view of Western logic, namely that all propositions can be reduced to the orthodox subject-predicate form. He instances the cases of propositions asserting relations (especially asymmetrical ones, e.g. A is greater than B), where the subject-predicate or substantive-adjective view is directly contradicted. The motive that inspires Russell to maintain that the subject-predicate form is not universal, is to refute absolutism, which, he thinks, is based on the fundamental misconception that all judgments predicate some quality or qualities of Reality. He thinks it best to refute this by showing that all judgments do not contain a subject and a predicate, and consequently all judgments do not express qualities; on the contrary, there are judgments which express relations between two entities, which are independent and not joined as substantive to a quality. But the motive of the Vedāntins in refuting the universality of the subject-predicate form is just the opposite. It is to pave the way for a type of absolutism which far outstrips that of Hegel and Bradley, who are the targets of Russell's poignant criticism.[2]

As for propositions like "A is greater than B," "A is before B," that (according to Russell) express relations which prevent their reduction to the orthodox form, the Advaitins will prefer to force them into that very form and interpret them in the ordinary substantive-quality way. But what they are interested in is the Vedānta texts, containing sentences describing the undifferentiated Absolute (nirguṇa Brahman), which is spoken of as being beyond all qualities and relations. They argue that these sentences cannot be interpreted in the ordinary subject-predicate way.

In order to prove this contention, the Advaitins draw attention to a distinction regarding the meaning of a sentence that is ordinarily forgotten. The meaning of some sentences involves, it is true, relations between two or more elements. Propositions which, we have seen, express the reference of an ideal content to Reality, i.e. an adjective to a substantive, surely establish some qualitative relations between two elements. Again, propositions like "A is before B," which Russell thinks do not come under the qualitative class, also express relations, it may be between two independent substantives. The meaning of both these kinds of sentences may be said to be *relational*, and a sentence of this type is called

1 *Our Knowledge of the External World*, Lecture II.

2 *External World*, pp. 38-39.

saṃsargāvagāhi-vākyam (a sentence signifying a relation). But there are other sentences spoken with the definite purpose of expressing a non-relaional meaning, which is not constituted by the relation of two or more elements. Such a sentence is called akhaṇḍārthaka-vākyam, a sentence with an indivisible or unitary or non-relational meaning.

6. Some Identity Propositions : Advaita View and Western Criticism

Propositions expressing true identity, and those defining a single object of thought, belong to this class. The illustration of a propostion expressing identity, according to the Advaitins is "This is that Devadatta." (saḥ ayam Devadattaḥ). This proposition if analysed reveals a *prima facie* absurdity. For "this" means here "as determined by the present time and space," as seen here and now, and "that" means "as determined by some other time and space," as seen at some other time and space. It is absurd that "this" should be "that," for they represent a pair of incompatible determinants. Still there is not the least doubt about the fact that we do mean something, and mean nothing short of an identity. By such a judgement it is not meant that the two incompatible determinants are related as identical, nor that the sunstantive Devadatta, as determined by the one determinant, is the same as the substantive as determined by the other; this latter alternative also is absurd because, determined in two different ways, the substantive yields two logically distinct terms which cannot be identical. The only way in which such a judgement can be considered valid is to understand the identity of the substantive Devadatta, by negating or deducting the determinants; in other words to understand that this Devadatta is that Devadatta, in so far as Devadatta is the same in spite of the differing determinants which, as unable to affect the identity of the person, may be regarded *as non est*. Similarly is to be understood the Vedic text, "Thou art that" (tat tvam asi), where "Thou" means an individual consciousness while "That" means universal consciousness, and where the identity meant is to be found by deducting, as before, the two incompatible determinants "individual" and "universal" from both sides, and retaining in thought only the common factor, consciousness.

In such a proposition, therefore, the meaning obtained consists only of one element that alone is retained, and not of two or more elements in any way related together. Such a vākya is, therefore, akhaṇḍārthaka.

The method by which we interpret such an apparently contradictory propositon by removing the contradictory elements and retaining the common factor is called jahad-ajahal-lakṣaṇā, of which we have already spoken in Chapter IV.

A student of Western logic would inevitably raise many objections against this theory of the Advaitins. And in India itself many objections were actually raised by some formidable opponents of the Advaitins. Before we can take up the other type of akhaṇḍārthakavākya, we must consider therefore some important objections against the Advaita position, as regards this first type of proposition.

The most fundamental objection that will be raised will be against the possibility of an identical proposition itself. Bradley says that "judgement is not the assertion that subject and predicate are identical or equal,"[1] and that a "judgement asserts the equality or sequence or position of two subjects, and it surely does not say that both are the same."[2] And Hobhouse goes a step further. He criticizes Lotze,[3] who favours an identity judgement, and quotes Hegel[4] to show that such a judgement is self-contradictory, as it "sets out to say something and ends precisely by saying nothing." He thinks, therefore, that the "study of identical judgements belongs, together with tautology, not to logic, but to the pathology of thought."[5] Thus the very existence of the identity judgement is threatened. Let us examine the real worth of these objections as applied against the Vedanta theory.

It should first of all be made clear that the Advaitins do not claim identity to be the general relation between the subject and predicate of every judgement, against which view the criticism of Bradley, and also to a certain extent that of Hobhouse, are levelled. On the contrary they maintain, as should be evident from what has been said before, that most judements do not signify identity. It is only a few judgements, as illustrated above, which do so. The illustrations which Bradley, as well as Hobhouse, takes to show that there cannot be a relation of identity between the subject and the predicate of a proposition are,

1 *Logic*, vol. i, p. 22.

2 Ibid., p. 28.

3 *Logic*, Book I, chap. ii, arts. 54-55.

4 *Wissenschaft der Logik*, Book II. *Vide* Wallace's *Logic of Hegel*, pp. 213-214.

5 *Theory of Knowledge*, p. 163.

"You are standing before me," "A is North of C," "B follows D," "All negroes are men," "Iron is a metal," "A is like B,"[1] "Some men are black," "Body has extension,"[2] etc. It will be seen at once that the Advaitins also join hands with these critics in maintaining that none of these judgements signifies identity. But this does not, of course, argue that there is *no* judgement which signifies identity.

How are we to understand a judgement like "A is identical with B"? We can, we hope, assume that no reasonable person will go to the absurd length of saying that such a judgement is impossible or meaningless. If then such a judgement can be seriously passed, what do we mean by the term "identical with"? If a word is used for its meaning, then we think there is no other alternative than to confess that identity and nothing but identity is meant by the phrase. If however such a usage implies any slipshod method of speaking or thinking, it has no place in philosophical criticism. For the very presupposition of criticism or argument is the significant use of words. But it may be said that the proposition, "A is identical with B," means only that there is one aspect from which "A is identical with B," while from other aspects A is also different from B. And if A is in no way different from B, such a judgement would have been quite unnecessary; nay, it would have been not a judgement at all but a tautology. There would then have been no meaning in using two different terms A and B, instead of one term, A or B.

This method of argument is inspired by the so-called Hegelian conception of identity-in-difference, which has been found to be the universal solvent for reconciling all contradictions in Philosophy. But we confess that this method, with its cheap paradoxical phraseology, casts only a mystic glamour over contradictions which are merely concealed and not explained. Let us see how. In the illustration, "A is identical with B," let us suppose that there is an element "m" common to both A and B, and that A is equal to am, B equal to bm, so that the proposition becomes on substitution "am is identical with bm." It will be found that the proposition in its present form, in spite of the common element being disclosed, is not a whit nearer to the explanation of identity than it was before. For if there is the common element "m" on both sides, there are also peculiar elements "a" and "b", which stand in the way of identity. So long as "a" and "b" are thought as real as "m," the only reasonable

1 *Logic*, vol. i, pp. 22-23.

2 *Theory of Knowledge*, pp. 160-161.

judgement can be one of similarity or even dissimilarity, and surely not of identity. If so, judgements like "Bradley, who is the author of *Appearance and Reality*, is the same as or identical with Bradley, the author of *Truth and Reality*," would have been impossible. We should have instead judgements like "Bradley, the author of *Appearance and Reality* is similar to Bradley, the author of *Truth and Reality*"; so that so long as difference is regarded as existing *pari passu* with community. there can be no question of identity at all. Identity is possible only when difference has been effaced or negated. If the paradoxical expression "identity-in-difference" means identical as different, we shall have no choice but to repeat the words of Hobhouse, that the study of such meaningful contradictions belongs "not to logic, but to the pathology of thought." The only rational meaning of this expression can be identity where there was apparent difference; that is to say identity established by the sublation of apparent difference. It is true that identity always presupposes difference. But how? Identity does not surely presuppose a difference that continues to be as real as identity. Identity presupposes difference, just as every negation presupposes an affirmation or every affirmation presupposes a negation, without implying that both are equally real to thought.

A second objection will then be raised. If the judgement "A is identical with B," implies no real difference between A and B, then the judgement is a mere tautology. The criticism of Hegel, that such a judgement is contradictory as failing to assert something which it desired to assert, applies to it.

To this we have to reply that identity, as we have seen, implies difference. But it is not necessary that this difference also should be real. Nay, if the difference also be real there can be no question of identity at all. The character of tautology is not peculiar to this kind of judgement alone. It is common to all judgements. As Hobhouse himself has shown, the proposition, "Some men are black," means nothing more than that only black men are black. "The dog drinks" also means that only the drinking dog and the dog while drinking drinks.[1]

The charge of tautology is due, however, to a misconception (as Hobhouse points out) as regards the function of a judgement. A judgement neither adds anything to reality nor does it take anything away from it. Metaphysically considered, therefore, there is no novelty in a judgement. But judgement concerns *knowledge* of reality; it is essentially a movement

1 *Theory of Knowledge*, p. 160.

of thought. Whatever was eternally real or even eternally false may only now be known to be so by the judging mind, and in asserting this a judgement really achieves something new for thought. Therein lies the fulfilment of its humble mission. If this view of a judgement is able to rebut the charge of tautology brought against other judgments, it also succeeds in the case of an identity judgement. For here the movement of thought begins with difference as the starting-point, and ends by negating the difference and reaching identity as its terminus. In the judgement, "A is identical with B," or "am is identical with bm," the different determinants "a" and "b" are first thought to be as real as "m." But in the end they are considered as nought, as only apparent, as unable to affect the identity of "m". Hence through their sublation the identity of "m" alone is asserted. Such a vākya may be called akhaṇḍārthaka, since in it the existence of a single content alone is asserted, and it is distinct from the ordinary type of judgements in which one ideal content is applied to another content, whether real or imaginary, and the two different elements are related together. Such a judgement will be possible only when the different determining elements "a" and "b" are *somehow* thought to be apparent, and not capable of affecting the identity of "m." Such accidental and apparent determinants (or rather mere marks) must, therefore, be distinguished from the real ones, which can modify the identity of the substantive they qualify. In vedāntic terminology they are called upalakṣaṇas, whereas the ordinary determinants are called viśeṣaṇas. As regards the vedantic text "Thou art that," which means that "the individual consciousness is the same as the universal consciousness," the term "individual" and "universal" are upalakṣaṇas, as they are held to be only apparent determinants the falsity of which is somehow proved, though it is irrelevant to our present topic to show how they are actually so proved.

We may now consider the second type of akhaṇḍārthaka vākyas. These are sentences containing the knowledge of a single object by definition or description. The definition of an object, it will at once be said, should show its relation to its genus and other co-ordinate species. A description also contains the relation of an object to various other things. How then can the meaning of such a sentence be non-relational? To this we must reply that we must distinguish between the *end* that a judgement is intended to achieve, and the *means* whereby that end is achieved. The import or meaning of a proposition is constitued not by the means, but by the end that is attained by the judgement expressed by that proposition. If this be not granted, then we cannot even distinguish between a positive judgment and a negative one, such as A is B and A is not B, which differ only in respect of their respective ends—affirmation and negation—the terms and relations being all identical. Now the definitive or descriptive proposition in question may express a relation of the unknown object to other objects. But the end to be achieved by such a proposition is not to show relations, but to show the object as it is , relation being used only as means to that end. Thus the import of such a propositon cannot be said to be relational. The illustration used for this purpose by the Advaitins is a sentence defining the moon. A man who does not know the moon, but only knows that it is a heavenly body to be seen at night, asks another, "Which is the moon"? (Kaḥ candraḥ). He is told, "The most resplendent is the moon," prakṛṣṭa-prakaśaḥ candraḥ.[1] Now this sentence is spoken not to express any relation of the moon to anything else but to indicate which the moon is. At first sight it would seem that in this sentence an adjective, "the most resplendent," is attributed to a substantive, "the moon." But really it is not so. A quality can be predicated of a substantive, only when the substantive is already known. But here the substantive itself is unknown. Besides, the enquirer does not want to know *what* the moon is, i.e. what quality it possesses, but *which* the moon is , i.e. which particular object it is, so that the answer, to be relevant to the question can only say *which* it is and not *what* it is.

It may be said that as an object without any attribute—i.e. characteristic—cannot be known, because without a distinguishing mark it cannot be differentiated from other objects of its kind, the knowledge of quality or attribute is necessary even for the knowledge of the object *as it is*. To this we reply that it is really necessary to use some distinguishing attribute even to point out an object; and it is exactly for this purpose that the adjective "the most resplendent" has been used. But this only implies that such a sentence points out the object only through the help of a distinguishing attribute. Thus it does not mean that the import of the sentence is either to predicate an attribute of the object, or to relate the object to any other object. If then we bear in mind the definite purpose of the sentence, the end it tries to achieve, as distinct from the means, we have no choice but to admit that the sentence means only one single

1 Advaita-siddhi, chap. ii, and Citsukhī, chap. i (on akhaṇḍārthaka vākya).

unrelated element. Though the sentence taken by itself can mean a relation between a substantive and adjective, yet when interpreted with reference to the motive of the speaker (and the question asked) it has to be taken in a modified sense (to suit the particular purpose) as meaning only the object enquired about and no relation, so that such a vākya also can be said to be akhaṇḍārthaka.

The Vedanta text, "satyaṃ jñānam anantaṃ Brahma" (the real, the conscious, the infinite is Brahman), which describes the Absolute, also comes within this class and should be interpreted in a similar way. From the context it is found that the Absolute is considered to be beyond all determinations and attributes, so that the meaning of this sentence cannot be the attribution of qualities (satya, jñāna and ananta) to Brahman. The sentence has to be taken in a secondary sense, as attempting to convey an idea of Brahman to the mind only by indirect suggestion. Satyam is used to indicate that the Absolute is not asatyam or unreal, jñānam that it is not ajñānam or unconscious or objective, and anantam to mean that it is not finite; thus the three apparent attributes are used only to indicate what Brahman is by saying what he is not. As Brahman is usually mistaken for the unreal, the objective and the finite, the use of all the three words where otherwise one might be sufficient is necessary to remove the three possible sources of confusion. This sentence indicates, therefore, the absolute, pure and simple, through the negation of negation and not through the positive predication of any attribute. So such a vakya also should be taken as akhaṇḍārthaka.

While conceding all that has been said above, the objection may yet be raised that such a definitive or descriptive sentence, as asserting only an isolated content—a mere identity—is a mere verbal expression; it is no judgement. As Hobhouse says : "There may be mental acts which predicate mere identity. There are such acts; every circular definition is an instance; but they are not judgements, they are simply the verbal expression of an attempt to make a judgement which has failed."[1] As the writer does not illustrate his statement, it is not quite clear what sort of definitions he has in view. But as for the definitive sentences we have given above, we may say that whether they can be said to contain any judgement or not would depend entirely on the conception of judgement. If it is held that the attribution of one content of thought to another is the

1 *Theory of Knowledge*, pp. 162-163.

essential requisite of a judgement, then of course such sentences, as containing no such *characterization*, are by definition barred from being judgements. But if we refuse to make the definition of a judgement so arbitrarily narrow, and consider, as some philosophers have done, any proposition of which truth or falsity can be significantly predicated as containing a judgement, then these difinitive sentences also can be said to contain judgements. Of a mere verbal exprssion we can predicate only grammatical correctness or incorrectness, and not truth or falsity.[1]

The common view in Indian logic that a vākya must contain an uddeśya and vidheya, as well as the common Western theory that *every* proposition must contain a subject and a predicate in the substantive-adjective relation, is based on a faulty generalization from the vast majority of cases where such a relation really holds. But this theory neglects the small minority of cases where, as we have seen, such a relation is not present. But even this incorrect theory has struck such deep roots into the mind, that when the neglected refractory cases are disclosed, rather than the long-cherished theory be sacrificed or modified to include the new cases, the Gordian knot is cut by declaring these cases to be merely verbal and not genuine enough to call for any reconsideration. We have observed how some modern Western logicians, like Russell, have tried to expose the folly of such a philosophic conservatism. We have also shown how in India the Advaitins also, from a different point of view,fought against the absolutism of this orthodox dogma and tried to establish the genuineness of the akhaṇḍārthaka vākyas. We shall end this discussion with a short reflection on an important point that will help us to understand the Advaita contention.

In all judgements containing a subject and a predicate, one content is applied to, or attributed to, or referred to, or related to another. Whether such a judgement is positive (S is P) or negative (S is not P) the ground is the same, namely, "P is referable to or relatable to S." We have before our mind a possible relation between P and S, and the relation is either affiemed or denied, giving rise to the entire series of judgements of the subject-predicate form. Thus the ground of all propositions of the subject-predicate form is "P is referable or relatable to S." If so, what should be said of propositions of which the ground is "P is not relatable to S"? The negative judgements of this class have to be distinguished from those of the former class. The illustrations of the former class would be "The

1 *Vide* Johnson, *Logic*, vol. i, p. 1.

flower is not white," "The square is not big," whereas the illustrations of the latter class would be "The flower is not honest," "The square is not circular," "The rope is not a serpent." Vedanta texts, where qualities and relations are denied of Brahman, should also come under this second class.

It will be remembered that Hegel[1] noticed this distinction, and called the former class of judgement simply negative and the latter negatively infinite. But he thinks that the latter are absurd. Thus he observes : "Examples of the latter are : 'The mind is no elephant,' 'A lion is no table,' propositions which are correct but absurd, exactly like the identical propositions, 'A lion is a lion,' and 'Mind is mind.' "Consequently he holds that "the negatively infinite judgement, in which the subject has no relation whatever to the predicate, gets its place in the Formal Logic solely as a nonsensical curiosity."[2]

Against this criticism we must say that such propositions are not at all meaningless or nonsensical. The very fact that an infinitely negative judgement is distinguished from the other class of judgements is a proof that they are neither absurd nor meaningless, in which case the author's statement would have been absurd and meaningless. As we said in a previous connection, the non-existence of a relation or even the frustration of an attempted relation may be the objective of the speaker as much as the affirmation of a relation. Thus a proposition which has such an objective is as full of meaning as any other. As Hobhouse observes : "It is not always absurd to deny a connection between things so remote that no connection between them should be conceivable. 'The soul is not an attenuated gaseous substance.' There is a stage of intelligence at which that denial is worth making, however superfluous it may seem later on."[3]

But it may be urged that even the rejection of a relation presupposes its possible affirmation, and without it the negation would be useless though not meaningless. To this we may say that it is true that the negatively infinite judgment, in which relation is rejected, logically presupposes a possible or suggested relation. But it does not mean that the presupposition of the judgement is identical with its immediate import

1 Wallace, *The Logic of Hegel*, p. 306.

2 Ibid.

3 *Theory of Knowledge*, pp. 154-155.

of objective. If it were so, the import of an affirmative judgement would be negation and that of a negative judgement, affirmation. Neither does it mean that the presupposed possibility of a relation should be real. The possibility may be merely subjective and illusory, and the negation would thus be highly useful as representing the correction of an error, possible, or actual. It is in this way that the Vedānta texts, containing the negation of determinations, as illusorily attributed to Brahman, become highly significant and useful[1].

Before we conclude this chapter we may sum up its main results in a few words. A vākya represents a signficant combination of isolated concepts as symbolized by individual words. The meaning of a sentence is derived from a constructive combination of ideas—a process that takes place under peculiar and specific conditions, which distinguish the knowledge of the meaning of a sentence from ordinary types of knowledge, e.g. perception, memory, memory-synthesis and inference. This peculiar kind of knowledge is called śabda-bodha. Again, vākyas are of two kinds, saṃsargāvagāhi and akhaṇḍārthaka, according as they express some relation between two contents or express a unitary unrelated content.

1 *Vide* author's Article, "The Import of a Proposition in Vedanta," *The Philosophical Quarterly*, January, 1929.

CHAPTER V

THE OBJECTIVE REFERENCE IN A SENTENCE

WE have confined ourselves hitherto to the epistemic or subjective aspect of a sentence, namely to the world of meanings alone. But the terminus of a declaratory sentence is not meanings or concepts, but existents or objects. On hearing a sentence like "The flower is red," we have not merely an idea of a flower characterized by the idea of redness, but we invariably have, under normal circumstances, belief in the objective existence of a flower with a perceptible physical quality of redness. It is only in exceptional cases like story-telling, joking or lying, where we are definitely aware on the contrary that the sentences spoken have no objective ground to refer to, that our belief is suspended. But for these exceptions, it would have been scarcely possible for us to know the abstract world of bare meanings and concepts, standing midway between words and objects, just as it is scarcely possible to know, through sight, the existence of a transparent medium like a piece of glass, unless vision is otherwise obstructed. Even while hearing a story like "There was a king. He had a vast kingdom, etc." we can scarcely help forming images of a king and his vast kingdom, and also referring them to some time and place in the objective world in which we move, though we are conscious that the reference has no objective ground. This is why even a fictitious story can arouse in us feelings of fear, love, hatred, joy and sorrow, which would otherwise have been out of place.

We have said in the last chapter that a vākya or a sentence, on being spoken, generates in the mind of the hearer a constructive knowledge of the combination of ideas or meanings, which is called śābda-bodha. But a vākya is not conceived as ending its function here. Unless positively obstructed by some deterrent factor, a vākya asserting a fact produces belief in the fact which forms its objective or intention (tātparya). A vākya comes, therefore, to be a source of knowledge about facts. Consequently, śabda, as vākya, is regarded as a pramāṇa or method of knowledge. This is called śabda-pramāṇa.

The relation between śabda-bodha and śabda-pramā, i.e. between the knowledge of the meaning of a sentence and the knowledge of facts as derived from a sentence, has to be clearly understood. Knowledge of meaning is an intermediate process that is indipensable to the knowledge of facts. But the former is organic to the latter and cannot be said to have any independent existence. In fact, in ordinary speech, words lead the mind directly to facts, and the intermediate process of the combination of ideas or meanings is no more known, even by a trained hearer, than is the formation of images on the retina in the case of visual perception. It is only when objective reference is held in abeyance by some factor that obstructs belief that we are conscious of the intermediate meaning-function. As Schiller rightly observes,[1] "the apparent paradox that meaning should be most intense when it is most obstructed is not unparalleled. Just as the strength of a current is revealed when it eddies over the rocks that obstruct its course, so the reality of our activities is manifested to us by the resistance they encounter.... It is natural enough, therefore, that cases of obstructed expression should yield the purest and intensest consciousness of meaning."

In ordinary cases words, meanings and facts are scarcely distinguished. The independence of meaning and expression (or words) is perhaps known first when a suitable expression for thoughts is not forthcoming, and we are conscious that we *mean* something which we fail to *express*, or that we do not *mean* exactly what the words seem to *express*. The independence of meaning and facts is known by the speaker when he uses words (in lying, joking, story-telling, etc.) which *mean*, but have no corresponding *facts*; and by the hearer when he has cause to suspect the veracity of the expression, and comes to think that the words though having meaning have no facts corresponding to the meaning. Nay, meanings and facts are perhaps still more indistinguishable to ordinary folk. They are regarded as almost identical. For when a man lies and jokes, his words are often said to be *meaningless*. The intermediacy of the meaning-function (between words and facts) from the stand-point of the hearer, as we have indicated, is to be looked upon as a mere logical abstraction. The psychological fact seems to be that the formation of meaning and reference to facts take place simultaneously in the mind of the hearer. As a sentence comes to mean, it means facts. In other words, in knowing the meaning of a proposition, "A is B," we also believe, under normal circumstances, that "A is B" is true. It would appear, therefore, that the Advaitins are right in holding that śābda-bodha (knowledge of the meaning of a proposition) is not a distinct phase of knowledge from śābda-pramā (the knowledge of facts as derived from

1 *Vide* Symposium, "The Meaning of 'Meaning.' " Mind, 1920, p. 396.

the proposition), but that the former is included in the latter.[1] The interdependence of meaning and objective reference has been rightly expressed by Russell in his *Analysis of Mind*.[2] "The objective reference of a proposition," he says, "is a function (in the mathematical sense) of the meanings of its component words."

We discussed in the last chapter the four conditions under which the knowledge of the meaning of a proposition i.e. (śābda-bodha) takes place. There we interpreted all the conditions from the subjective standpoint, since we were concerned only with the subjective aspect, i.e. the understanding of the meaning of a proposition. Of these four conditions, tātparya-jñāna (or the knowledge of the speaker's object in speaking) and yogyatva (compatibility) have also their objective aspects, which determine the mental attitude of the hearer to the proposition. When, for example, the speaker is telling a story, the hearer is conscious that the object of the speaker is not to state facts; consequently belief in objective facts corresponding to the ideas expressed by the words is obstructed, and there is a positive disbelief. This also is the case when the speaker is known to be lying. When the object of the speaker is known to be jesting, belief may be merely suspended, and the mental attitude may be one of vacillation or doubt; and in ordinary circumstances, when there are no positive grounds for supposing that the speaker is deviating from the normal object of speaking (i.e. statement of *facts*), there is implicit belief in the truth of his statement.

Similarly, compatibility, which subjectively means ideal compatibility, is also understood in its objective aspect to be compatibility with facts. When we are told, "The square is circular," want of ideal compatibility between the subject and predicate prevents the very consciousness of meaning. But when we are told, "The man has two horns," there is no ideal incompatibility; we can very well imagine a man with horns. Thus though the sentence is not altogether meaningless, there is a positive obstruction to the belief in the truth of the statement, since it is incompatible with experienced facts.

To sum up all that has been said here, we always implicitly believe in the truth of a statement made by someone, if there be no positive ground for doubting or disbelieving him. We come thus to the Vedantic theory of śabda-pramāṇa, namely that a vākya or sentence whose import

1 *Vide* Citsukhī, chap. i (discussion on anvitābhidhānam and abhihitānvayaḥ).

2 P. 271.

(subjective or objective) is not contradicted in any other way is a valid source śabda of knowledge. Thus belief in the truth of one's words is primary and śabda direct. Doubt or disbelief is secondary and indirect; it is otherwise śabda caused by some positive hindrance to belief.

The main reason why we have undertaken the foregoing psychological analysis of the process of verbal knowledge is to prepare the ground for a thorough understanding of the logical problem regarding the validity of the claim of śabda as an independent and ultimate source of knowledge. Thus the chief object of our investigation still remains unattained. In the next chapter, therefore, we must enquire into the logical grounds for treating śabda as an independent method of knowledge, and consider the chief objections against it.

But before we do so, we should note that though the Advaitins generally follow the Mīmāṃsakas in Epistemology, there is a very important difference between the two schools regarding the object of the Vedas the authority of which both accept as verbal testimony *par excellence*. According to the Mīmāṃsakas the Vedas teach ritual duties; they are a body of commandments. As such ritual knowledge can be obtained only from the Vedas, they are a *unique* source of knowledge which no other method can yield. It is but logical, therefore, for this school to attach primary importance to the imperative or mandatory sentences (vidhi-vākyas) in the Vedas. All other Vedic sentences which state facts and describe the nature of realities (siddhārthas) are regarded as being only of instrumental value, their sole purpose being to help and encourage the performance of rituals.[1] It will be seen, therefore, that for this school the question of objective reference has little value. For the knowledge of a commandment it is enough to understand the *meaning* of the sentence containing it.

On the other hand, the Vedāntins (and Advaitins in particular) attach greater importance to the Vedas as containing the sentences that assert or declare the nature of the World, Self, God, etc. The problem of objective reference discussed in this section has great importance, therefore, for these thinkers. They are interested in the Vedas primarily as the source of the knowledge of truths. Though they also recognize the subsidiary utility of the mandatory texts in so far as they lay down the path of action, that purifies the heart and paves thereby the *way to* the knowledge of truths, as Śaṃkara points out.[2]

1 *Vide* Jaimini's Mim. sūt. 1, 2, 1-7.

2 Com. on Brahma-sūt, 3, 4, 36.

CHAPTER VI

THE VALIDITY OF VERBAL KNOWLEDGE

THE very purpose of speaking is to convey information. Lying is rightly condemned as a great sin—it serves to destroy, through abuse, the security of speech, which is one of the greatest factors that have made human society possible. We have seen that the tendency of a person is to believe in the truth of what he hears, unless there is any special cause for doubt or disbelief. "We accept on trust," says Montague, "nine-tenths of what we are told to be true. Man is a suggestible animal and tends to believe what is said to him unless he has some positive reason for doubting the honesty or competence of his informant."[1]

But in spite of this fact it may be asked : "Whatever be the primary object of speech, now that lying and deceiving also are so common, what reasons have we to accept the validity of verbal knowledge (i.e. the authority or testimony of other persons) unless we are prepared to confuse mere psychological belief with logical certainty?"

This objection has compelled some Indian philosophers—e.g. the Buddhists and the Vaiśeṣikas—to reject verbal testimony as a source or method of knowledge. They believe that as the validity of information received from others has ultimately to be established or rejected through inference from the trustworthiness of the speakers (or any other data), the independence and ultimacy of śabda cannot be supported; it must be brought, therefore, under anumāna or inference. Similarly also, Western logicians, almost without any exception, hold that authority cannot stand as an independent source of knowledge and is really a case of inference.

In order that we can correctly and clearly judge the claim of śabda to be considered a method of knowledge, we must consider the fundamental conditions that are regarded as necessary for a method to satisfy. By analysis it is found that the following three problems are involved in the consideration of a method of knowledge :—

1. Whether the alleged method is a *source* for the attainment of knowledge of facts.

2. Whether the validity of the knowledge attained by the alleged method is *constituted* by the very conditions which make the knowledge itself possible, or whether it is constituted by any external condition.

3. Whether the validity of the knowledge is also *known* or *ascertained* by the conditions that constitute that knowledge, or by any external condition.

1 *The Ways of Knowing*, chapter on "Authoritarianism."

In Indian epistemology these three problems were critically distinguished. They were dealt with separately as the problem of pramāṇa (the source or cause of true knowledge), that of prāmāṇyasya utpattiḥ (the genesis or the objective constitution of validity), and that of prāmāṇya-grahaḥ or prāmāṇyasya jñāptih (the knowledge or ascertainment of validity). This analytic grasp of the three distinct problems, which are ordinarily confused, was a source of much accurate thinking.

If we remember these three distinct questions, we shall understand better in what sense (or on what ground) a particular method of knowledge is accepted or rejected by a particular school of thinkers.[1]

To apply the result of this analysis to the method under consideration, we at once find that those who think that verbal testimony cannot be considered a method of knowledge, because the validity of such knowledge has to be ascertained through inference and therefore this method becomes reduced to inference itself, confuse the problems (1) and (3).

Any source, which gives us information about facts, can be and should be considered a method of knowledge, irrespective of the question whether its validity is ascertained intrinsically or by some external method. For otherwise even perception cannot stand as an independent method. When the validity of a perception is doubted, it has to be established through inference; then perception also has to be brought under inference. Neither can it be said that as the validity of perception is not always doubted, at least in those cases of absence of doubt, it can be accepted as a method. For, if this be granted, exactly for a similar reason verbal testimony, the validity of which also remains very often undoubted and unchallenged, should also be accepted as a method at least for those cases. And if inference or perception is necessary to validate testimony, testimony also is, at times, employed to validate inference and perception. Nay, at times either of them may be rejected in deference to testimony. We perceive the sun to be moving, but in deference to the authority of astronomers we disbelieve our perception. Thus we find that the grounds on which śābda, as a method of knowledge is discarded lead us to absurdities. In fact, however, for a method to be so considered it is sufficient that it should give some information which *is* not derived from (even though it may be *derivable* from) other sources. When I am told by a friend that he is suffering from a headache I may believe him, but the belief may also be

1 *Vide* author's Article, "Testimony as a Method of Knowledge," *Mind*, vol xxxvi, N. S., No. 143.

the result of an inference from his trustworthiness or truthfulness. But this inference gives me only the knowledge that his statement is true, *not* the knowledge that he is suffering from a headache. The object of this inference is the establishment of truth or falsehood and that of the verbal statement the *information* which is to be subjected to the judgment of truth or falsehood. If this distinction be remembered, we find that the information yielded by verbal testimony, being itself not derived from inference, cannot be reduced to the latter. On the contrary, verbal testimony can be regarded as an independent method of knowledge as much as perception or inference. There are many cases such as the knowledge of the questions, wishes, requests, commands, feelings and ideas of other persons for which their own words are the *only source* for us.

In some cases, it is true, the knowledge derived from verbal testimony can be obtained also from some other source. But in a similar way in many cases the knowledge obtained through perception can also be obtained through inference, and *vice versa*. This point cannot be said to vitiate the independence of śabda if it does not do so in the case of perception or inference. For the method to be considered independent it is sufficient that it yields information that is *new* for the *hearer* in that context. To ascertain the particular source from which knowledge has been derived we must see from what source it has been *actually* derived, and not from what source it can be derived; and in this work of ascertainment the Indian philosophers believed that subsequent introspection (anuvyavasāya) was our chief guide. If the authority of memory-introspection were not accepted we should be unable to ascertain whether the knowledge of a flower, I had a moment ago, was got through perception or memory, or inference or testimony. It is on the strength of such memory that we are able to say "I perceived the thing," or "I inferred it," or "I remembered it," or "I heard of it," where the thing *can* be known through each of these many sources.

On the above-mentioned grounds the Naiyāyikas accepted śabda as a method of knowledge, though they held that the validity of verbal knowledge was neither constituted by, nor known from, the intrinsic conditions of the knowledge itself. The validity of every method of knowledge, whether perception or inference or verbal testimony, was according to them to be ascertained by inference. The Sāṃkhyas also accepted the words of scripture as an independent source of knowledge, though they confined their allegiance only to those texts the validity of which was otherwise ascertained to be unassailable.

Of modern Western logicians or epistemologists very few have devoted any attention to a searching consideration of verbal knowledge. Those who have incidentally considered authority have summarily rejected its claims. But it is interesting to find that a Western writer, W.P. Montague, has bestowed a little attention on this neglected topic. To a certain extent his veiw resembles that of the Naiyāyikas. For he thinks that, though the validity of testimony can be ulitmately established only by some other method, yet a testimony that is open to free and honest study remains as legitimate a source of knowledge as any other.[1]

It would appear, then, that even though the validity of verbal testimony must be known through some other method, there is no reason whatever why it should cease to be considered a method of knowledge. On the contrary, the fact that the testimony can yield some *new* information that is not derived from some other source is sufficient reason for considering testimony a distinct method that is not reducible to any other method. Introspection also supports this view by showing the memory of verbal knowledge to be distinct from that of perception or inference. These considerations alone are sufficient for rejecting any theory that tries to reduce śabda to inference, and for holding on the contrary that it is a legitimate method of knowledge.

But the Mīmāṃsakas and the Advaitins, who also accept testimony as a method, go further. For according to them even the validity of verbal knowledge is constituted by, and also *known* or ascertained through, the intrinsic conditions of verbal knowledge itself. Thus though the Naiyāyikas and Sāṃkhyas on the one hand, and the Mīmāṃsakas and the Advaitins on the other, all accepted śabda as a pramāṇa, there was this important difference in the exact senses in which they accepted it. This difference between these two opposing schools of thought was not peculiar to the theory of verbal knowledge alone; it was the result of their views on the validity of knowledge in general. It is necessary to mention it briefly in this connection.[2]

According to the former school of thinkers,[3] no knowledge is valid on its own account. The validity of knowledge, whether perceptual, verbal

1 *Ways of Knowing*, p. 49.

2 For a discussion of this problem *vide* Citsukhī (chap. i), Sarva-darśana-saṃgraha (Jaimini-system).

3 *Vide* Tattva-cintāmaṇi, Prāmāṇya-vāda.

or inferential, is derived from some special conditions which must operate in addition to the conditions which caused the knowledge itself. If the validity of knowledge was conditioned by the very conditions which condition the knowledge itself, then no knowledge could turn out to be false. As this is not the case, we must assume that in addition to the intrinsic conditions of knowledge itself, there must be some special conditions which make the knowledge valid, and others which make it false.

Again, validity is *known* also from an *external* source, i.e. by inference based on the presence of the special conditions which *make* knowledge valid.[1] Similarly falsity also is inferred from its own special conditions. If the knowledge of validity was intrinsically conditioned by the conditions of knowledge itself, there could be no possibility of doubt in any case of knowledge. The very fact that knowledge is sometimes doubted and sometimes belived is a proof that truth and falsity are known through some special *external* conditions which are present in some cases of knowledge and absent in others.

This doctrine is called prāmāṇya-paratastva-vāda, as it holds that knowledge is both *made* true and *known* to be true by special conditions, which are *external* to those that condition knowledge itself. As against this line of thought the Mīmāṃsakas and the Advaitins hold a theory called prāmāṇya-svatastva-vāda, which means that validity is *conditioned* by the conditions *intrinsic* to knowledge itself, and that validity is *known* also from the conditions of knowledge itself. The reasons for holding such a view are briefly the following [2] :—

Knowledge, whether perceptual, inferential or verbal, is essentially a process directed to the attainment of truth. Thus truth is an intrinsic characteristic of knowledge. If knowledge sometimes fails to attain truth, it is because some special hindrance stands in the way of knowledge itself. Falsity, therefore, is due to or constituted by some special conditions that are external to (and that interfere with) the conditions which make knowledge possible, and the fulfilment of which alone would otherwise make for truth. So it is falsity that is externally conditioned, whereas validity is conditioned by the conditions of knowledge itself. For validity, the only external condition that can be conceived is perhaps the negative fact of the absence of the special vitiating factors that make knowledge

1 *Vide* Tattva-cintāmaṇi, Prāmāṇya-vāda.

2 *Vide* author's paper, "The Source of the Knowledge of Validity," *Proceedings Indian Philosophical Congress*, 1928.

false. But it is no positive condition, and it should account rather for the negative fact of the absence of falsity than for positive validity.

We may remark here that the difference between the two opposing views points to a fundamental difference in the conception of the meaning and function of knowledge. According to the former view the differentia of knowledge would be belief; and as belief may be both true and false, knowledge also is neutral to truth and falsity. This tendency of thought does not seem to be very happy. Neither belief nor knowledge is a neutral attitude towards both truth and falsity. The very aim and purpose of knowledge is truth. Belief essentially means "believing to be true." Thus truth is organic to both knowledge and belief, and falsity is only an accidental case of their frustrated purpose. So the connection between falsity and knowledge is not organic but purely accidental. It is, therefore, unfair and inaccurate to think of knowledge as being impartially present in both truth and falsity. The Advaitins and the Mīmāṃsakas, who emphasize the fact that truth is intrinsic to knowledge while falsity is externally conditioned, recognize, therefore, an important truth.

To turn now to the second point, namely the knowledge or ascertainment of validity or truth. As against the view that validity is ascertained through inference, the Mīmāṃsakas and the Vedāntins argue that this view leads to an infinite regress. For if the validity of knowledge (say a perception) is ascertained through another knowledge, i.e. inference, the validity of the second knowledge also being not self-evident has to be ascertained through a third knowledge, and that by a fourth and so on *ad infinitum*. If, to avoid the regress, it is said that the validating inference may be self-evident, it may be asked, then, why the validity of the first knowledge also should not be self-evident. We are forced, therefore, at some stage or other to admit that knowledge must also certify its own validity.

It may be asked, however, if that be so, how could doubt at all arise, and why is argument at all required for certifying the validity of knowledge? To this it is replied that doubt arises only when there is positive knowledge of conditions or facts which seem to contradict the *knowledge* we have; and arguments are necessary not for the positive work of establishing the validity of knowledge, but for the negative work of removal of doubt or the chances of contradiction. That knowledge carries with it an inherent guarantee of its own truth can be established by introspection, and can also be inferred from the behaviour of persons who act unquestioningly on their knowledge of things as soon as they acquire it, without waiting till its truth is certified by a validating inference. Thus it is the falsity and the doubtfulness of knowledge that are inferred (from the presence of conflicting facts), and not its validity, which is inherent in the knowledge. Non-contradiction is the only guarantee of validity, and this guarantee does not forsake knowledge until it is positively contradicted or doubted.[1]

Many objections can be raised against this theory of the self-evidence of the validity of knowledge. But as the consideration of the general problem of validity is only incidental to our main purpose, we can afford only to consider briefly the chief objections in this connection.

The most fundamental objection will be that such a theory confuses logical certainty with mere psychological belief, as Russell would say. "Some of our beliefs seem to be peculiarly indubitable,"[2] yet they very often turn out to be false. Thus belief is no sure index of truth; it is not the same thing as certainty.

This distinction, though apparently sound and in a way really useful, is in the ultimate analysis untenable and unintelligible. For the knowledge of judgment of validity (as distinct from the objective conditions of validity, which we considered first) is mainly a subjective question. Certainty is nothing but a quality of knowledge. It is belief itself which has been strengthened by a logical process of reasoning. But on being strengthened belief does not cease to be psychological. Still, it would have been useful if we could ascertain the degree of strengthening, or the amount of reasoning, that was necessary to turn a mere belief into a logical certainty. But that is possible neither psychologically nor logically; because different persons require different degrees of certification for the validity of their knowledge and because no objective or logical limit can be set to the degree of strengthening that is required for establishing certainty. According to the correspondence theory, there can be no talk of any absolute "criterion," which is "chimerical," but there "may be relative criteria" for the determination of truth. Consequently "there is no way hitherto discovered of wholly eliminating the risk of error."[3] According to the theory of systematic coherence, as held by Joachim,[4] the suggestion of absolute truth and absolute certainty for our fragmentary knowledge is altogether out of the question. The process of the ascertainment of truth

1 For a full discussion of this topic *vide* Citsukhī on svataḥprāmāṇyam (ch: i).

2 *Analysis of Mind*, p. 262.

3 Russell, *Analysis of Mind*, p. 269.

4 In his *Nature of Truth*.

cannot stop until the whole system — the Absolute itself — is known. The theory of consilience, as held by Hobhouse,[1] is akin to the coherence theory, in so far as it also holds that the probability of truth increases the greater the system of judgments is, with which the particular judgment is consilient. Thus according to these various theories ascertainment of validity cannot be said to be logically complete at any stage. If so, when is truth known, and judgment of validity passed? We must say that the judgment of validity is nowhere possible. But if it is possible at any stage of the process it should be possible at the first stage of knowledge also. For even the initial belief that is inherent in an act of knowledge (not yet externally certified) possesses a degree of probable truth, though it may be of the smallest degree. What is more important to note is that though knowledge may be more and more certified to be true, and subjective certainty also may gradually increase, the logical judgment of validity, "A is B is true," remains the same throughout—beginning from the primary case of what is called mere belief through all the attitudes of increasing logical certainty. Moreover, if it is true, as Russell confesses, that even logically established certainty may also eventually turn out to be erroneous, the special and only disqualification pressed against primary belief, that it often turns out to be false, should be withdrawn for the sake of fairness and consistency.

On all sides, therefore, it is found that knowledge of validity takes place simultaneously with the act of knowledge itself which is implicitly believed. And if no amount of external certification is logically complete, we have to treat and accept any kind of knowledge as true if it is not as *yet* doubted or falsified. Thus it would appear that non-contradiction has ultimately to be resorted to as the guarantee for a judgment of validity. The positive and primary guarantee of the truth of the knowledge of a thing is the knowledge itself. As I look at the table I believe in the truth of the visual knowledge of the table, and judge the knowledge to be valid, primarily on the positive basis that I am seeing it (or having visual knowledge), and secondarily on the negative basis that I have no reasons to doubt or disbelieve my knowledge. Verification of the visual knowledge through knowledge of touch (which is as liable to error as vision) is, only partly, possible. But the judgment of validity does not wait till verification takes place; neither is the judgment changed after it takes place. When positive grounds for doubting or disbelieving the truth of knowledge are

1 In his *Theory of Knowledge.*

known to exist, the doubtfulness or falsity of the knowledge is of course inferred. Judgment of validity is primary and that of falsity is secondary. If knowledge were not somehow previously believed to be true, known to be valid, there would have been no occasion for declaring it to be false, no meaning in judging it to be not valid.

Sooner or later, knowledge itself should vouch for its own truth, make its validity self-evident, or there is no escape from relativity, no stop to infinite regress. But it may be asked, if validity is self-evident how is it that a self-evident truth turns out to be a falsity? and how then can self-evidence still be considered to be a faithful criterion? We have already said that falsification is not peculiar to self-evidence alone; it is the common danger to which every other method is liable. Besides, *if knowledge ceases to be self-evident, it so far ceases to be knowledge itself*, and it is not the case that when self-evidence ceases to certify knowledge, knowledge is left behind to be certified by some other method. When there is positive knowledge of causes which make a particular belief false or doubtful, what we are aware of is not merely that the knowledge is not self-evident, but that we had no knowledge at all. As I take a rope for a serpent, but subsequently know it to be a rope, I do not merely find that my knowledge of the serpent is no more self-evident, but that my knowledge of the serpent was no knowledge at all, that I did not perceive the serpent though I *seemed* to perceive it. And when I merely doubt whether the thing is a serpent at all, I am uncertain whether I am perceiving the serpent, though I seem to perceive it. It is clear, therefore, that doubt or positive contradiction is not levelled directly against self-evidence but against knowledge itself; and self-evidence as an inseparable quality of knowledge vanishes only indirectly with the vanishing of the knowledge itself. When, in any instance, doubt or contradiction standing in the way to knowledge is removed, knowledge is made possible and with it self-evidence also returns. It is true that validating inference is sometimes resorted to. But that does not prove, as Russell believes, [1] that self-evidence fails to resist "the assaults of scepticism," but only that knowledge itself is at stake, and the attempt at ratification or verification is only an attempt at reinstating knowledge by removing obstacles that threaten to undermine knowledge. When ten different arguments are adduced to ratify a particular knowledge, what

1 The Analysis of Mind, p. 263.

is achieved is not directly the ascertainment of validity (which is congenital with knowledge itself), but the removal of ten actual or possible sources of doubt or contradiction which stand in the way of knowledge itself.

The only consistent procedure for the real believer in relativism would be complete silence. The judgment that would establish relativism would be self-contradictory. Unless self-evidence of some sort is resorted to, arguing, and still more so philosophizing, has to be abandoned.

We find, therefore, that the Advaita view that the conditions of knowledge itself are the grounds both of its validity and the knowledge of its validity is reasonable. The conditions of knowledge will be different in different cases. We have seen already the special conditions under which verbal knowledge occurs. It would follow, therefore, that when these conditions are satisfied we have not only knowledge from some verbal statement, but also belief in the validity of that knowledge. This belief in verbal knowledge is as much justified as that in any other knowledge derived from any other source, though the belief may perchance turn out to be false, as that in any other knowledge also may. So long as there are no positive grounds for doubt or contradiction, like any other knowledge verbal knowledge also must be considered valid. And as in any other kind of knowledge, so also here, validating inference may be necessary only to remove doubts as regards the satisfaction of the conditions of the knowledge itself. If what has been said above is clearly understood, it will be found that the arguments that are generally advanced against testimony or authority as a method of knowledge are wholly untenable. Before we conclude we may notice a few objections raised by Montague, who is perhaps the only modern writer who considers it necessary formally to state the objections against testimony.

"The weakness of the authoritarian method," says this writer, "consists first in the fact that authorities conflict, and there is consequently an internal discrepancy in the method, which makes it difficult of application."[1]

We have tried to show that the fact that knowledge derived by a particular method may sometimes come into conflict with some other knowledge and even definitely turn out to be false, is no reason why the method should be discarded for ever. If this principle were consistently followed, neither perception nor inference could stand as a method. For

1 *Ways of Knowing*, p. 39.

perceptions also sometimes conflict, and still more so inferences. As the writer himself has to confess later on: "This difficulty however is not peculiar to authoritarianism, it is present, though to a less extent, in each of the other methods."[1] Accuracy demands a statistical proof for the statement that the knowledge derived from authority comes into conflict more than that derived from any other source. And even if that proof is given, it is necessary first of all to determine the maximum amount of conflict that may be tolerated in a method. But granting that all these conditions are satisfied, the distinction that will be based on such statistical calculations will be merely practical and convenient, and not logical or even psychological.

Again, if conflict points to any internal discrepancy in the method, since conflict is present in the knowledge derived from other methods also, even though to a less extent, those methods also may be equally accused of the same fault. But a searching enquiry into the internal causes of the conflict between the statements of two or more speakers (or of the same speaker at different times) would tell against other methods rather than against testimony. In most cases, except those of wilful lying, that two speakers speaking in good faith come to conflict is due ultimately to a difference in observation (perception) or inference or both. And it is not unlikely that the cause of lying itself may be traced back to errors of observation and inference and a consequent miscalculation of ultimate results.

A more weighty objection which, though sparing testimony as a method, tries to deprive it of primacy and ultimacy has been raised by Montague. "The second and more serious source of weakness," he says, "is due to the apparent impossibility of treating authority as an ultimate source of truth."[2] This is due, he states, to the fact that whenever two authorities conflict we must advance beyond the authoritarian method to ascertain truth.

As against this objection we may say, first, that it is not always the case that conflict of authorities drives us to a foreign method. Another authority may be able to remove the conflict. And besides, this difficulty in so far as it is true of authority is true of other methods as well. On waking from sleep I find the street wet and infer that it rained. Another

1 Ibid.

2 Ways of Knowing, p. 40

man with the same data infers that the street was watered. How can this conflict be removed and truth ascertained? Either by perceiving that not only the street, but also the trees and houses, are wet, for which raining alone may be responsible, or by *hearing* from a man who observed that it had rained. Sometimes when perceptions conflict, inference or authority may remove the doubts. And if in spite of these facts perception and inference can be considered ultimate and primary sources of knowledge, there is no reason why testimony also should not be so considered. From the Vedāntic standpoint, however, external verification removes only doubts and cannot establish the validity of any kind of knowledge, as knowledge itself furnishes the grounds for the judgement of validity.

We may sum up the important results of the foregoing discussion.

The knowledge derived from a vākya *is* not really derived from any other source, though in some cases it *can* be so derived and in other cases it cannot. This fact alone entitles śabda to be a method of knowledge (pramāṇa). Inference may at most establish the *validity* of the knowledge derived from a vākya; it does not yield the knowledge itself. Thus it is wrong to suppose that testimony is reducible to inference. Even if the truth of knowledge derived from śabda be known through inference, śabda would not cease to be a source of knowledge. But the Vedāntins have shown that the truth of knowledge also is vouched for and known by the inherent conditions of the knowledge itself. Thus the truth of verbal knowledge, also, has not to be established by an external method like a validating inference, which can only remove doubts. Moreover, in some cases like the knowledge of the questions, wishes, requests etc., of other persons their *words* are our primary, and sometimes the only, source of knowledge for us. It follows, therefore, that śabda should be accepted as an independent and ultimate method of knowledge in the fullest sense of the term.

The final object of the Advaita theory of knowledge is to show with the help of the different methods (pramāṇas) that the world of multiplicity cannot be consistently explained without admitting one underlying unity which transcends all changes and diversities and which, therefore, is the highest Reality. The Vedas including the Upaniṣads (—also known as Vedānta, i.e. end of the Vedas) contain the great declarations of unity—called the mahā–vākyas (great sayings)—which are the reports of the direct realization of unity by the seers (ṛṣis).[1] He who desires to liberate

1 Pañcadaśī . Chap. 5

himself from the delusive appearances of multiplicity, and realize the One Brahman behind all, and realize also the unity of his own self and Brahman, can utilize the teachings of the seers. These are, to start with, mediate (parokṣa) knowledge for him, but by constant meditation they can be turned into immediate (aparokṣa) knowledge.

The Advaitins illustrate the possibility of the conversion of mediate knowledge obtained first from authority (śabda-pramāṇa) into immediate knowledge with a story. Ten persons, having crossed a river, count themselves. Every time the counter forgets to count himself and finds only nine. They mourn the loss of the tenth person. The error is corrected by a passer-by who counts all, and tells the counter, "You are the tenth". This mediate knowledge from authority afterwards becomes immediate knowledge when, counting again and including himself, the counter comes to realize, "I am the tenth."[1]

One who would realize his unity with Brahman should, first of all, go through the fourfold mental and moral discipline (sādhana-catuṣṭaya),[2] namely, discrimination between the eternal and the non-eternal, giving up desires for enjoyment of fruits of actions here or hereafter, acquisition of self-control, powers of endurance, concentration etc., and ardent determination for liberation. Prepared thus one should enter upon the three-step path under the guidance of a master who himself has realized Brahman. The steps are : (*a*) Listening (Śravaṇa) to the Upanishadic teachings, (*b*) reasoning (manana) about their truth, and (*c*) intensive meditation (nididhyāsana) on the truths rationally accepted. By long and continued contemplation the truths known from authority attain maturity (paripāka), and immediacy (aparokṣatva). Brahman shines forth as the only REALITY in all outer things and the inner self. It is thus that the teacher's precept, "Thou art Brahman", comes to be realized by the pupil in an immediate consciousness of the form, "I am Brahman." This is the crowning phase of Vedāntic knowledge.

1 *Ibid*, 7, 22 f.

2 Śaṃkara on Bṛ. Sūt. 1, 1, 1.

INDEX

("*f.*" means "*following pages.*")